Restraining Air Power

RESTRAINING AIR POWER

ESCALATION MANAGEMENT BETWEEN PEER AIR FORCES

Robert C. Owen
With
Lazar Berman, Benjamin S. Lambeth,
Forrest E. Morgan, and Steven Paget

Copyright © 2022 by The University Press of Kentucky

Scholarly publisher for the Commonwealth,
serving Bellarmine University, Berea College, Centre
College of Kentucky, Eastern Kentucky University,
The Filson Historical Society, Georgetown College,
Kentucky Historical Society, Kentucky State University,
Morehead State University, Murray State University,
Northern Kentucky University, Spalding University,
Transylvania University, University of Kentucky,
University of Louisville, University of Pikeville, and
Western Kentucky University.
All rights reserved.

Editorial and Sales Offices: The University Press of Kentucky
663 South Limestone Street, Lexington, Kentucky 40508-4008
www.kentuckypress.com

Library of Congress Cataloging-in-Publication Data

Names: Owen, Robert C., 1951– author.
Title: Restraining air power : escalation management between peer air
 forces / Robert C. Owen [and four others]
Other titles: Escalation management between peer air forces
Description: Lexingtton, Kentucky : The University Press of Kentucky,
 [2022] | Includes bibliographical references and index.
Identifiers: LCCN 2022040043 | ISBN 9780813196015 (hardcover) | ISBN
 9780813196039 (pdf) | ISBN 9780813196022 (epub)
Subjects: LCSH: Air power—History—20th century—Case studies. | Air
 warfare—History—20th century—Case studies.
Classification: LCC UG625 .O94 2022 | DDC 358.400904—dc23/eng/20220823
LC record available at https://lccn.loc.gov/2022040043

This book is printed on acid-free paper meeting
the requirements of the American National Standard
for Permanence in Paper for Printed Library Materials.

Manufactured in the United States of America

Member of the Association
of University Presses

Contents

Foreword   vii

Introduction   1

1. The Principles of Escalation and Escalation Management   6
   Forrest E. Morgan
2. A Distant Mirror: Exercise Sagebrush 1955   36
   Robert C. Owen
3. The Yom Kippur War 1973   62
   Lazar Berman
4. The Angolan War 1975–1988   90
   Robert C. Owen
5. The South Atlantic War 1982   126
   Robert C. Owen and Steven Paget
6. India's Kargil War 1999: Conventional Air Operations under a Constant Nuclear Shadow   166
   Benjamin S. Lambeth
7. Escalation Management in Practice   209
   Forrest E. Morgan and Robert C. Owen

About the Authors   221
Index   225

Foreword

To the average citizen, the notion of escalation as it applies to military force employment is an esoteric and highly specialized subject that, starting in the latter half of the twentieth century, has related principally to nuclear weapons and to various strategies for the control of their potential use. The classic work in this regard is Herman Kahn's *On Escalation* first published in 1965. In that work, Kahn addressed forty-four successive rungs of a notional conflict escalation ladder. It was he who first introduced the term "escalation dominance," a concept positing that, if a side in a particular dispute holds a position of advantage over an adversary, that side commands a greater likelihood of achieving a successful outcome should deterrence fail and an actual armed conflict ensue. However, interest in this subject receded after the end of the Cold War. Yet today, there could be no subject more important to study and understand than the effective management of military force application, not only as it might relate to nuclear conflict, the least likely of situations, but more appropriately to conventional wars, including so-called gray-zone conflicts.

The experience of actual armed conflicts around the world in recent years has revealed not just an inability of either side to fine-tune the measured taking of steps up and down a theoretical conflict escalation ladder, but even uncertainty as to the practicality and likelihood of either side achieving clear escalation dominance during the course of an unfolding conflict. This work offers insights as to why this seems to be true through an examination of actual past experiences of escalation and attempted escalation management in conflicts involving peer air forces.

As today's information age continues to show ever more progress in the richness and ready availability of information, the rapid exchange of information regarding global events and how it is assimilated is heightening the potential for armed conflict. For example, the likelihood of the People's Republic of China conducting a hostile assault to seize physical control of Taiwan is apparently becoming greater every day. By the same token, Russia continues its provocative acts against Ukraine. North Korea likewise remains a wild card, and Iran continues its reckless but determined pursuit of nuclear weapons.

Operations in air, space, and cyberspace are also proliferating around the globe as modern technologies have now become readily available to anyone with access to the internet and a credit card. This greatly expanded ability to create effects in the third dimension is exemplified by the proliferation of cheap drones and by the explosion of their use by both state and non-state actors for achieving lethal outcomes. Information has always been a powerful force in driving people to action, but today more than ever before, information itself has become weaponized and able to attack physical resources and incite people to act. For example, hostile operations in cyberspace have now become a preferred means for creating strategic effects by actors seeking non-attribution. Accordingly, *Restraining Air Power: Escalation Management between Peer Air Forces* is a very timely work that provides insights on issues that are of concern to national security leadership.

In the chapters that follow, Editor Robert Owen and his able contributors taken together offer an informed and discerning exploration of the dynamics of actual past conflicts in which air forces of roughly equivalent capability have played a key role. Of special note is the general preference of this compendium's authors to speak in terms of "escalation management" rather than of "escalation control," on the premise that when it comes to real-world conflicts, the process of escalation never follows clear-cut steps up and down a well-defined "ladder" of the sort envisaged by Kahn and others. Instead, it is far more complex and rarely so systematic in its progression over time.

Starting out with a general review of the principles of escalation and escalation management, this compendium explores a number of selected real-world conflicts between peer states that allow for a practical testing of various theoretical propositions regarding the dynamics of escalation. In so doing, it provides insights that should be of value for future leaders in the planning and execution of contingency operations. In addressing a subject vitally important in illuminating the various considerations bearing on the likelihood of success in armed conflict, *Restraining Air Power* offers insights that every military professional involved in joint-force operations must understand. At the same time, it is written with a clarity of expression that renders it equally accessible to readers beyond the uniformed services with roles in national security. *Restraining Air Power* provides much of lasting value from its many informed observations and insights.

David A. Deptula, Lt Gen USAF (Ret.)
Dean, Mitchell Institute for Aerospace Studies

Introduction

This book juxtaposes theory and experience to ask whether or not escalation can be managed in conflicts between opponents possessing mutually dangerous air forces. In so doing, it addresses the question of whether opponents in several peer-on-peer conflicts were or were not able to conduct limited air warfare. Given the emerged possibility of major conflicts in Europe and the Pacific between powerful air forces on both sides, this question of manageability has great contemporary importance for civil and military leaders thinking about how to keep things from getting out of hand. While the scale of such wars would be vastly greater than those discussed here, the evidence in these case studies suggest that the elements of culture, politics, technology, geography, assessments of risk, and so on that influenced leaders in these smaller conflicts will also be in play in larger conflicts.

For perspective, "peer opponents" in this study means combatants possessing strong air forces that gave them realistic options of escalating conflicts between them in terms of pace, scale, or targeting. To make a conflict "limited," such opponents must have consciously restrained air operations in reflection of their strategic objectives, doctrinal guidelines, domestic and international political circumstances, uncertainties about the consequences of escalation, or other considerations. Put another way, both combatants have the capability to escalate in a militarily effective manner, but at least one chooses to hold back.

In terms of methodology, this study will correlate theoretical and empirical assessments of restrained air warfare. It will begin with a discussion of the theoretical principles of escalation and escalation management, with particular attention to conventional (non-nuclear) warfare. There will follow five case studies, including one of a relevant military exercise and four conflicts between countries possessing capable air forces. Thematically, these case studies will respond to three general questions: Why did or did not the political and military leaders of opposing air forces consciously seek to expand or restrain air operations? What were the causes of success or failure of their efforts? What were the consequences of those successes and failures? Finally, the study will revisit the theoretical argument in light of the answers to those questions.

Surprisingly, the number of wars between peer air forces capable of mutually significant escalations since the end of World War II is small. The great majority of military air operations conducted since 1945 have involved relatively small air forces on at least one side that did not have the force structure or doctrines to escalate operations, whether their leaders wanted to or not. The dozens of colonial wars and conflicts between militarily weak states fought in this era almost always involved profound imbalances in the air warfare capabilities of one or both sides. These imbalances rendered the question of escalation management and risk largely moot. In the case of great powers, the United States, the Soviet Union, and now Russia and China have postured for peer air wars among themselves, but have never actually taken the risk of picking direct fights with one another. The United States, for example, faced opponents such as Iraq (1991 and 2003), Serbia (1999), and Libya (2011), that possessed comparatively insubstantial or incompetent air warfare capabilities or, in the cases of Korea and Vietnam, that fielded small air forces of quality but had neither the intent nor the capabilities to escalate their operations beyond local air defense. A review of post–World War II Soviet/Russian experiences in places like Afghanistan, Chechnya, Georgia, and the Ukraine reveals that they too have not fought anything close to a peer air force since the end of World War II.

The air wars examined in this study constitute a substantial portion of the list of conflicts in which opposing nations fielded air forces of equivalent capabilities and options to escalate their strategic objectives and operations. Importantly, all of the conflicts examined—the Yom Kippur War (1973), the Angolan War (1976–1982), the South Atlantic War (1982), and the Kargil War (1999)—involved one opponent in possession of nuclear weapons. So, while all of these wars were fought with conventional tactical forces, the potential for escalation all the way up to the nuclear threshold was a background threat to all of the participants and to the world at large. Because humanitarian and grand strategic considerations held back the states involved in these conflicts from even threatening the use of nuclear weapons, this study also includes a discussion of Exercise Sagebrush (1955). Sagebrush stands as an example of what might have happened, had those considerations not restrained military commanders from employing nukes on an as-needed, almost wholesale basis. The strategic and operational contrasts between Sagebrush and the lesser conflicts examined here offer contemporary insights into the things that might restrain or constrain escalation from intense conventional operations to nuclear exchanges between great states in the future.

It is worth noting that this study enters a discourse stretching back well over a century. The contracting powers of the First Hague Convention (1899) opened the diplomatic discourse by prohibiting aerial bombardment for the next five years. In *The War in the Air* (1908), the novelist H. G. Wells provided a cautionary tale of escalation, revenge, and cultural dislocation consequent to unrestrained aerial warfare. Given the profound dangers of being second to strike, Wells visualized that now-or-never urgency, surprise, and totality would be keynote strategic premises of air war.[1] Air warfare theorists of the 1920s, including Giulio Douhet and William Mitchell, argued that the power and reach of air forces mandated offensive-mindedness and preemptive attacks as the only logical courses of action in air warfare, given the devastating consequences of enemy first strikes with weapons of mass effect, namely pattern bombing, gas, and chemicals. The assured penetration of nuclear-armed bombers and missiles and the frightful potentials of escalatory misjudgments inspired a new generation of researchers and theoreticians in the 1950s and 1960s to seek formulas for preventing out-of-control escalations that might carry Armageddon-scale consequences. More recently, beginning in the 1990s, the strategically decisive potentials of mass air strikes employing precision weapons, and the reemergence of great-power conflict centered again on the United States, China, and Russia in the 1990s prompted the present wave of interest in escalation management, particularly at the threshold between large-scale, *non*-nuclear strikes and decisions to employ nuclear weapons.

Given its history, the collaborators of this study believe it makes an important start at filling a void in the ongoing discourse of escalation and escalation management.[2] As Forrest Morgan reflects in the next chapter, most of the recent literature is based on theoretical modeling or, in the case of some American theorists at least, hope that their country's enemies will assess the motives and risks of escalation in the same way they do. Empirical case studies are present in this literature, but not ones that systematically examine the experiences of peer opponents who actually dealt with the challenge of prosecuting wars in the face of air forces capable of harming them, perhaps decisively. Not constrained by or perhaps even unaware of the neatly crafted theories of escalation management in the literature, these warring states dealt with the unpredictable realities of weapons, human foibles, strategic concerns, outside stakeholders, and the chances of geography, weather, and battle to restrain or escalate their air wars as they thought appropriate. Sometimes they succeeded, and sometimes they failed. The collaborators in this study believe that, in sum, the variable contexts of these successes and failures offer more refined theoretical visions of the possibilities and challenges of managing escalation in a powerful mode of warfare between opponents who believe they face choices between sacrificing major interests and risking escalated destruction of their economies, military forces, and governing authority.

The increasingly complex context of air warfare makes this a timely, as well as an important, study. The global proliferation of space, cyber, precision-guided, and artificially intelligent weaponry; distributed information technology; and the rise of trans-regional, non-state political and military powers have great implications for an understanding of "peer competitor" and "escalation." States or organizations that cannot confront larger air forces in the air and space may now compete with them as peers through cyber disruption, Special Forces or fifth-column operations, information attacks, and other strategies. These approaches to war have the potential to vitiate the advantages of strong air forces almost as surely as by shooting down their aircraft. These variegated opponents also present a wider array of escalation calculi than earlier air warfare theorists and practitioners were obliged to consider in their concepts. An expansion of target lists, for example, will mean different things to secular leaders concerned with preserving their national economies and holds on power or theocratic leaders bent on pleasing God. Their different perceptions of risk, reward, and obligation, in turn, will beget differing and often unpredictable reactions and exploitations of non-traditional and asymmetric modes of counter escalation. Put another way, we live in a world of unprecedented military complexity, and it is our hope that our writings as a team will update our understanding of air warfare in that context.

Notes

1. H. G. Wells, *The War in the Air* (London: George Bell and Sons, 1908), 105, 176–207, and 345–56.

2. After some wrangling, the authors decided to address this subject as one of "management" rather than "control." "Control" we feared would lend support to the hidebound

notion that escalations occur on something like a ladder, upon which opponents can control their steps and their results with a degree of precision and premeditation. The evidence in this study, we believe, speaks to a much more complex dynamic, involving many influences, that can leap out of control as a consequence of even minor, or what were perceived as minor, escalatory actions. So, we like "management" better, since the real art of making escalation work is to identify escalatory thresholds through the eyes of enemies and avoid taking actions that will make conflicts get bigger than we want them to be. The notion of taking proactive actions that will entrap enemies at lower levels of escalation, we believe the evidence suggests, has always lacked theoretical credibility and does not have support in the historical record.

1

The Principles of Escalation and Escalation Management

FORREST E. MORGAN

This chapter presents a theoretical foundation for understanding escalation and how escalation management operates in nuclear and conventional (non-nuclear) warfare. In doing so, it will lay a foundation for assessing the conflict studies that form the core of this report. To begin, escalation can be described as *the tendency of combatants to increase the force or breadth of their attacks to gain advantage or avoid defeat.*[1] This dynamic has characterized limited wars throughout history. Prussian military theorist Carl von Clausewitz had it in mind when he proposed that war, being a contest between interacting human beings would, in theory, culminate in each opponent's maximum exertion of strength.[2] Of course, Clausewitz went on to explain that factors present in the physical world, such as difficult terrain, the inability to employ all of one's forces instantly, the presence of uncertainty, and the limited value of some objectives, tend to constrain the pace of military operations and the magnitude of violence, keeping war from escalating to its theoretical extreme.[3]

Such insights indicate that not only is escalation naturally constrained in many respects; they suggest that the risks of unwanted escalation can be managed if military and political leaders understand the phenomenon and take the necessary steps to do so. Surprisingly, however, a body of theory on how to manage escalation did not emerge until the Cold War, when the nuclear capabilities of the superpowers threatened to make the costs of uncontrolled escalation in any military conflict between them horrific. This body of theory grew and matured for several decades but largely stagnated after the collapse of the Soviet Union, when the risk of nuclear war receded. To U.S.

leaders, it appeared that the West would have clear dominance in any future conflict at both conventional and nuclear levels, so escalation would not be a serious concern.

Yet even early in the post–Cold War era there were indications that dangerous escalation could still occur in limited conflicts, and escalation management should remain an important consideration in all military operations. Unexpected developments in the Middle East, Somalia, and the Balkans suggested that escalation could emerge along dimensions not previously considered and deliberately employed by adversaries not cowed by U.S. conventional and nuclear superiority. And as China began its ascent as a great power at the turn of the twenty-first century, U.S. Air Force leaders again became concerned about risks of escalation in any conflict with that state or other opponents. As a result, they commissioned a study by the RAND Corporation that resulted in a fuller understanding of the phenomenon and prompted the development of a new generation of escalation management theory.[4]

This chapter briefly examines the evolution of theory regarding escalation and escalation management. It reviews the history of thinking about this dangerous phenomenon and offers a new framework for understanding it—along with insights on how to manage it.

Escalation Theory during the Cold War

Escalation is not a new phenomenon, or even one particular to the modern age, but systematic thought about how to manage it did not crystallize until the Cold War. Serious thinking about escalation first emerged in terms of using the threat of it to deter the Soviet Union from invading Western Europe. Early in his first term in office, President Dwight D. Eisenhower worried that the NATO allies could not afford to generate enough conventional forces to offset the Soviet buildup in Eastern Europe. At the same time, however, he was unwilling to take the burden of Europe's conventional defense on U.S. shoulders. As a fiscal conservative, he was convinced that the United States' long-term security depended on limiting spending on Defense and other government programs, thereby freeing national resources for economic development.

Eisenhower met the challenge of providing for European security in an affordable manner by crafting a policy dubbed the "New Look," which relied on threatening the use of strategic nuclear weapons to deter conventional and nuclear threats from the Soviet Union and the Warsaw Pact. In January 1954, Secretary of State John Foster Dulles unveiled this new policy in a speech in which he said, "Local defenses must be reinforced by the further deterrent of massive retaliatory power," and in order to deter aggression, the free community would have to be "willing and able to respond vigorously at places and with means of its own choosing."[5] Although Dulles did not make the threat explicit, the implication was clear: the United States would answer any Soviet attack with nuclear *massive retaliation*.

While this policy seemed to provide a ready solution to a serious threat, it quickly came under fire from security analysts in academia. A threat of massive retaliation might be credible in response to a nuclear attack, but how could the United States make Moscow believe it would really respond to a conventional invasion with nuclear weapons, knowing that the Soviets also had nuclear weapons with which to answer such an escalation? More seriously, how could the United States make a threat of massive retaliation credible in response to minor provocations? These questions were raised in a series of scholarly books and articles published in the mid-1950s, which proposed that strategies incorporating measured reprisals would have to be developed and limited nuclear war contemplated to make deterrent threats credible.[6] Yet these arguments only raised more doubts. If the United States used limited nuclear strikes to blunt a Warsaw Pact invasion of Western Europe, why would Moscow not respond with its own limited nuclear strikes to return the advantage to its superior conventional forces? Would the United States then escalate its nuclear strikes and risk an even greater escalation from the Soviets? Where would it end? Given these considerations, would limited nuclear war even be possible? And would not even posturing nuclear forces in Western Europe in a crisis risk triggering a Soviet preemptive strike?[7]

Herman Kahn and Escalation Dominance

In the midst of the debate, Herman Kahn emerged as the outspoken proponent of nuclear warfighting; arguing that limited nuclear threats could be made credible, nuclear wars could be fought and won, and escalation could be controlled. Beginning in about 1960, Herman Kahn conducted a series of studies exploring strategic options available to the United States in nuclear war and their possible effects. Using systems analysis and mathematical and scientific tools to forecast the outcomes of extreme threat scenarios, he concluded that the United States would need a mixed strategy that would include enough first-strike capability to reduce casualties should war appear inevitable—a strategic approach that would be labeled "damage limitation" in later debates—and enough survivable retaliatory capability to impose unacceptable losses on the Soviet Union should Moscow contemplate conducting its own first strike.[8] Over the course of his work, he examined the strengths and risks of fourteen alternative strategies, ranging from the renunciation of war at one extreme to launching a preventive war at the other, in an exercise aimed at thinking about ways to avoid war, as well as how to "fight, survive, and terminate a war, should it occur."[9] Nevertheless, a host of critics remained unconvinced that escalation could be controlled in such extreme circumstances. In 1965 he met their challenges head on with the publication of a book entitled: *On Escalation: Metaphors and Scenarios*.[10]

In that work, Kahn proposed that U.S. leaders envision crisis and war in terms of a metaphorical *escalation ladder* with each *rung* representing a different level of intensity in the confrontation or conflict. The lowest escalatory rung of Kahn's ladder represented the onset of a crisis, with higher rungs corresponding in turn to shows of force, limited conventional conflict, full-blown conventional war, limited nuclear warfare, and, at the top of the ladder, an all-out strategic nuclear exchange. Kahn acknowledged that in an actual conflict the ladder might include many more levels of escalation. In fact, the notional ladder around which he organized his book was composed of no fewer than forty-four rungs, more than half of which involved at least some use of nuclear weapons.[11]

With this metaphorical ladder in mind, Kahn maintained that the United States could *control* escalation, thereby keeping wars limited, by achieving what he called *escalation dominance*. As he conceived it, escalation dominance described "a capacity, other things being equal, to enable the side possessing it to enjoy marked advantages in a given region of the escalation ladder."[12] It would involve posturing and employing forces to give one the ability to escalate a conflict in ways that would be disadvantageous or costly to the enemy, while the enemy could not do the same in return, either because it would have no escalation options or because those available to it would not improve its situation. Once enemy leaders have realized one has achieved escalation dominance, they should be deterred from taking the conflict to a higher rung where they would suffer greater costs with no comparable advantage. Moreover, later analysts have maintained that once escalation dominance is achieved, the threat of further escalation should become a particularly powerful coercive lever for bringing the enemy to favorable terms.[13]

The escalation ladder metaphor is a powerful one, being easy to visualize, and concepts of escalation control and escalation dominance are attractive to military leaders and planners. As a result, these terms have become common parlance in strategic discourse, and the concepts have been embraced in military doctrines in the United States and elsewhere. However, prospects of achieving escalation control face considerable obstacles in the real world, and strategies aimed at establishing escalation dominance entail serious risks. Given the significance of these challenges, we shall examine them in some detail.

Problems with Kahn's Conception of Escalation Control and Dominance

While Kahn's concept of escalation control is perfectly rational in an abstract sense, it suffers from several serious defects when one attempts to apply it in real-world strategy making. First, the escalation ladder metaphor bears only a passing resemblance to the dynamics of actual conflict. It suggests that escalation occurs in discrete steps, observable to both sides and that the belligerents share a common perception of where each of them is standing on the ladder at any given time. Just as seriously, it assumes they have sufficient control of their forces to move up or down the ladder at will. Anyone who has studied crisis and war in depth knows that such assumptions are unrealistic. Wars such as those in Korea and Vietnam illustrate how difficult it can be for adversaries to understand at what levels of conflict their opponents are attempting to fight and whether lulls or flare-ups in intensity are deliberate or circumstantial.[14]

In fact, confrontations between dangerous states are fraught with uncertainty, misperception, and miscalculation.[15] Clausewitz recognized the inherent uncertainty in war and devoted considerable attention it, discussing how incomplete, misleading, and contradictory intelligence leads to confusion and contributes to friction.[16] Indeed, the "fog and friction of war" is now spoken of so commonly that the phrase has become almost cliché. In truth, war is a very uncertain affair in which only limited knowledge even of one's own forces is available at any given time. Battle management is always a challenge. In the heat of combat one's forces frequently do not do what is expected of them, either because communications have broken down, plans have disintegrated in the face of enemy resistance, or subordinate commanders have seized upon unexpected opportunities (or have simply chosen not to do what was planned).[17] With so much uncertainty regarding what one's own forces are doing, how much more difficult would it be to accurately determine at what "rung" an opponent is attempting to scale its efforts, especially once some number of nuclear detonations have occurred? Even Kahn admitted that the escalation ladder metaphor was far from perfect. He devoted an entire chapter to "Defects in the Escalation Ladder Metaphor" in which he discussed such issues as discontinuities in the importance of rungs and the spacing between them; the fact that Soviet leaders would not likely envision the same ladder or put the same importance on certain rungs as U.S. leaders; and that the concept might put undue faith in each side's rationality, clarity of understanding, and ability to communicate, particularly in conflicts at higher rungs.[18]

Second, the ladder metaphor suggests that escalation occurs along but a single dimension, vertical—i.e., increases in the *intensity* of conflict—and that it takes a conscious effort to step up to each new rung. In fact, escalation can occur along multiple dimensions, as wars in the Balkans have demonstrated, and opponents often escalate over the course of a conflict without meaning to and sometimes without even realizing they have done so.[19] During the Vietnam War, when U.S. and South Vietnamese forces attempted to eliminate communist sanctuaries in Cambodia and Laos, they drove their adversaries ever deeper into those countries, escalating the conflict horizontally in a way that ultimately contributed to the destabilization of the governments there. Meanwhile, communist leaders used those sanctuaries and employed other tactics to deliberately prolong the struggle in recognition that the asymmetry in stakes—defeating the insurgency was not nearly as important to the United States as expelling the Western powers and reunifying Vietnam under Hanoi's governance was to North Vietnamese and National Liberation Front leaders—gave them an advantage in motivation that would prove decisive over time.[20] As Fred Iklé points out, the escalation ladder metaphor fails to address this important consideration, the ability to escalate in the temporal dimension. Ultimately, contrary to what the escalation ladder metaphor implies, it often takes a greater effort to de-escalate a conflict than to escalate one, and the damage caused by escalation often cannot be undone.

Finally, true escalation dominance is rarely attainable in any challenging confrontation. It clearly was not achievable in any meaningful way during the Cold War, although both sides attempted to build arsenals at various stages of the competition that they hoped would give them that advantage in the event of war. Granted, the United States quickly achieved escalation dominance in its interventions in Granada (1983) and Panama (1989), and in fairly short order in its wars against Iraq and Serbia.[21] However, escalation control had little relevance in those conflicts, given the inability of the opponents to do much harm to U.S. or coalition forces, much less the U.S. homeland. In a war between the United States and a near-peer opponent, such as China or Russia, escalation dominance would likely be a fleeting goal, considering the many dimensions of conflict and options for inflicting costs that would be available to them.

Even given the dramatic asymmetries of power between the United States and lesser states in the post–Cold War world, such as Iran or North Korea, most enemies will have some ability to escalate. Though the options may not be very attractive once the potential costs are taken into account, an adversary who finds its back against a wall often becomes remarkably inventive in discovering new ways to prolong the contest and inflict costs on the opponent in hopes of eroding its will over time. Therefore, while escalation dominance is always desirable, it is more useful to treat it as a philosophical aspiration than as a concrete policy objective.

Thomas Schelling and Brinkmanship

As debates continued in the mid-1960s regarding the viability of Kahn's approach to escalation control, the economist Thomas C. Schelling offered another school of strategy—*brinkmanship*—based on game theory.[22] Drawing from that field of research, Schelling proposed that crises and conflicts between nuclear-armed adversaries were actually contests of coercive diplomacy in which tacit bargaining was a central feature. Because neither opponent could achieve victory at an affordable cost should the contest turn into a nuclear conflagration, both shared a common interest in keeping the confrontation below the nuclear threshold. That shared interest provided a space in which they could engage in coercive bargaining: each using threats and limited applications of force to pursue its objectives at the other's expense.[23]

Unlike Kahn, who made insufficient allowance for the possibilities of misperception and lack of control, Schelling made uncertainty a virtue. He argued that since nuclear-armed opponents shared the risk of escalation, leaders could manipulate that risk to their advantages by demonstrating willingness to escalate conflicts in a way that might get out of control if adversaries did not comply with coercive demands. The opponent most committed to taking the confrontation to the brink of nuclear war by binding himself to irreversible action and using "the threat that leaves something to chance" would win this contest of brinkmanship—or as Schelling sometimes described it, "game of 'chicken' "—by forcing the adversary to back down to avoid catastrophe.[24]

The preeminent example of brinkmanship can be seen in the 1962 Cuban missile crisis. In that episode, President John Kennedy and Premier Nikita Khrushchev postured nuclear and conventional forces and exchanged several letters, each warning the other that a confrontation between those forces might result in events getting beyond their control. When, after several tense days, U.S. Attorney General Robert Kennedy met privately with Soviet Ambassador Anatoly Dobrynin and warned him that the President might not be able to hold back a U.S. attack on Cuba if the crisis did not end very soon, Khrushchev lost his nerve and backed away from the brink.[25] The Cuban missile crisis is frequently extolled as an example of successful crisis management due to President Kennedy's skilled use of brinkmanship, and rightfully so. Yet there are several reasons why brinkmanship was not used in subsequent crises and will probably be avoided in future conflicts.

THE PROBLEMS WITH BRINKMANSHIP

While Schelling's approach was more realistic than Kahn's in that it acknowledged the uncertainties present in confrontations between states, brinkmanship shares some of escalation dominance's defects and also exhibits other shortcomings. Like Kahn, Schelling envisioned the dynamics of escalation mostly in one-dimensional terms and occurring in a contest between two opponents relatively symmetrical in capability. Neither theorist should be condemned for such assumptions. Bipolarity was the prevailing condition of the Cold War era in which they worked, and the specter of nuclear war made other escalation risks so pale in comparison that it is not surprising that they were overlooked. Nonetheless, such shortcomings limit these concepts' utility in a world in which multiple potential adversaries, widely disparate in power, are emerging. But brinkmanship is limited even as a means of managing vertical escalation against a single opponent. Envisioned principally in terms of managing confrontations approaching the nuclear threshold, it provides little guidance for managing escalation in conflicts well below that threshold or those that have moved above it. In essence, to employ brinkmanship as a means of escalation management, one would have to deliberately take the confrontation or conflict to the brink of nuclear war.

Probably due to this last limitation, the United States and the Soviet Union tended to avoid brinkmanship as an approach for escalation management and crisis management after the Cuban missile crisis. Although shades of it can be seen in the 1973 Yom Kippur War, with the United States raising nuclear alert levels in response to Soviet nuclear threats in the face of Egypt's imminent defeat, the dangers encountered in the Cuban missile crisis had so frightened U.S. and Soviet leaders that they were no longer inclined to go very far in such high-stakes games of chicken. Military leaders on both sides continued planning for conventional and nuclear war throughout the remainder of the Cold War, but political leaders had little interest in engaging in direct confrontations, much less issuing threats that might leave something to chance. Instead, the predominant means of escalation management employed by both sides during the remainder of the Cold War became the avoidance of direct superpower conflict. The United States and Soviet Union fought a number of proxy wars between 1965 and 1990—in Southeast Asia, Southwest Asia, Africa, and Latin America—but both were careful to avoid situations in which their own military forces might be pitted directly against each other.

Rising Concerns about Inadvertent Escalation

By the closing decade of the Cold War, Washington and Moscow had become relatively confident that they could avoid escalatory confrontations by prohibiting direct contact between U.S. and Soviet forces. Moreover, a growing number of U.S. analysts had become convinced that, should the United States and Soviet Union find themselves at war, both sides would understand conventional warfare and the risks of escalation well enough to control them.[26] However, not all analysts were so sanguine. National security scholar Barry Posen, having considered U.S. Navy arguments that, in the event of war, it should be allowed to conduct conventional air and missile attacks on Soviet forces in the Barents Seas and Kola Peninsula, worried that such strikes might be perceived as threats to the Soviet Union's ballistic missile submarine force based at Murmansk. Moscow might interpret the attacks as an attempt to destroy that element of its nuclear deterrence force, creating "use-or-lose" anxieties that could result in inadvertent escalation.[27]

While security analysts in the Reagan administration largely dismissed such concerns, discussions with former Soviet officials after the Cold War revealed that this was a very real danger. In 1983, with tensions rising amidst a sharp increase in U.S. Defense spending and President Reagan's rhetorical campaign against the Soviet "evil empire," some Soviet intelligence officials believed that NATO command-post exercise Able Archer 83 was a ruse to cover military deployments for a surprise attack on the Soviet Union. They lobbied their superiors for a preemptive, damage-limitation strike on U.S. forces, but fortunately, cooler heads prevailed.[28]

One might suggest that an important lesson lies in this history. As conflict avoidance constitutes the safest, most reliable means of escalation management, and as there is an ever-present risk of inadvertent escalation between dangerous, distrustful rivals, Western leaders ought to embrace conflict avoidance as the strategy of choice for the current age. But that would be a mistake. Conflict avoidance worked for the superpowers in the stability of a bipolar world, one in which Moscow and Washington had other actors available to posture against each other as pawns in a larger chess game, and even then, it did not fully eliminate the risk of war. Even had it done so, those conditions do not describe today's world. With the breakup of the Soviet Union, the dissolution of the Warsaw Pact, and a substantial loss of influence in the developing world, the Russian Federation has no more pawns to move and is now struggling to find its own place in the international order. Recent efforts to regain some measure of its former power have challenged Western interests in Russia's "near abroad," and Moscow may assert itself more aggressively there in the future. Meanwhile, China is emerging as a great power and becoming more assertive in its claims over territories in the East China Sea, South China Sea, and, of course, Taiwan.

To employ conflict avoidance as a means of escalation management would mean abandoning U.S. and allied interests in the face of those challenges. That might be an acceptable solution in cases in which U.S. stakes are small. It probably would not be, however, were Russia or China to threaten the independence or safety of states to which the United States has made security commitments. Then U.S. leaders would need to find a new approach to escalation management.

Escalation Theory in the Twenty-First Century

By 2004, strategic planners at U.S. Air Force Headquarters, cognizant of threats represented in emerging Chinese military developments, had become concerned that they did not adequately understand escalation risks in the contemporary security environment. An increasing number of war games conducted by the various military staffs in the Pentagon since the late 1990s had ended in uncontrolled escalation: games in which the scenarios called for only limited U.S. military intervention against notional adversaries that were clearly outmatched by U.S. forces. How could such operations get out of control, given conditions in which the United States should have had clear escalation dominance? At first, game analysts assumed the outcomes were spurious, the result of overly aggressive "red teams," or perhaps the advanced systems being postulated in some of the futuristic scenarios were somehow escalatory by nature. But the increasing frequency with which the games turned escalatory and the wide range of participants and scenarios involved suggested something else was at work, something that Air Force planners did not understand.

Consequently, the Air Force tasked the RAND Corporation to examine the twenty-first century security environment for possible escalation risks and offer recommendations on how it could best manage any that might be found. In the study that followed, RAND determined not only that significant escalation risks did indeed exist, but that escalation management concepts developed during the Cold War would probably be inadequate for managing those risks. The study observed that, whereas Cold War escalation management approaches focused solely on managing confrontations between nuclear superpowers, new methods would be needed to manage risks in a security environment that had become much more complicated, with potential adversaries falling into three relatively distinct but interrelated categories: large nuclear powers, such as China and Russia; new and emerging regional nuclear powers, such as India, Pakistan, North Korea, and Iran; and transnational networks of insurgents, terrorists, and criminals.[29] The study then proceeded to examine the escalation dynamics that might arise in conflicts between the United States and opponents in each of those categories and offer recommendations on how to manage the risks that such conflicts would present.[30]

More importantly, since escalation in war begins at levels below nuclear crisis, even when the principal belligerents are both nuclear-armed states, the study focused on understanding the mechanisms and dynamics of escalation in conventional warfare and how to manage those phenomena. This perspective led the RAND team to examine the nature of escalation thresholds and identify how three mechanisms, working independently or in combination, can drive conflict over those thresholds. It then proposed approaches for managing the mechanisms of escalation in ways that would enable combatants to attain military and political objectives in war while keeping the conflict at an acceptable level of violence. The study observed, however, that no matter how skillful political and military leaders may be in managing escalation mechanisms, they will be working at a distinct disadvantage if their state's stakes in the issue in question are notably less than those of the opponent. Therefore, it admonished those involved in escalation management planning—indeed, *all* strategic planning for war—to begin with an objective assessment of the balance of interests between opponents. Leaders should then tailor their objectives and modulate their efforts accordingly. What follows is a synopsis of the findings of the work done at RAND in the aforementioned study and subsequent efforts. It begins with a closer look at the nature of escalation.

A More Precise Definition of Escalation

A first step in developing a deeper understanding of escalation is to define it a way that is more precise and analytically useful. In that regard, escalation can be defined as "*an increase in the intensity or scope of conflict that crosses threshold(s) considered significant by one or more of the participants.*"[31] Contrary to what the narrow Cold War conceptions suggest, conflicts can intensify or expand in many ways. Some prominent examples include attacking types of targets previously considered to be off limits, opening new theaters of operations against an enemy, or employing weapons not previously used in the conflict. Further, when one examines historical cases, other less frequently considered forms of escalation emerge, such as the expansion of military objectives, the enlargement of political demands, and even increases in the vehemence of political rhetoric.[32] Yet not every rise in threat or increase in the intensity or breadth of conflict is escalatory. Escalation only occurs when at least one of the belligerents believes that the new development has introduced a qualitative change in the crisis or conflict and behaves accordingly.

Escalation usually manifests as an interactive process between two or more opponents, each increasing its threats or use of force in response to the actions of others. But it can be unilateral as well, with one belligerent escalating to gain advantage or increase its pressure on another, independent of that actor's behavior. In such cases, the enemy might not respond because it does not have a comparable avenue of escalation, as, for example, when the United States began firebombing Japanese cities in 1945. Alternatively, an opponent might consciously choose not to answer a provocation, as was the case when Iraq began firing SCUD missiles at Israel in efforts to bring that country into the first Gulf War, or it may choose to escalate in a different way. But generally, when one actor in a conflict violates an escalatory threshold, it is reasonable to expect its enemies to follow suit. A threshold breached tends to lose its saliency. Yet even this is not always the case, particularly in conflicts between adversaries who are markedly dissimilar in capability. For several years during the Vietnam War communist forces violated the neutrality of Cambodia and Laos to move supplies, train and reconstitute forces, and launch operations into South Vietnam before U.S. and South Vietnamese forces launched major operations into those states. Yet the international community and even the U.S. public viewed the latter actions, when they finally did occur, as a significant escalation.

Escalation in armed conflict is a very diverse phenomenon. It can occur quickly or slowly. A belligerent can escalate in dramatic moves that are visible to almost any observer or in incremental steps so small that they are unrecognized as constituting significant escalation until after the fact, even by the one doing the escalation. Given this diversity, to recognize escalation and understand it more fully, we must examine the nature of thresholds more closely.

The Nature of Escalation Thresholds

An escalation threshold is an identifiable point in the intensity or scope of events which when crossed is recognized by at least one of the belligerents as constituting a significant change in the nature of the conflict. Thresholds are socially constructed elements existing purely in the minds of the parties involved, so they come in many forms. Some escalation thresholds are symmetrical in that all parties to a conflict recognize them and tend to view them similarly. Examples might include being the first to initiate hostilities in a crisis or employ nuclear weapons in a war. But sometimes thresholds that are important to one actor may seem trivial or even be invisible to another. This subjectivity is one of the reasons why escalation can be difficult to recognize, control, manage, and exploit.[33]

The subjective nature of thresholds creates serious risks of misperception and miscalculation. If one party knows that another considers a particular threshold to be important, that threshold is likely to be significant in its own eyes as well. But the adversary's perspective is not always well known or understood, nor is it always clear whether the enemy knows where one's own thresholds lie or what importance one places on those thresholds. In general, the thresholds that will be the easiest to anticipate are those that are geographically prominent—such as a river recognized as the boundary of one's territory—or those involving strongly held international norms, such as the taboos against the use of nuclear, chemical, and biological weapons. National policies firmly established before a crisis or conflict arises can also offer signposts regarding what actions an opponent might consider escalatory in war. Escalation thresholds might be relevant to a wide range of adversaries and in a broad set of circumstances, such as the use of nuclear weapons, or they might be particular to specific cases, such as the nineteenth century agreement between the European great powers guaranteeing Belgium's independence and neutrality. Thresholds thought firm in peacetime may be viewed differently when their violation actually occurs. An international ban on unrestricted submarine warfare, widely supported in the interwar years, quickly dissolved after the outbreak of World War II. Yet assuming that thresholds have grown weak with age can be dangerous, as German leaders discovered when they violated Belgian neutrality in 1914, thinking Britain would surely not go to war over a mere "scrap of paper."[34]

Given the subjective nature of thresholds, states sometimes attempt to manipulate them to their own advantage, either to strengthen or create new thresholds to better deter an enemy from undertaking an undesired action, or to reduce the significance of established thresholds to make crossing them less risky. Achieving the former objective may involve employing exaggerated rhetoric to demonize the use of certain weapons, or more concerted political approaches such as formally outlawing them.[35] Strengthening a threshold in peacetime is challenging in that it requires building an international consensus on an issue that would likely advantage some states at the expense of others, but persuading members of the international community that a threshold is less important than they previously believed is even more difficult. States hold thresholds to be important because their violation puts them at greater risk.

Thresholds that emerge during a conflict are the most difficult to anticipate, as they typically arise in response to events the possibility of which are unforeseen before they occur, or capabilities the threatening nature of which are unappreciated before they are employed. Post–Cold War conflicts have revealed that the vast conventional superiority that Western forces now enjoy increases chances that opponents facing those capabilities will perceive some actions escalatory that Western military leaders consider routine. For example, early in NATO's 1995 air campaign against the Bosnian Serb Army, an insufficient number of Allied strike aircraft were available to service targets across all of Bosnia, so Allied planners confined their efforts to the country's southeast zone of operations (ZOA). When additional aircraft arrived in theater, the Allies wanted to engage a greater number of targets, but Serbian air defenses in the northwest ZOA were particularly dense, so planners decided to employ F-117A stealth fighters and U.S. Navy Tomahawk Land-Attack Missiles (TLAMs) to "soften them up" before sending in non-stealthy strike aircraft. That decision was based purely on these weapons' availability and operational utility, yet Serbian leaders interpreted their use as a major escalation in NATO's prosecution of the war.[36]

The Mechanisms and Motives of Escalation

While attention to thresholds is an important prerequisite for managing escalation, that alone is not enough. Leaders must also understand the mechanisms through which escalation manifests and why parties to a conflict sometimes choose to intensify or broaden the scope of their attacks, even while hoping to keep the conflict limited. Escalation in confrontation and war occurs through three mechanisms: *deliberate*, *inadvertent*, and *accidental*. While these mechanisms are theoretically distinct, escalation in an actual conflict can result from the interaction of more than one of them at once, and escalation of one type can sometimes trigger escalation through one or both of the other mechanisms as well.

Deliberate Escalation

Deliberate escalation occurs when a party to a confrontation or conflict intentionally undertakes some action that it knows will cross one or more of an opponent's escalation thresholds. There might be any number of proximate motives for taking such action, but they can all be generally described as either *instrumental* or *suggestive* in nature or some combination of both. In instrumentally motivated escalation an actor believes that increasing the intensity or scope of the fight will work to its advantage by raising its prospects of success. A belligerent might throw in an extra division to turn the tide in a land battle,[37] broaden the list of bombing targets to overwhelm an enemy's capacity to resist, or launch an attack in a region previously unthreatened to cut off the enemy's access to important resources or force it to divide its forces. Escalation of this type often prompts the opponent to try to match or surpass the increase in effort, or escalate in some other dimension, to counter the advantage accrued to the escalator. Alternatively, in suggestively motivated escalation a belligerent deliberately increases the intensity or scope of conflict in efforts to signal an opponent that it ought to change its behavior in some way. This form of deliberate escalation is akin to the kind of coercive bargaining that Schelling described, in which an actor punishes its opponent, not primarily for the direct military benefit that might result from such action, but to suggest that more punishment will come if the opponent does not comply with coercive demands.[38]

Operation Rolling Thunder, the U.S. bombing campaign against North Vietnam between 1965 and 1968, is probably the most frequently mentioned example of this kind of coercive escalation. Critics often cite the failure of Rolling Thunder as condemnation of strategies that use "graduated escalation" for purposes of signaling or otherwise restraining the employment of air power.[39] Their arguments have merit to the extent that Rolling Thunder was indeed overly restrained, at least in the early phases. However, it is important to understand that using deliberate escalation for coercive signaling does not imply that attacks need to be gradual or excessively restrained. The systematic firebombing of Japanese cities in 1945 was an example of deliberate escalation for suggestive motives. It signaled Japanese leaders that until they complied with Allied demands for unconditional surrender, they could expect such horrendous costs to mount, day after day. The atomic bombings of Hiroshima and Nagasaki constituted another deliberate and dramatic escalation to reinforce that signal.[40]

Avoiding deliberate escalation is partly a matter of self-restraint. Leaders should resist the temptation to escalate a conflict in ways that might offer temporary tactical advantages at risk of suffering serious long-term strategic costs.

But self-restraint in war can be exceedingly difficult. The more restrained one is, the more difficult it is to achieve one's military objectives. Efforts to exercise restraint often pit military leaders, who tend to argue for more operational freedom, against their political superiors, who worry that granting such freedom might result in a more intense and costly conflict or bring other belligerents into the war. In the 1962 Cuban missile crisis, for instance, U.S. military leaders lobbied for an invasion of Cuba or, at least, air strikes against the Soviet offensive missiles being installed there, but President Kennedy wisely resisted those pressures.[41] Similarly, the U.S. experience in the Korean War, when General Douglas MacArthur's 1950 penetration into North Korea prompted Chinese intervention and a costly three-year war of attrition, made President Lyndon Johnson resistant to U.S. military pleas for permission to launch a more intense bombing campaign against North Vietnam in 1965.[42]

But containing deliberate escalation requires more than just self-restraint. As war is a struggle between two or more adversaries, one must also deter other actors from escalating the conflict by convincing them that doing so would not work to their advantage. Deterrence involves threatening to punish the opponent for some prospective escalation, posturing and employing forces in a way that convinces it that the escalation would not be successful, or some combination of both approaches. The objective is to influence the opponent's decision calculus, leading enemy leaders to conclude that the costs of escalation would ultimately outweigh whatever benefit they might hope to gain from it. Deterring deliberate escalation often involves threats of counter-escalation. In some relatively easy cases, simply threatening to match the escalation symmetrically might be enough to deter it. The presence of a powerful bomber force might be enough to deter an adversary from embarking on a campaign of city bombing. Similarly, the vulnerability of an enemy's heretofore-unmolested province might be enough to deter it from escalating a conflict into a region in one's own country not yet affected by the war. In more challenging cases, however, greater or different threats might be required to offset the advantages the enemy expects to gain by escalating. France's nuclear doctrine during the Cold War, "deterrence of the strong by the weak," offers an example of such an asymmetry in its reliance on the imbalance of interests favoring the defender to deter the aggressive designs of more powerful potential adversaries.

Whether instrumental or suggestive, deliberate escalation is the mechanism most naturally associated with the metaphor of climbing a ladder.

Therefore, it is what military and political decision makers tend to envision when they think of escalation, leading them to assume they can control it. Unfortunately, escalation often gets out of control despite the best efforts of leaders on all sides to contain it. This is because not all escalation is deliberate in nature. Sometimes it occurs inadvertently or due to accident.

INADVERTENT ESCALATION

Inadvertent escalation occurs when one belligerent deliberately undertakes an action that it does not consider escalatory, but the action is perceived as such by an opponent. In other words, the action crosses a threshold that is important to the adversary, but that appears insignificant or is unknown to the escalator. Incidents of inadvertent escalation typically result from not anticipating how an opponent will view certain actions, either due to a lack of intelligence or simply not considering how the opponent's view of the conflict, and particularly its vulnerabilities, will likely affect its perception of thresholds. It can also result from an inability to anticipate the reactions of third parties or other second- or third-order consequences.[43]

Numerous cases of inadvertent escalation can be found in past wars. Several, such as Germany's 1914 violation of Belgian neutrality, MacArthur's 1950 drive into North Korea, and the U.S. expansion of the Vietnam War into Cambodia and Laos have already been mentioned. Among the many insights these cases offer is that inadvertent escalation cannot be directly deterred because it occurs as a result of decision makers not understanding the degree to which the actions they are embarking upon are escalatory. Therefore, a straightforward approach to reducing the risk of inadvertent escalation would be to, first, inform adversaries of where one's important escalation thresholds lie then issue threats or take other actions to deter them from violating those thresholds. Yet this too is easier said than done. Inadvertent escalation often occurs because neither side has fully considered where even its own escalation thresholds lie until one of them is crossed. In other cases it occurs because one side considers a threshold to be so obvious that it need not warn the other side of its existence.[44] Complicating matters, thresholds often change over the course of a conflict, and belligerents may resist revealing where their critical thresholds lie, because to do so would acknowledge certain political or military vulnerabilities. A threshold illuminated provides a focal point for deterrence, but it also exposes a weakness that enemies might choose to exploit. A deliberate effort to keep one's critical thresholds vague is illustrated in France's nuclear doctrine, which declares that states that threaten its vital interests are at risk of nuclear retaliation without specifying what those vital interests are or even whether they would have to be overtly attacked before France would strike.[45]

Given these challenges, managing risks of inadvertent escalation requires a balanced strategy incorporating several features. The first step is to make a considerable effort in advance to identify potential paths of escalation. This requires not only collecting and analyzing intelligence about each adversary's capabilities, vulnerabilities, and potential attitudes and behaviors, but also those of important third parties and an assessment of one's own thresholds as well. Next, analysts must sensitize planners and decision makers to the risks of inadvertent escalation, both generally and in terms of specific escalation thresholds relevant to the contingency at hand, so they can consider those elements in their planning. Finally, strategic plans need to incorporate features designed to avoid critical escalation thresholds of other actors and steer enemy actions away from one's own thresholds, either by announcing their existence and issuing threats to deter their violation or by visibly posturing forces in ways that deter enemy exploitation by denying benefits of that behavior.

Accidental Escalation

Perhaps the most difficult form of escalation to manage directly is that which occurs totally by accident. Like inadvertent escalation, accidental escalation is unanticipated, but instead of being an unexpected result of deliberate action, it is the consequence of events that were not intended in the first place. Such events might be the results of pure accident, such as sinking a ship belonging to a neutral state due to misidentification, or bombing the wrong target due to a navigation error or outdated map. But accidental escalation can also result from military forces acting in ways not authorized or intended by national leaders, either because the combatants do not understand their leaders' intent or because they do, but disregard it and act on their own.

Twentieth century wars offer numerous examples of accidental escalation. Those of the first type—that is, escalation resulting from *pure* accident—are often exemplified by the escalation in strategic bombing that occurred early in World War II after the Luftwaffe accidentally bombed London on

August 24, 1940. According to some historians, Britain's retaliation against Berlin the following night enraged Adolf Hitler, contributing to his decision to launch the Blitz, the bombing campaign against London and other British cities that lasted into 1941.[46] An often cited example of accidental escalation resulting from a combatant commander deliberately exceeding his superior's intent occurred late in the Vietnam War, when U.S. 7th Air Force commander General John D. Lavelle authorized aircrews to engage surface-to-air missile (SAM) sites in North Vietnam before those sites fired on U.S. aircraft, a violation of the standing rules of engagement (ROE), and told aircrews to report that the SAMs had fired first.[47]

Since accidental escalation, like inadvertent escalation, is not intentional, one can do little to deter the enemy from doing it. The best leaders can hope to do is recognize that isolated incidents of enemy provocation might not be deliberate and modulate their responses to those events accordingly. That does not mean that they should ignore all provocations believed to be accidental. Failing to respond firmly to undue aggression, even when that aggression was not done deliberately, might signal a lack of resolve that emboldens even greater escalation. But military and political leaders do need to evaluate each incident in context and respond to it in a judicious manner.[48]

Regarding one's own forces, military leaders need to identify those factors that might raise risks of accidental escalation in any confrontation or war and manage them. Approaches for managing these risks depend on the nature of possible accidents. Those emanating from potential mechanical failures can be reduced by designing systems in ways that allow for high degrees of reliability and by creating procedures and ROE that minimize such risks. Risks of accident arising from human error or carelessness can be minimized by training, exercise, and closer leadership attention. Risks of escalation resulting from subordinates misunderstanding commanders' intent or deliberately defying the limitations placed upon them can only be reduced by developing reasonable and coherent ROE and communicating and enforcing them more effectively. In sum, minimizing the risk of accidental escalation requires effective leadership in all phases of a military operation and at all levels in the chain of command.

Even when strong leadership and discipline are applied, however, such risks can never be completely eliminated. After all, some accidents will always happen. When they do, allied leaders will have to promptly assess their potential impacts and take whatever actions are needed to mitigate their escalatory effects. Such actions might include informing the adversary that the act was unauthorized and will not be repeated. Some accidents might also require issuing threats or posturing forces in efforts to deter the adversary from escalating in response to them. But in some cases, leaders will simply have to accept the fact that the adversary will likely escalate in response to the accident, endeavor to establish a new upper-escalation threshold, and resolve to fight on to victory, albeit at higher costs. As Clausewitz argued, friction in war is an inescapable reality. Only practice, experience, and the unrelenting will of a competent commander can overcome it.[49]

Escalation Management and the Balance of Interests

No matter how skillful a nation's military and political leaders are in employing force in a measured, judicious manner, they will find it difficult to obtain their objectives at affordable costs if their interests in the dispute are substantially less than those of the opponent's. Wars result from conflicts of interest, however defined. And as Clausewitz stated, "The political object—the original motive for the war—will thus determine both the military objective to be obtained and the amount of effort it requires."[50] As the value of the political object also determines the level of motivation to pursue that object and the resolve to carry on in the face of resistance, the relative stakes in the conflict—that is, the balance of interests between the adversaries—also influences each side's perception of escalation thresholds and their tolerances for costs and risks.[51]

Unfortunately, some of the wars in which the United States has engaged since World War II have demonstrated that U.S. leaders tend to overestimate their interests, vis-à-vis those of the adversary, early in the conflict, even while underestimating the levels of effort that will be required to obtain those interests. Vietnam offers the archetypal example. In that conflict U.S. leaders initially believed that stopping the spread of communism there would be crucial to the success of the policy of *containment*, which was considered a core U.S. national security interest. Conversely, they assumed that North Vietnam's interests in the dispute derived simply from an ideologically motivated ambition for conquest—and the interests of the National Liberation Front were dismissed as being subservient to Hanoi's—failing to grasp that both actors, though communist, were primarily motivated by nationalist aspirations and anti-colonial resentment. As a result, although military superiority enabled the United States to escalate the conflict in ways that inflicted enormous costs on its opponents, as the war ground on, the U.S. public grew disillusioned regarding U.S. interests there and increasingly intolerant of the costs the nation was paying. Ultimately, the communists enjoyed an asymmetry of interests that translated into an asymmetry of motivation, making them much more persistent and cost tolerant than U.S. citizens or their government.[52]

Similar dynamics can be seen in some of the stability operations in which the United States has engaged, such as those in Beirut, Lebanon (1982–1984), and Mogadishu, Somalia (1992–1994). In these episodes, the United States and UN forces intervened for a variety of motives, ranging from humanitarian concerns to desires to eliminate or contain sources of instability before they further jeopardized regional economic and security interests. Yet, in both of these efforts, local actors' interests were much greater than those of the intervening powers, and they achieved escalation dominance by demonstrating their willingness and ability to inflict casualties on stability forces at levels that exceeded the cost tolerances of Western governments and publics at home.[53]

Considering these examples, one might conclude that the United States will be at an inherent disadvantage in most future conflicts because it will likely be conducting expeditionary operations against opponents on their own territories. In such settings, U.S. forces would be attempting to wage limited wars for limited stakes against adversaries who would have much greater stakes in the outcomes and therefore feel less bound by the same constraints. That has indeed been a problem in many past conflicts, and it will likely continue to be a troubling dynamic in some future cases, particularly those in which the United States intervenes in civil wars or attempts to stabilize failed states in regions in which U.S. economic and security interests are only marginal.

However, there is no reason to assume *a priori* that such would be the case in the kinds of future conflicts in which the United States would be most concerned about managing escalation—those with nuclear-armed states. Granted, in any war against such an opponent, U.S. forces would likely be conducting expeditionary operations, but that, in itself, does not indicate Washington would not perceive vital interests to be at stake. After all, the United States and other states in the Western Hemisphere concluded that their interests in Europe and Asia were great enough to mount considerable expeditionary operations and pay substantial costs in two world wars during the twentieth century, even though their homelands were not directly threatened. Moreover, the

United States might not be the only side embarking on expeditionary operations. Depending on what interests are at stake, a future nuclear-armed adversary might be sufficiently motivated and emboldened to conduct military operations outside its home territory as well. Whether a significant asymmetry of interests would emerge should the United States confront such a move, and if so, which side would perceive greater stakes in the issue (and manage to sustain those perceptions in the face of costly resistance) would depend on a wide range of factors. One important consideration would be which side is trying to change the status quo and which is trying to preserve it. Beyond that, were third-party territory to be fought over, the cultural orientation and political preferences of the government and citizens of that territory would doubtless play important roles in shaping local, regional, and international perceptions regarding which side had greater moral justification in attempting to change or defend the status quo.[54]

In any event, before intervening in a regional conflict against a nuclear-armed opponent—indeed, before embarking on any military expedition in the face of potential resistance—U.S. leaders should do a serious, dispassionate assessment of each side's interests in the issue at hand and scope their objectives accordingly. Such an assessment would be an essential element of the threshold analysis, as thresholds are closely related to perceptions of interest as well as to vulnerabilities. Once each side's stakes and potential escalation thresholds are understood, U.S. and allied or coalition leaders should craft and execute an operational plan aimed at defeating the opponent's conventional forces, but only to the extent needed to obtain their limited objectives. Ideally, that plan would respect the opponent's higher-level interests and thresholds, while holding them at risk as part of a carefully crafted escalation management strategy.

Finally, as any conflict unfolds, events will inevitably deviate from expectations, and plans and operations will have to be adjusted. The fortunes of war could go either way, but leaders must maintain a steady hand regardless. They should resist the temptation to escalate their political objectives in the face of unexpected military success.[55] Conversely, in the event of serious setbacks, military leaders will want to increase their efforts to avoid defeat. This is permissible—indeed, the opponent will likely expect it—so long as such increases do not violate important escalation thresholds. Should it appear that defeat is unavoidable without a serious escalation, political and military leaders should assess the implications of such an escalation in terms of the risks involved and weigh them against the interests at stake before embarking down a path on which the potential costs might ultimately exceed even the benefits of victory.

Concluding Thoughts

It follows from this discussion that controlling escalation can be and often is an insurmountable challenge. The stakes, uncertainties, and passions of wars tend to push mutually dangerous participants toward escalatory decisions. This will be particularly true in future conflicts between strong peers with high, even existential, stakes in their outcomes. A powerful belligerent facing an equally powerful opponent has good reason to preemptively escalate its diplomatic posturing and military operations, rather than wait for the enemy's next and stronger blow. This would be particularly true when neither side understands or trusts the other and the next step of escalation could involve the employment of nuclear weapons or capabilities banned by international convention, such as chemical and biological weapons. Further, the passions of war; whether sparked by religion, secular ideologies, nationalism, racism, ethnic hatreds, fears of conquest and genocide, and the like, tend to escalate conflicts—even when such escalations reflect poor risk/benefit calculations *in the eyes of opponents*. Of course, passions can give asymmetric advantages to materially weaker combatants whose emotional and principled interests exceed those of their stronger opponents. In such cases the weak-but-dedicated may simply pay the butcher's bill necessary to wear out strong-but-irresolute enemies.

So, this chapter recommends that political and military leaders inform their war strategies with the best understanding possible of each side's stakes, objectives, potential strategies, escalation thresholds, and escalation tolerances. These calculi will require many considerations, only the first of which will be each side's military capabilities and restraints. Others will include the passions discussed in the preceding paragraph, the preconceptions and personal interests of key leaders, and whether one can understand and trust the "signaling" of opponents. Of course, as discussed throughout this chapter, the subtleties, subjectivities, and uncertainties of these considerations, combined with the sure risks of miscalculation, reduce many escalation strategies to little more than uncertain gambles with the destiny of nations, movements, and ideals.

In the end, therefore, escalation management is much easier to articulate in theory than to do in practice. Indeed, the discussion in this chapter leads to a conclusion that *there is no such thing as escalation control*—at least, not against any adversary or combination of adversaries dangerous enough to make it necessary. As long as dangerous adversaries have free agency—and if they did not have it, there would be no war—then they will have the freedom to escalate, even though it may be to their detriment. One can attempt to deter them from doing so, warn them to avoid one's critical thresholds, avoid crossing theirs (to the extent they can be divined), and try to avoid escalatory accidents. But when all is said and done, the adversary will still have to choose whether and how to escalate. It will do so if it believes its survival is at risk or some other vital interest will be lost otherwise. So, in conflicts between committed and mutually-dangerous adversaries, the realistic mindsets and goals of escalation strategists should be maintaining effective analytical processes within, clear communications with their opponents, avoidance of undesired escalatory actions, and mitigation of the risks inherent in any escalation. In many cases, escalation will not be avoidable and forces will simply have to continue fighting, but at a new level.

Notes

1. We shall define it more precisely later in the chapter.

2. Carl von Clausewitz, *On War*, edited and translated by Michael Howard and Peter Paret (Princeton, N.J.: Princeton University Press, 1976), 77.

3. Clausewitz, *On War*, 78–86.

4. For the findings of that study, see: Forrest E. Morgan, Karl P. Mueller, Evan S. Medeiros, Kevin L. Pollpeter, and Roger Cliff, *Dangerous Thresholds: Managing Escalation in the 21st Century* (Santa Monica, Calif.: RAND Corporation, 2008).

5. John Foster Dulles, *Massive Retaliation*, Speech to the Council on Foreign Relations, January 12, 1954.

6. See for instance: William W. Kaufmann, *The Requirements of Deterrence* (Princeton, N.J.: Center of International Studies, Princeton University, 1954); Bernard Brodie, "Unlimited Weapons and Limited War," *The Reporter* 11, no. 9 (November 18, 1954); William W. Kaufman, ed., *Military Policy and National Security* (Princeton: Princeton University Press, 1956); Henry A. Kissinger, *Nuclear Weapons and Foreign Policy* (New York: Harper and Row, 1957); Robert E. Osgood, *Limited War: The Challenge to American Security* (Chicago: University of Chicago Press, 1957); Morton Kaplan, "The Calculus of Deterrence," *World Politics* 11, no. 1 (October, 1958), 20–43.

7. Albert J. Wohlstetter, *The Delicate Balance of Terror* (Santa Monica, Calif. RAND Corporation, November 6, 1958), 1472; Bernard Brodie, *Strategy in the Missile Age*

(Princeton: Princeton University Press, 1959), 335–57; Henry A. Kissenger, *The Necessity for Choice: Prospects of American Foreign Policy* (New York: Harper, 1961). For a fuller analysis of the evolution of the Cold War-era limited war debate, see Robert E. Osgood, *Limited War Revisited* (Boulder, Colo.: Westview, 1979).

8. Herman Kahn, *On Thermonuclear War* (Princeton, N.J.: Princeton University Press, 1961), 39.

9. Herman Kahn, *Thinking About the Unthinkable* (New York: Horizon, 1962), 19. In interviews following the publication of this book, Kahn was notorious for declaring, "Nuclear wars are winnable!"

10. Herman Kahn, *On Escalation: Metaphors and Scenarios* (New York: Praeger, 1965).

11. Kahn, *On Escalation*, 39. Kahn's ladder could have been much larger, as it included few rungs involving purely conventional uses of force, and none featuring the use of chemical or biological but not nuclear weapons.

12. Kahn, *On Escalation*, 290.

13. Daniel L. Byman, Matthew C. Waxman, and Eric Larsen, *The Dynamics of Coercion: American Foreign Policy and the Limits of American Might* (Cambridge: Cambridge University Press, 2002), 40. Also see Daniel Byman, Matthew Waxman, and Eric V. Larson, *Air Power as a Coercive Instrument* (Santa Monica, Calif.: RAND Corporation, 1999), 30–36.

14. At several points in the Vietnam War, Viet Cong and People's Army of North Vietnam attacks declined in frequency, suggesting to U. S. leaders that the communists were losing either the resolve or the ability to continue fighting, when, in fact, they were simply hoarding supplies in preparation for renewed offensives. For an in-depth analysis of the difficulties each side had in interpreting the actions the other during the Vietnam War, see Wallace J. Thies, *When Governments Collide: Coercion and Diplomacy in the Vietnam Conflict, 1964–1968* (Berkeley, Calif.: University of California Press, 1980).

15. A great deal of research was done during the Cold War on the risks of misperception. Some of the more notable works of that era include: Fred Iklé, "Can Nuclear Deterrence Last Out the Century?" *Foreign Affairs* 51, no. 2 (January, 1973), 267–85; Robert Jervis, *Perception and Misperception in International Politics* (Princeton, N.J.: Princeton University Press, 1976); Robert Jervis, "Deterrence and Perception." *International Security* 7, no. 3 (Winter, 1982–1983), 3–30; Richard N. Lebow, *Between Peace and War: The Nature of International Crises* (Baltimore, Md.: The Johns Hopkins University Press, 1984), 101–228.

16. Clausewitz, *On War*, 1976, 117–21. Also see page 140, where he says the "general unreliability of all information is a special problem in war" of such prominence that he names it as one of three principal attributes of all military activity.

17. A classic example of several of these elements coming to play at once can be found in the opening days of World War I when the German General Staff lost contact with its western-most armies as they attempted to envelop the Allied armies in Belgium. When commander of the German First Army Alexander von Kluck saw what he believed to be an opportunity to entrap the British Expeditionary Force before it could withdraw below the Marne, he veered to the southeast, deviating from the operational plan and unknowingly exposing his army's flank to the French Sixth Army forming up north of Paris. Only discovery of this vulnerability at the eleventh hour enabled Kluck to pull his forces back in time to avert disaster. See Larry H. Addington, *The Patterns of War Since the Eighteenth*

Century, Second Edition (Bloomingdale, Indi.: Indiana University Press, 1994), 140; Barbara W. Tuchman, *The Guns of August* (New York: Random House, 1962, Ballantine edition, 1992), 470–91.

18. Kahn, *On Escalation*, 214–29.

19. Examples of adversaries escalating along unexpected dimensions can be found in the Balkan wars, where Serbian forces resorted to shelling civilian market places, holding UN safe areas hostage, systematically raping Muslim women, and the ethnic cleansing of Kosovar Albanians. An example of an inadvertent, unknowing escalation can be found in Operation Deliberate Force, when limitations in available air assets led NATO forces to focus on select targets with advanced weapons that Serb leaders considered escalatory. We shall discuss this in more detail later in the chapter.

20. Fred Charles Iklé, *Every War Must End, Second Revised Edition* (New York: Columbia University Press, 1991), 41.

21. Byman, et al., argue that Operation Deliberate Force compelled Bosnian Serb leaders to negotiate a ceasefire in 1995 because U. S. airpower imposed escalation dominance on them, being able to conduct airstrikes at will without exposing U. S. forces to counterstrikes of any kind. The same argument could be made regarding how Slobodan Milosevic was forced to terms in the 1999 Kosovo conflict. See Byman, et al., *The Dynamics of Coercion*, 36.

22. In 2005 he and Robert J. Aumann were jointly awarded the Nobel Prize in Economic Sciences for their Cold War-era work in game theory.

23. Thomas C. Schelling, *The Strategy of Conflict* (Cambridge, Mass.: Harvard University Press, 1960), 53–80; Thomas C. Schelling, *Arms and Influence* (New Haven, Conn.: Yale University Press, 1966), 1–34 and 131–41.

24. Schelling, *Arms and Influence*, 92–125. In his class at the University of Maryland in the mid- 1990s, Schelling was fond of posing and answering the following question: "How do you win a game of chicken on the highway? When your car and the opponent's come careening toward each other, pull off your steering wheel and throw it out the window! *Just make sure the opponent sees you do it.*" Although Schelling is most famous for developing the brinkmanship concept, Kahn addressed it and even used the highway-chicken game metaphor, complete with the steering-wheel removal strategy, in the introduction to his 1961 book, *On Escalation*. See Kahn, *On Escalation*, 7–11.

25. Graham Allison and Philip Zelikow, *Essence of Decision: Explaining the Cuban Missile Crisis, Second Edition* (New York: Longman, 1999), 360; Laurence Chang and Peter Kornbluh, eds., *The Cuban Missile Crisis, 1962* (New York: The New Press, 1992, 1998), 378. In Robert Kennedy's memoirs he said he delivered an ultimatum to Dobrynin in that meeting, a claim that Dobrynin later denied. Nevertheless, Dobrynin did admit that, based on intelligence available to him on U. S. military preparations, he believed an airstrike or even an invasion was "very likely in the coming days." See Alexander L. George, "The Cuban Missile Crisis" in *Avoiding War: Problems of Crisis Management*, ed. Alexander L. George (Boulder, Colo.: Westview Press, 1991), 252.

26. Morton Halperin argued as such as early as 1963. See Morton Halperin, *Limited War in the Nuclear Age* (New York: John Wiley, 1963), 64.

27. Barry R. Posen, "Inadvertent Nuclear War?: Escalation and NATO's Northern Flank," *International Security* 7, no. 2 (Fall, 1982), 28–54.

28. Benjamin B. Fischer, "A Cold War Conundrum: The 1983 Soviet War Scare," CIA, Center for the Study of Intelligence, July 7, 2008.

29. Morgan, et al., *Dangerous Thresholds*, 3–4.

30. Due to resource limitations and the focus of client interest, the RAND study examined escalation risks in a conflict with China, but not one with Russia. Later, the study's principal investigator did work for the French Institute of International Relations exploring how to manage escalation risks in a war between NATO and the Russian Federation. For the findings of that study, see: Forrest E. Morgan, *Dancing with the Bear: Managing Escalation in a Conflict with Russia* (Proliferation Papers, French Institute for International Relations, Paris, Winter, 2012).

31. Morgan, et al., *Dangerous Thresholds*, 8.

32. One might not think of the last example as constituting a dangerous form of escalation. But consider how, on the eve of the first Gulf War, when Saddam Hussein indicated a willingness to reach a negotiated settlement, President George H. W. Bush escalated his public rhetoric making it impossible for the Iraqi leader to back down without losing face in the Arab world.

33. See Schelling, *Arms and Influence*, 153–68 and 283–86.

34. This was part of German Chancellor Theobold von Bethmann-Hollweg's indignant response when Ambassador Sir Edward Goschen delivered Britain's ultimatum for Germany to cease hostilities against Belgium within 48 hours. See Tuchman, *The Guns of August*, 153–54.

35. The Chemical Weapons Convention exemplifies an effort to strengthen an established threshold by formally outlawing a class of weapons. Alternatively, declaring that chemical, biological, and nuclear weapons collectively constitute a single category of "weapons of mass destruction," despite the obvious differences in their destructive power, is a prominent example of efforts to raise a threshold via demonization.

36. Mark J. Conversino, "Executing Deliberate Force, 30 August-14 September 1995" in *Deliberate Force: A Case Study in Effective Air Campaigning*, ed. Robert C. Owen (Maxwell AFB, Ala.: Air University Press, 2000), 150–53. Also see Richard L. Sargent, "Weapons Used in Deliberate Force," Owen (2000), 264.

37. Committing additional units to a battle is not necessarily escalatory. If a conflict has already escalated to the point at which each side expects the other to do whatever it possibly can to win at the conventional level of war, then neither is surprised when the other commits forces previously held in operational or strategic reserve. However, if both sides have previously withheld the employment of forces below a given threshold in hopes of keeping the conflict limited then one opponent commits additional forces exceeding that threshold, the opponent is likely to consider the move escalatory and react accordingly. In sum, the commitment of additional force is escalatory if and only if either of the opponents believes doing so has crossed an escalation threshold.

38. Schelling, *Arms and Influence*, 172.

39. See for instance A. L. Gropman, "The Air War in Vietnam, 1961–73" in *War in the Third Dimension: Essays in Contemporary Air Power*, ed. R. A. Mason (London: Brassey's Defence Publishers, 1986), 37–39. Robert Pape also condemns Operation Rolling Thunder, but the root of his criticism is not that the strategy was overly restrained. Rather, he argues that North Vietnam was largely immune to conventional coercion during that period because

conventional bombing was ineffective in defeating a guerilla warfare strategy and Hanoi was willing to bear whatever costs the United States was willing to inflict to achieve its territorial ambitions in South Vietnam. See Robert A. Pape, *Bombing to Win: Air Power and Coercion in War* (Ithaca, N.Y.: Cornell University Press, 1996), 174–95. Also see Robert A. Pape, Jr., "Coercive Air Power in the Vietnam War," *International Security* 15, no. 2 (Fall, 1990), 103–46.

40. It is important to note that, while the atomic bombings represented a dramatic escalation in that they introduced a terrifying new weapon, they were not escalatory in terms of the levels of destruction or suffering they caused as compared with the fire bombings. For instance, the March 9, 1945, firebombing of Tokyo inflicted 185,000 casualties in a single attack. In comparison, the combined casualty toll from the bombing of Hiroshima and Nagasaki was about 110,000 people killed with an estimated 90,000 more people injured. See *United States Strategic Bombing Survey: Summary Report (Pacific War)*, (Washington, D.C., 1946), reprinted as *The United States Strategic Bombing Surveys (European War), (Pacific War)*, (Maxwell AFB, Ala.: Air University Press, 1987), 92 and 100–101.

41. We now know that some of the missiles became operational during the crisis, were armed with nuclear warheads, and launch authority had been delegated to the Soviet military commander in Cuba. Graham Allison and Philip Zelikow, *Essence of Decision: Explaining the Cuban Missile Crisis, Second Edition* (New York: Longman, 1999), 215–17; Lyle Goldstein, *Preventive Attack and Weapons of Mass Destruction: A Comparative Historical Analysis* (Stanford, Calif.: Stanford University Press, 2006), 45.

42. Mark Clodfelter, *The Limits of Airpower: The American Bombing of North Vietnam* (New York: The Free Press, 1989), 53; David Halberstam, *The Best and the Brightest* (New York: Fawcett Crest, 1972), 424.

43. As previously mentioned, Barry Posen did the seminal work on the risks of inadvertent escalation during the Cold War in Posen, "Inadvertent Nuclear War?" 28–54. He further developed his argument in Barry R. Posen, *Inadvertent Escalation: Conventional War and Nuclear Risks* (Ithaca, N.Y.: Cornell University Press, 1991).

44. This raises questions about why thresholds are sometimes perceived by one side and not the other or perceived differently by opponents. A range of causes might be involved, such as cultural differences, bureaucratic routines, and various forms of cognitive bias. The causes doubtless vary from case to case, and they probably operate interdependently in some cases.

45. David S. Yost, "France's New Nuclear Doctrine," *International Affairs* 82, no. 4 (2006), 701–21.

46. See, for instance, Christopher Catherwood, *Winston Churchill: The Flawed Genius of World War II* (New York: Berkeley, 2009), 72; Terry Copp, *No Price Too High: Canadians and the Second World War* (Whitby, Ontario: McGraw-Hill Ryerson, 1996), 50. Other historians argue that Hitler would soon have ordered the bombing effort to shift from RAF airfields to London, anyway, because time was running out for executing Operation Sea Lion, the invasion of Britain, before fall weather would make a channel crossing infeasible. Breaking the resistance of RAF Fighter Command was a prerequisite to the invasion, and Luftwaffe leaders believed that only attacking London would draw British fighters up in sufficient numbers to enable Fighter Command's destruction. See R. J. Overy, *The Air War: 1939–1945* (Chelsea, Mich.: Scarborough House, 1980), 34–36; John Ray, *The Battle of Britain: Dowding and the First Victory, 1940* (London: Cassell & Co., 2000), 92–93.

47. When this practice was exposed in the news media, General Lavelle was relieved of command and forced to retire in disgrace at a reduced grade. However, on August 6, 2010, President Barack Obama, after an extensive review of the Lavelle case, exonerated the general and posthumously restored him to his full military rank and honors. The investigation revealed that General Lavelle's conduct had been consistent with secret orders from President Richard Nixon, who had, for political reasons, elected not to speak up for him when the scandal erupted. See http://www.arlingtoncemetery.net/jlavelle.htm, accessed June 19, 2011.

48. An example of a peacetime accident that could have escalated into an international crisis is the April 2001 collision between a U. S. Navy P-3 Orion reconnaissance aircraft and a Chinese F-8 fighter over the South China Sea. Fortunately, military and political leaders on both sides kept cool heads, and the issue was resolved with the U. S. aircrew's return after 11 days and the aircraft about three months later. For an analysis of this episode, see Shirley A. Kan, Richard Best, Christopher Bolkcom, Robert Chapman, Richard Cronin, Kerry Dumbaugh, Stuart Goldman, Mark Manyin, Wayne Morrison, Ronald O'Rourke, and David Ackerman, *China-U. S. Aircraft Collision Incident of April 2001: Assessment and Policy Implications,* CRS Report for Congress, Washington, D.C.: Congressional Research Service, 2001, October 10.

49. Clausewitz, *On War,* 119–21.

50. Clausewitz, *On War,* 81.

51. Alexander L. George, "Theory and Practice," in *The Limits of Coercive Diplomacy, Second Edition,* eds. Alexander L. George and William E. Simons (Boulder, Colo.: Westview, 1994), 15.

52. See William E. Simons, "U. S. Coercive Pressure on North Vietnam," in eds. George and Simons, 1994, 133–73; and Alexander L. George and William E. Simons, "Findings and Conclusions," in George and Simons, 1994, 281–82. Also see Wallace J. Thies, *When Governments Collide: Coercion and Diplomacy in the Vietnam Conflict, 1964–1968* (Berkeley, Calif.: University of California Press, 1980), 6–13.

53. For case studies examining the escalation dynamics that occurred in these operations and an analysis of the escalation dynamics of irregular warfare more generally, see Morgan, et al., *Dangerous Thresholds,* 117–58 and 197–220.

54. For instance, consider differences in world reaction to the Anschluss, Hitler's 1938 annexation of Austria, a Germanic nation whose citizenry included an outspoken pro-Nazi, pro-unification minority, and the German annexation of Czechoslovakia and especially the invasion of Poland in 1939.

55. Iklé, *Every War Must End.*

2

A Distant Mirror

Exercise Sagebrush 1955

ROBERT C. OWEN

> The Air Force's nuclear deterrent and conventional precision strike forces can credibly deny adversary objectives or impose unacceptable costs by effectively holding any target on the planet at risk and, if necessary, disabling or destroying targets promptly, even from bases in the continental United States.
>
> —David A. Deptula, *Beyond the Bomber* (Washington, DC: Mitchell Institute, 2015), 18.

The war recommenced with that old cliché: "It was a dark and stormy night." Bombers of the Sixth Air Army broke the faltering truce on November 15, 1955, when they flashed across the ceasefire line. Coursing like wolves, they raced across the hinterlands of central Louisiana, each carrying an atomic bomb destined for a United States Air Force (USAF) base. At around 1840 hours they pulled up into the darkness and climbed to their bombing altitudes, some as high as 45,000 feet. Their rising blips lit up USAF air defense radars immediately. But, on such a night, tactical commanders in the operations centers of the defending Twenty-Ninth Air Force (provisional) could only watch and wait for the enemy's blows. A squadron of balky F-86D interceptors was all they had to send into the darkness and clouds to attempt interceptions. The rest of the American air fleet consisted of F-84F fighter-bombers and some aging B-26s. The F-84s lacked intercept radars to find the enemy, and had no instrument landing systems to get all of them back on the ground

Though a fast and agile aircraft for its time, the F-84F Thunderstreak still lacked night and poor-weather navigation and attack systems. (United States Air Force. https://commons.wikimedia.org/wiki/File:92d_Tactical_Fighter_Squadron_-_Republic_F-84F-45-RE_Thunderstreak_-_52-7114.jpg)

before they ran out of fuel. The B-26s did not have attack radars and could not carry nuclear weapons anyway. So the Americans watched and listened to reports as one base after another "died" under atomic fireballs. By 1930, seventeen of the Twenty-Ninth's nineteen forward bases had been destroyed. Sixth Air Army F-86Hs got the last ones in the morning. In all they delivered fifty-two nuclear weapons in the first day of operations, some of them with yields of up to 200 kilotons. Twenty-Ninth Air Force counterstrikes on the sixteenth took out most aggressor bases as well. But, by evening, the Air Force's offensive capabilities consisted only of a flight of B-61 Matador cruise missiles, while the Sixth Air Army possessed ample offensive capabilities to block the return of any USAF base to operational status, with sorties left over to beat up the American Ninth Field Army as it retreated before the enemy's Eleventh Mechanized Army. In a week, the Eleventh was across the Red River and poised to continue its advance to the northeast. With that, the umpires had seen enough and paused Exercise Sagebrush to give both sides a week to reset their forces for the American counteroffensive.[1]

These opening gambits gave Exercise Sagebrush relevance to air warfare theorists and operators today.[2] With ground operations encompassing most of central Louisiana, and air operations spread across the southeastern US, Sagebrush involved 110,000 soldiers and 30,000 airmen—still the largest U.S. military exercise conducted since World War II. On its part, the Tactical Air Command (TAC) committed over 600 combat, about forty tanker, and eighty troop carrier aircraft to the exercise (table 2.1). The modern relevance of Sagebrush, however, lies in the Army and Air Force's almost unrestrained employment of *hundreds* of simulated nuclear bombs, cruise missiles, tactical ballistic missiles, and artillery projectiles during its two operational phases. Like Mardi Gras krewes scattering beads, Sagebrush umpires detonated dozens of mushroom-cloud-producing "atomic simulators" all over the exercise area to mark the annihilations of air bases, command centers, bridges, infantry companies humping through the swamps, and just about any place else that might present a target.[3] For the first time, American tactical commanders were obliged to systematically address the doctrines, strategies, and tactics of warfare in a weapons-of-mass-effect (WME) context, where either side could defeat the other in a matter of hours. Thus, the experience of Sagebrush presents useful insights to modern airmen contemplating future WME warfare, such as by waves of aircraft and missiles from both sides delivering thousands of precision-guided weapons in a night. Given the common possibilities of more-or-less instant victory or defeat, current air war theorists and practitioners will do well to review the insights gained or even those overlooked by their professional ancestors about things like preemptive strikes, escalation management, air dominance, target priorities, and so on. Things were different in 1955, but in some ways *not that* different. So, putting a little historical depth behind our thinking about future air warfare is a good idea.

This report uses the term Weapons of Mass Effect (WME) to emphasize a conceptual linkage between the tactical and strategic concepts applied to a theater nuclear war exercise in 1955, and those that might well be relevant to future wars in which the United States seeks to win victories over nuclear-armed enemies, but without the use of nuclear weapons. Here, then, WME applies to any weapon system or set of weapon systems that offer the possibilities of quick victory or defeat in wars between strong peer opponents. The term is distinct from the earlier one of Weapon(s) of Mass Destruction (WMD). Technically, only nuclear weapons merit that designation, since

Exercise Sagebrush Air Order of Battle Combat Aircraft—Squadrons	
USAF Twenty-Ninth Air Force (provisional)	**Aggressor 11th Air Army**
F-84F—6	F-86H—6
RF-84—2	F-86D—1
F-86D-1	RF-84F—2
B-26–2	F-100A—2
RB-66–2	B-57–2
KB-29–4	
TM-61—one flight	
Shared Troop Carrier Forces	
Eight squadrons C-119, Six squadrons C-124, One squadron H-19, One squadron H-21, some C-123s.	

Table 2.1 Tactical Air Command, *History of the Tactical Air Command 1 July 1955–31 December 1955,* vol. 8, 33. (See note 3 on page 59)

their extreme physical and moral effects likely would coincide with the destruction of cities and military base areas, and the rendering of whole territories uninhabitable. In comparison, precision-guided munitions, chemical and biological weapons, and various forms of electromagnetic attack were too limited in their individual effects to be realistically considered as WMD. In the early 2000s, however, the range, precision, and effects of these systems reached the point that they could impose rapid and potentially decisive effects if used in mass. These mass effects can present civil and military leaders with strategic and escalation management challenges similar in scale and quality to those posed by limited numbers of nuclear strikes. These similarities, in turn, place advanced non-nuclear weapons employed in mass and nuclear weapons used in limited fashions into a common category based on their impacts on conflict outcomes and escalation strategies.

The conceptual similarities between Exercise Sagebrush and future wars, pursued at least initially with masses of advanced non-nuclear weapons, reside mainly in the war-initiation and escalation-management calculations each would require of civil and military leaders. Whether national leaders were anticipating a devastating WME attack or considering retaliation to

Umpires detonated atomic simulators routinely. (United States Air Force, Ninth Air Force, "Evaluation of Exercise Sage Brush 1955," in *History of the Ninth Air Force 1 July—31 December 1955*, Vol. VII [Shaw AFB, SC: Headquarters Ninth AF, 1955], 16–17.)

one already delivered, they would be engaged in complex risk-benefit calculations. Their calculations would have to address the profound dangers of allowing their enemies to strike first, the probabilities of subsequent strikes, their own abilities to preempt or retaliate, and the possibility that their responses might trigger further escalation of the conflict. Subjectively, they would have to consider things like the national mood, the long-term impact of the destruction suffered already, what more could be lost in continued conflict, and the importance of the interests they would have to trade to avoid further combat. As a test of limited theater nuclear conflict strategy and tactics, therefore, Sagebrush offers valuable insights into that type of war and the non-nuclear conflicts the United States more likely will face in the future.

The Exercise

Sagebrush was predicated on a nuclear-armed enemy invading the southern United States. The zone of ground operations was central Louisiana. Air operations spread over the entire southeastern US. Operational planning began on the assumption that the invader had halted on a truce line, but was poised to renew its advance.[4] Based on guidance from the Pentagon, the Commander of the Tactical Air Command and also the Sagebrush Maneuver Director, General O.P. Weyland, instructed his field commanders to focus their exercise participation on "tactical air operations against an enemy who possesses and employs nuclear weapons, and on mobile nuclear strike force operations."[5] The mobile nuclear strike force concept was then under development by TAC as a method of reinforcing beleaguered theaters of operation in future conflicts with a compact air strike force ready to commence nuclear attacks within hours of arriving at overseas bases.[6] Old TAC hands will recognize that this concept soon evolved into the composite air strike forces (CASFs) employed in 1958 during the Lebanon and Quemoy-Matsu crises. Exercise play would also include tests of Air Force nuclear planning concepts, service and joint command and control procedures, intelligence and targeting, communications, and the capabilities of different types of frontline aircraft to perform their missions under nuclear combat conditions. In parallel, the Army would test its ability to conduct and support defensive and offensive operations on nuclear battlefields. As a major focus, the Army planned to test and refine the organizations of its Atomic Field Test Army (ATFA) units, most importantly the 1st Armored and 3rd Infantry divisions. The ATFA was an interim step in the army's quest for a new organizational structure that would allow it to fight with tactical units designed to disperse widely for survival on a nuclear battlefield, quickly concentrate for specific missions, and then re-disperse to avoid nuclear counterstrikes.[7] In short, Sagebrush was both an exercise of unprecedented scale and complexity, and also one of transformational importance to the development of U.S. warfighting capabilities and strategies that presaged modern warfighting concerns.

Recognizing that simulated nuclear weapons would be as able to shut down an exercise as real ones could destroy nations, the organizers of Sagebrush shackled their operational play from the beginning. The most telling artificiality was the exercise scenario itself, which did not address the realism of a nuclear-armed enemy getting onto the shores of a nuclear armed America

Though something of a maintenance "pig," the F-86D "Sabre Dog" was the best the USAF had for night and poor weather interceptions. (National Museum of the United States Air Force. https://www.nationalmuseum.af.mil/Visit/Museum-Exhibits/Fact-Sheets/Display/Article/198076/north-american-f-86d-sabre/)

or its allies without quick employment of those weapons. But, if real-world logic had prevailed and nuclear weapons had popped off in the first phase of the exercise, there would have been no further opportunities for theater air and ground forces to practice their trades. Also, though key rear support bases were in range of enemy aircraft, exercise rules declared them off limits to attack. England AFB, at the center of the ground exercise area, was also off limits to attack, since its role was to serve as a base for reconnaissance and troop carrier forces utilized by both sides of the exercise.[8] Only one Air Force had the privilege of initiating operations in any given exercise phase. Exercise rules required the other Air Force to wait until attacking enemy aircraft appeared on its radar scopes before responding, a procedure that left it with only minutes before bombs started falling. Moreover, to keep play going, umpires returned air bases obliterated by nuclear attacks to operational status only one to three days after all their people, planes, and facilities had theoretically been annihilated. Since no aircraft in TAC at that time had accurate high-altitude, night and all-weather bombing radars, exercise rules ascribed those capabilities to the Sixth Air Army's B-57s, so that such operations could be evaluated.

Constrained by these same artificialities, the second operational phase of Sagebrush reprised the outcomes of the first. Given the honor of the first volley, Major General E. J. Timberlake launched an all-out surprise attack on the morning of November 28. In possession of an Air Force that, except for his Matador missiles, could only make accurate attacks in clear weather, he sent in as many atomic-armed F-84Fs and conventionally armed B-26s, as he could to destroy enemy air bases. By the end of the day, his squadrons had delivered fifty-one atomic weapons and only one of the Sixth Air Army's nineteen bases was still functioning. Twenty-Ninth AF strikes got that one the next morning. Before losing all of their bases, however, Sixth Air Army crews got off enough counterattacks to kill fifteen of the Twenty-Ninth's twenty-five bases. From that point on, the Air Forces were in a "struggle for survival" as the Sixth Air Army engineers pushed to get bases back into operation, and the Twenty-Ninth AF repeatedly attacked them to prevent counterstrikes. The danger of atomic strikes was so profound that exercise evaluations assessed that just one night's operations by the Sixth Air Army's B-57s from a reconstituted base could have tilted the operational balance back in its favor.[9] Meanwhile, the Twenty-Ninth provided atomic and conventional strikes in support of the U.S. Ninth Army's offensive across the Red River and southwards. But, for the main, the Army relied on its own extensive atomic arsenal to destroy anything that got in the way of its advance.

Had all those weapons been real, Louisiana would have been glowing in the dark, and not from the bright lights of New Orleans.[10] The employment and effects of atomic weapons in Exercise Sagebrush were pervasive enough to perhaps startle current readers. Exercise rules allocated 275 nuclear bombs and warheads to the Twenty-Ninth Air Force and 230 to the Sixth Air Army, with yields ranging from 20 to 200 kilotons of TNT.[11] In all, air and land forces released something like 19,000 kilotons of weapons during the exercise.[12] Moreover, the Air Force tactical commanders had almost unlimited release authority over their weapons, apart from 15 percent reserved for employment at the theater commander's discretion.[13] The Army pushed release authorities down to division commanders, who then used them "extensively."[14] Having adjudged that two B-57s dropping atomic bombs on an air base had a probability of kill (PK) of .986, the umpires declared that the first wave of Sixth Air Army attacks destroyed eighteen Twenty-Ninth Air Force bases in just two hours.¹⁵ The resulting destruction left the Twenty-Ninth with only the ability to launch a handful of Matador missiles per day. But, these missiles were proven in live tests to put warheads consistently within about 3,000' of their targets out to a 250-mile range and, so, they accounted for half of all Twenty-Ninth counterstrikes during the first operational phase.¹⁶ Army units floundering and bunched up on the narrow and rain-sloppy roads and bridges over flooded rivers served mainly to provide targets for atomic strikes of all kinds. Most significant ground movements, consequently, ended with detonations of one of those damned atomic simulators nearby.

The conduct of troop carrier operations turned out to be a major operational and doctrinal challenge during the exercise. Troop carrier's primary role was to support movements of air and ground forces within theaters of operation under combat conditions. But the ability of troop carrier forces to operate in combat zones was questionable. As discovered as early as Exercise Swarmer in 1950, transport aircraft were acutely vulnerable to and almost impossible to defend against attacks by jet fighters.¹⁷ By Sagebrush, Army planners presumed that jets and atomics meant that airborne operations "would not be successful . . . if troop carrier aircraft were marshalled in large numbers . . . or if . . . more than two battalions were dropped in the same area."¹⁸ Troop carrier doctrines echoed this evaluation, placing greater faith in passive measures, such as dispersion and flying at night, than on friendly fighters for protection.

There also was not enough airlift to go around. By committing every squadron it had, the Eighteenth Air Force, TAC's troop carrier command, provided both sides of the Sagebrush exercise with a common pool of about eighty C-119s, two helicopter assault squadrons, and as much C-124 support as it could break away from real-world missions. This small force restricted the airborne portion of the exercise to separate air drops of combined arms battle groups, each of between 1,000 and 1,500 troops.¹⁹ It also fell far, far below the 400 C-124s and 800 new C-123s the army's recent Project Vista study had assessed were needed to support a single corps of three divisions maneuvering on atomic battlefields.²⁰ TAC wasn't happy either. Moving a fighter wing, it estimated, required about fifty to sixty C-124 loads, and its new dispersal tactics called for moving a lot of wings often.²¹ This was a lot to ask from a troop carrier force that fielded only about a hundred C-124s in the entire Continental United States and no more than around thirty in any major overseas theater. Even if added to these active forces, the Air Force

Partial solution—coming on line only a year after Sagebrush, the B-66 Destroyer gave the Air Force an all-weather tactical bomber of substantial range but did not mitigate its dependence on long runways or the pressure to preempt in theater nuclear war. (United States Air Force. https://upload.wikimedia.org/wikipedia/commons/a/a7/Douglas_RB-66B_Destroyer_in_flight_%28SN_53-422%29_061102-F-1234P-027.jpg)

Reserve's twelve troop carrier wings only offered about 200 old and operationally awkward C-46s to the mix.[22]

Lessons Observed

Given the newness of atomic warfare at the time, it is not surprising that Sagebrush was grist for the ongoing debate on the implications of nuclear weapons for the future. The Army estimated (probably conservatively) that the notional release of the explosive power of *950* Hiroshima-equivalent bombs in just a few thousand square miles of Louisiana would have produced over 20,000 military casualties, destroyed 2,700 vehicles, and rendered all large units ineffective.[23] Additionally, the tactical Air Forces involved destroyed themselves several times over. No official estimates of potential civilian casualties appear to have been made. But all those blasts and the resulting fallout almost certainly would have created some ghost towns. Viewing these effects, the Army Chief of Staff, General Maxwell D. Taylor, suggested that "if Sagebrush had been a war ... it is unlikely that the Army—as we know it today—could have continued to fight as a coherent, integrated combat force." Noting Taylor's assessment, military commentator Hanson Baldwin declared at the time that the whole notion of relying solely on nuclear weapons in lesser conflicts and theaters, other than perhaps Europe, was dangerously inflexible and likely to make small conflicts into global ones. America's future, he proposed, "may depend upon our ability to win small wars without turning them into large ones."[24]

In contrast to the building moral debate, lesson one for the air commanders was more pragmatic—that restraint or delay in a confrontation with another atomic air force likely would be fatal. Indeed, had they known of the three escalation mechanisms described by Forrest Morgan in the first chapter, Sagebrush commanders would have embraced the idea that escalation in nuclear war must be deliberate and total at the start, with no incremental steps between looking ugly at each other and launching first strikes. Like gunfighters in a showdown, air forces in those circumstances could not afford to be second on the draw or to allow their opponents a fair chance of getting back into the fight. "The core of the air commander's job," declared the chief planner of the exercise, 'was to find means of rendering ineffective the enemy's special weapons capability while retaining an appreciable degree of his own like capability."[25] For Major General Timberlake, the extreme danger of an enemy air force pulling itself back together and getting off a retaliatory strike justified an "over expenditure of weapons" without waiting for battle damage assessments to determine if a base remained inoperative or not.[26] Convinced that, in atomic war, "over killing presents less danger than under killing," his attack planning called for three nuclear strikes against each base initially, followed by more attacks against any base that seemed ready or just *could* be getting ready to resume operations. In other words, shoot 'em down and then shoot 'em again every once in a while, just to keep 'em dead.[27] Bases, indeed were the primary targets of all counterair attacks, since they determined an enemy's ability to counterattack. Given that, Sagebrush air commanders considered destruction of enemy aircraft and personnel just a "bonus feature" of air base attacks.[28] Indeed, TAC commanders fairly ached to propose preemptive attacks in future confrontations, but they were held back by official policy. So, the position they took was that "the force initiating the attack attained a tremendous advantage . . . able to attain and maintain air superiority . . . [so] while initiating an attack has not been recommend, it has become necessary to establish an operational concept which will give friendly forces the chance of survival."[29]

Air commanders also gained operational insights from Sagebrush that were new to them but more familiar to airmen today. First, they saw that active dispersal of forces would be essential in atomic air battles. Until then "dispersal" mainly meant scattering and hiding aircraft and support elements on or near their airfields. Now, in the presence of atomic weapons that could wipe out entire bases and their environs, the term meant running a shell game of moving packets of one to two squadrons "forward enough to reach the target, yet rearward as possible to deny the enemy attack," and then shifting those packets from base to base as often as possible.[30] This was done for some fighter units during Sagebrush but, though recommended *after* the exercise, not for air refueling and airlift aircraft.[31] Second, the devastating potential of even a few atomic attacks changed the practical definition of "air superiority." In previous air wars the term meant freedom to accomplish missions while preventing enemies from doing the same. A few enemy aircraft leaking through own defenses now and again was undesirable, but of little relevance to the ultimate outcome of a conflict. But, in the context of atomic war, TAC's report assessed that "air superiority has a different connotation as a result of Exercise SAGE BRUSH. No longer does the force with numerical superiority necessarily enjoy air superiority. Air superiority has not been established as long as the opposing force retains any bases from which to launch a strike force."[32] Put another way, in their first engagement with notional WME, air commanders saw more-or-less instantly that air superiority was now a zero-sum game and that "complete elimination of the enemy air force's ability to retaliate is the goal."[33] Finally, air commanders argued that the speed and geographic dispersion of atomic air operations necessitated a reappraisal of the relationship between field armies and tactical Air Forces. Reflecting the findings of his commander, the TAC director of plans, declared that "present air-ground doctrine which ties a tactical air force . . . to a field army denies the Air Force of one of its most valuable assets—flexibility.[34] Given TAC's existence as the Air Force's guarantee of its commitment to support the Army, this call for greater independence in targeting and release of nuclear weapons was ironic and a potential violation of interservice agreements.

Not surprisingly, exercise leaders recognized that interservice, or *joint*, doctrines were inadequate for the operational demands of nuclear warfare. Except for truths about the fundamental nature of war, doctrines otherwise are expressions of how things should be understood or done under given circumstances—and nuclear weapons definitely had changed circumstances. Confronting those new circumstances, army ground commanders and tactical airmen had been squabbling over the control of nukes for several years prior to Sagebrush and had come to no agreement. Reflecting long-standing service interests and self-identities as the decisive arms of battle, Army assessments recommended that supported ground commanders have general authority over supporting air efforts, including target selection, durations of supporting actions, and munition requirements.[35] Sagebrush air commanders represented their service visions in their assertions that tactical Air Forces "must have control and direction of their weapons . . . whether these weapons are delivered on Air Force or Army requested targets."[36] This doctrinal division almost stopped preparations for Sagebrush altogether, when General Weyland refused to participate in an exercise that did not give the Air Force absolute control of its own tactics and weapon release decisions. Ultimately, the Army and Air Force chiefs gave Weyland, as the maneuver director, authority to set up whatever control procedures he wanted for the exercise, but only if he indicated in his reports that they did not reflect established service doctrines.[37] In the event, General Weyland gave theater air and ground commanders limited control of their weapons and did not require them to plan nuclear operations jointly. Post-exercise evaluations, indeed, recognized that the two services continued to "fight" without any jointly approved procedures for atomic warfare and coordinated their operations only when required to by a specific operational task.[38]

The airlift shortfalls experienced during the exercise led Sagebrush evaluators down another doctrinal rabbit trail. A key innovation during the Korean War, which had ended just two years before Sagebrush, had been the consolidation of virtually all theater airlift forces under a general officer reporting directly to the theater air force commander. The theater air commander, in turn, provided airlift support to the Air Force, Army, and general transportation efforts in accordance with apportionment decisions handed down from the theater commander.[39] In an atomic environment, however, Sagebrush Air Force commanders concluded that "an effective type of organizational airlift aircraft" should be assigned directly to tactical air strike units, and that any other arrangement was unacceptable.[40] Direct assignments, they argued, would speed up deployments and reduce the great number of flight hours expended just to get transports from their bases to the units they supported and back again.[41] But, while, the handiness of having transport aircraft sitting around waiting to deploy their fighter units was obvious, the proposal to actually set up such an arrangement was ironic coming from a command wedded to a fundamental doctrine that, in General Timberlake's own words, "the component parts (of tactical Air Forces)... 'cannot be effective if they are compartmented or parceled out to many various agencies or commanders who feel that they have a requirement for their own piece of tactical air.'"[42]

Lessons Overlooked

Exercise Sagebrush reports reflected the context of their writers. Consistent with the exercise's charter, they focused on the tactical and doctrinal requirements for winning an atomic conflict in a localized area. They did not address broader operational issues, such as improving force survival under nuclear attack and balancing forces and deterring enemies from pulling their nuclear triggers. After action reports did address other tactical air force roles, such as control of the air, situational awareness of enemy positions and targets, and mobility. But, they did so in very general terms and did not offer detailed suggestions for fulfilling those roles in the vicinities of exploding nuclear weapons. Moreover, the official reports did not reveal awareness of or sensitivity to the grand strategic, political, and moral issues inherent in weapons of such power. These oversights were *not* a consequence of intellectual shortfalls. General Weyland and his subordinate Air Force commanders were officers of significant combat and leadership experience and, probably, as astute a group of tactical air leaders as the Air Force has ever had. Weyland was a tireless advocate of tactical aviation and, when writing or speaking to USAF audiences, he revealed a broad and detailed view of global security issues and the likely characteristics of future wars. He never backed down from his belief that tactical air forces could deter nuclear enemies from attacking American allies or escalating such conflicts beyond theater-of-operations boundaries and that they could augment the striking power of the Strategic Air Command in general wars. But, when speaking to a national-level audience just months before Sagebrush, he more modestly declared that "as... an air commander—I am neither qualified nor inclined to speculate on our foreign policy, or on the possibility of future war."[43]

Weyland's circumspection reflected cautious, if probably not wholly sincere, good judgement, since his enthusiasm for tactical forces was out of step with the strategic views of most senior national defense and military leaders. Weyland commanded TAC at a time when President Eisenhower had issued the New Look security policy, which wedded American defense strategy to nuclear weapons. As articulated by his secretary of state, John Foster Dulles, the Administration sought to promote global stability and security, by depending "upon a great capacity to retaliate, instantly, by means and at places of our choosing" to block Soviet or Soviet-sponsored attacks on the United States and its allies.[44] Enthusiastic about the new strategy and faced by increasingly austere budgets, Air Force leaders focused their efforts on building up the strategic bomber force and continental air defenses.[45] Viewing ground operations as increasingly irrelevant in an atomic world, Air Force leaders reduced the size and budgets of tactical Air Forces to help fund the strategic buildup.[46] Seeing both a professional obligation to support national strategies and an existential threat to their part of the Air Force, TAC commanders wasted no time launching their own program to integrate atomics into theater warfare. Sagebrush was a key milestone in that program.

In the context of this national strategy, quickly labeled "Massive Retaliation," and TAC's own institutional interests, therefore, TAC leaders had little incentive to invest much thought into how they might manage escalation. In the first place, senior Air Force leaders didn't believe in self-restraint. In a 1955 interview revealing titled "We Must Avoid the First Blow," SAC Commander General Curtis E. LeMay opined that "only a foolhardy nation would ever base its power strategy upon the doubtful assumption that what it started as a localized conflict would remain localized . . . therefore . . . you dare not instigate limited actions unless you are ready to accept the possible consequences of all-out war."[47] This statement carried several implications; (1) other countries wouldn't start wars if the United States was ready to escalate, (2) the United States should be ready to escalate, and (3) responding to a limited conflict in a limited way was a risky and probably unrealistic strategy. Indeed, as the participants in Sagebrush had recognized, preemption and go-for-broke offensives made sense even at the theater-level of fighting. The promise of instant victory and the danger of instant defeat were two sides of the same atomic coin, and the latter option was simply too dangerous to risk by hesitancy or graduated applications of force.

But, in a broader context, the Air Force's thinking on nuclear warfare was losing *its* strategic credibility and was drifting out of alignment with the general body of academic and civil government thought on the matter. No sooner had the Administration articulated the massive retaliation strategy, than many prominent national security analysts began to call its basic premises into question. As Forrest Morgan discusses at length in the first chapter of this study, this body of publications was complex and nuanced, but a common theme was the question of how Soviet leaders could be made to believe that the United States was willing to trigger a mutually destructive nuclear conflict over even small and localized aggressions.[48] In the views of an increasing number of defense thinkers, the United States would continue to need non-nuclear forces to give its leaders options to deal with lesser contingencies and conflicts without having to choose between accepting defeats and risking national destruction. Air Force leaders were aware of this line of discourse, responded to it at times, and conducted numerous internal workshops and conferences to explore the employment of nuclear weapons in response to attacks by nuclear powers in limited conflicts. But, from his detailed examination of the Air Force's internal ruminations on the issue, historian Robert F. Futrell concluded that many, probably most, senior leaders in the Air Force and government remained committed to the policy of relying on nuclear weapons to deter or settle conflicts of any type.[49]

Returning to Exercise Sagebrush, a surprising void in the Air Force's post exercise reports was the absence of discussion about how to mitigate the vulnerabilities of bases and the forces on them to nuclear attacks. After all, the 800-pound gorilla of the exercise was the frustrating habit of bases to suddenly disappear under atomic blasts. But the exercise reports largely limited their discussion of these issues to veiled proposals of striking first, engaging in races to destroy bases, toughing out massive casualties, and shuttling fighter squadrons around with inadequate airlift forces. Some engaged wings also practiced "vertical dispersal," launching aircraft into holding patterns or on retaliatory strikes when warned of inbound attacks.[50] What the reports failed to say, however, was that these combined actions still resulted in the incineration of almost all engaged forces. Only in a few scattered comments did exercise commanders recognize that the real problem was the dependence of unsheltered tactical forces on developed and easily targeted bases. Only the

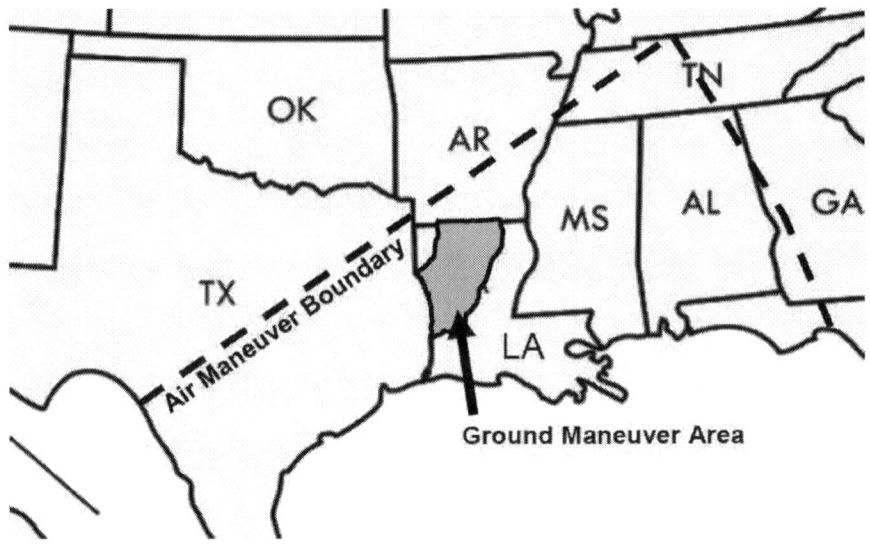

Map of USAF and Aggressor bases. The ground exercise area is the crosshatched zone in the middle. (United States Air Force. USAF, Ninth Air Force, "Evaluation of Exercise Sage Brush 1955," in *History of the Ninth Air Force* 1 July—31 December 1955, Vol. VII [Shaw AFB, SC: Headquarters Ninth AF, 1955], 15.)

public report by the TAC director of plans, Major General Stevenson, reflected that "as long as tactical Air Forces are required to use lengthy (7,000 to 10,000 feet) runways, they will be almost totally dependent upon radar detection of enemy approach and the ability of the air defense system and ground fire to neutralize initial attack." Otherwise, there were no discussions of developing combat and support aircraft that would not be tied to large air bases, or to airbase fortifications, such as those provided through the TAB VEE program that would not start until 1968.[51]

The Air Force reports also made no efforts to discuss the air war from the Army's perspective. This was an odd oversight, given the tactical air community's obligation to provide airlift and close air support to the Army, and the Army's often-expressed dissatisfaction with what it saw as the Air Force's disdainful neglect of those missions. Even as Sagebrush was underway, Army Chief of Staff General Taylor advised delegates at a National Defense Transportation Association meeting that "the Army's firepower is growing steadily, but the development of adequate mobility is lagging behind."[52] In the next year, 1956, Army commanders advised the Senate that the Air Force's provision of theater and intertheater airlift support to the Army was "uncertain" and "totally and completely inadequate."[53] The Army also began in 1956 to intensify its development of battlefield missiles to make up for what it perceived to be inadequacies in Air Force close air support (CAS), a perception reinforced by repeated statements by senior airmen that continued diversion of resources to CAS risked "national survival" in a general war.[54]

Current Reflections

Although it might at first appear to be ancient history, the record of Exercise Sagebrush suggests more relevance to current circumstances than might at first appear. Indeed, Sagebrush planners and leaders would have been on familiar doctrinal ground dealing with circumstances of today; rising enemies, proliferating weapon systems of mass effect, and threatened base networks from the homeland to forward-most operating locations. They likely would also not be surprised to find that the Army and Air Force in 2020 were desperately short of funds and searching for affordable concepts and technologies that would preserve their effectiveness and institutional credibility in future wars. They might be impressed with the maturation of our joint command structures over the past sixty years, but they certainly would not be surprised that *jointness* has not eliminated fundamental inter- and *intra*service doctrinal and budget disagreements. They might be surprised, however, that some land power and air power advocates are still making preposterous pronouncements about the independent decisiveness of their modes of warfare, and that two of the most serious bones of contention between the Army and the Air Force remain airlift and close air support. Looking back from the present, the old guys might also wonder how they could have missed the fact that the underlying presumptions of Sagebrush planning were already falling out of step with emerging realities. Spasm launches of nuclear attacks, for one, may have made some sense in conflicts characterized by American nuclear superiority, but less so in the looming reality of enemy parities in these areas. They also would note their oversight of the key question of what would enemies really do about their options of preemptive attack and escalation, as they merged in a theater of operations and either side thought it could gain irreversible advantage and avoid sure defeat by launching a massive first attack with hundreds, maybe thousands, of precision guided weapons. Also, given the potential of a theater "victory" to expand into a nuclear exchange under such circumstances, they might want to talk to us about the proper sharing of authority between theater and national command echelons. So, after just a few hours of brainstorming, the air planners of the 1950s and 2020s likely would be stunned by the realization that so much has changed tactically and technically over the past seventy years, while there has been so little *net* change in strategic context and operational concepts.

Perhaps the most important insight that air planners of today should take from these net continuities is that keeping operational concepts and strategic context aligned is a never-ending challenge. Both elements of this alignment, concepts and context, are dynamic; either can change dramatically in short-term cycles. These cycles may not disrupt the tendencies of strategic context and operational concepts to center back to persistent patterns, but they can cause them to disconnect at strategically and politically awkward times. For example, an extrapolation of operational concepts developed by the USAF in wars against the essentially helpless air forces of Iraq, Serbia, and Libya—concepts characterized by reliance on developed and secure bases, virtually unhindered access to vast quantities of military information, and increasing use of precision munitions—may not work against local peer air forces, like those of Russia and China. In their conflicts with Lilliput air forces, American airmen had the luxury of building up their forces and developing attack plans, while awaiting the outcomes of lengthy and always unsuccessful diplomatic exchanges with dictators who lacked the security of office or imagination to give political ground. Once free to strike, American air and naval aviation forces conducted systematic and prolonged campaigns that placed great emphasis on minimizing own casualties and enemy collateral damage and on preserving international endorsement of their operations. In contrast, modern air planners probably will find such a leisurely and restrained notion of air campaigning dangerous when confronting peer air forces that can find and strike bases with assurance, intercept inbound aircraft (particularly transports), quickly degrade or destroy most space-, aircraft-, and web-based information systems, and can strike overwhelmingly with precision weapons.

Indeed, air planners of the 2020s find themselves in much the same position as their professional ancestors faced in the 1950s; they live in a world where both they and their enemies are incentivized to strike first and massively. The challenge of course, is that the successful outcomes of such preemptive attacks by conventional weapons will put both sides in the position of either giving up the vital interests that presumably led them to war in the first place, or of escalating to the next level of military technology or targeting, such as nuclear counterforce strikes or even counter-homeland attacks. As strategists of the 1950s concluded, we will not be able to conceive of actually going to war with such enemies, but it is absolutely essential that they believe that we are just that crazy, and the essentials of that perception are brinkmanship and willingness to risk escalation.

There are other insights from Sagebrush worth noting, but they are offered here in the cautious understanding that the author does not have access to classified information and, consequently, does not know specifically what American, let alone other air force leaders and planners, are actually doing at the moment. But, such planners should ensure that their exercises conform to the full scope of current and emerging military contexts, such as enemy political characteristics, the strategic and operational logics of anticipated weapon systems, own vulnerabilities, and so on. They should be cautioned by the experience of Exercise Sagebrush, when planners recognized that equality in nuclear weapons mandated preemptive spasm attacks with everything available and, then, for exercise purposes, they only allowed one side or the other to initiate operations. Worse, when they discussed (or ignored) those fudged results with the Congress and others, they asserted that the key to success in the country's preparations for future wars would be more funding and more squadrons. In essence, having failed small, they proposed a solution that would only have resulted in failing bigger.

As history transpired, the strategic and political myopia of this self-delusion came to roost during the Cuban Missile Crisis of 1961, when the hardline brinkmanship and suggestions of preemptive attack coming from the Joint Chiefs of Staff startled the members of the Executive Committee (EXCOM) that President Kennedy assembled to help him contain the crisis and preserve the existence of the United States. Ultimately, President Kennedy declared in private conversation that he had a "positive lack of admiration for all the generals and admirals in the JCS . . . except for Chairman General Maxwell Taylor."[55] Taylor, of course, was the most influential military proponent of flexible response at the time. Whatever the merits of Kennedy's assessment, the wedge that Cuba drove between American civil and military defense leaders would have profound impact on American diplomacy, wars, and economics for years to come. Most important, after Cuba most strategic thinkers and at least senior civilian leaders concluded that nuclear strategy would have to be more about avoiding and deterring nuclear war than winning it. Non-nuclear escalation management also became important, as military planners realized that the outcomes of conventional wars against nuclear powers could trigger escalations up to and including employments of nuclear weapons. Ultimately, both the United States and the Soviet Union came to rely on proxy conflicts to achieve their ends and assiduously avoided direct confrontations that they might not be able to control.

Since the discussion has turned to issues of credibility, it is useful here to remind modern planners of the complacent failure of Sagebrush planning and reports to recognize and respond to the Army's frustration with the Air Force's neglect of its airlift and close support concerns. The evidence of the Air Force's disinterest in the Army's concern was overwhelming. Other than General Weyland's frequent declarations that TAC was committed to army support, virtually every other relevant public pronouncement by Air Force leaders extoled nuclear weapons as the Swiss army knives of modern wars of any kind and explicitly or implicitly predicted continued reductions in tactical combat and airlift forces.[56] Air Force programming actions were undeniable proof of its lack of appetite for handling Army problems. In 1952 and later, the air service converted several congressionally authorized orders for C-124s, which were of moderate use to the Army, into orders for C-118s, which served Strategic Air Command mobility needs but which had miniscule application to Army mobility problems.[57] In that same year, the Air Force cancelled development of the C-132, which would have been able to carry a tank over the Atlantic nonstop, in favor of the C-133, which could carry ICBMs but no heavy armored vehicles. When the Army protested before Congress, it was reminded by Air Force and defense department speakers that "American war strategy does not contemplate airlifting of large ground forces," and that "people who then express the feeling that we do not have [sufficient airlift] capability do not understand the magnitude of the problem."[58] Also in the late 1950s, the Air Force committed to the F-105 as the core of its future tactical strike fleet. The *Thunderchief* was an exquisite design for laying down a nuclear weapon at supersonic speed, but it did not require an aeronautical engineer to see that it was not intended for the low altitude turning maneuvers and on-target endurance required for close air support. In the end, the Air Force's fixation on limited nuclear war became a self-fulfilling prophecy since its programming actions robbed itself and the

C-119s were the backbone of the Air Force's theater airlift capabilities in 1955 and fell far short in the numbers and capabilities needed to support land and air operations in theater nuclear wars. (United States Air Force. https://commons.wikimedia.org/wiki/File:Fairchild_C-119B_of_the_314th_Troop_Carrier_Group_in_flight,_1952_(021001-O-9999G-016).jpg)

Army of their ability to conduct large-scale conventional wars against peer forces. The only warfighting option the Air Force had and believed practical was immediate recourse to atomic warfare.

In summary, then, the ultimate implication of Exercise Sagebrush is that the possession or posturing of nuclear and non-nuclear WME oblige modern air planners to think realistically and broadly about some key issues. Most important, such weapons in peer-on-peer conflicts drive both sides to this thinking. In the context of Sagebrush there really wasn't much room for considerations of other escalation triggers and the questions of inadvertent and accidental escalations were largely moot. So, if they are not to be merely the facilitators of such disasters, airmen must understand and respect the full scope of warfighting options and concepts available to them. For example, rushing B-21s and carrier battle groups across the Pacific to confront a Chinese aggression may be logical in terms of the nature of those aircraft and their weapons. But a less dangerous response might be posturing Army air defense units and non-aviation surface combatants first. The arrivals of such units would show resolve but not present Chinese leaders with an immediate existential threat which, hopefully, could keep diplomatic channels open. Also, if conflicts do escalate, the presence of such units would provide some protection for forward bases and logistics centers, which could come under attack the minute American offensive forces went "feet wet" over the California coast. To be respected contributors to the development of such complex strategies and the forces needed to enable them, airmen must cultivate an intellectual appetite for understanding a practically limitless range of things that will shape future wars. In the author's view, the things modern airmen must cultivate include deep and enthusiastic understandings of what the other services, the branches of their own services, and civilian agencies, like the State Department and CIA, can do and how. These understandings must also be grounded on broad and real-time appreciations of American and global geopolitics, technology and cultural futures, crisis leadership studies, and how identifiable enemies likely *will* react to our strategic concepts and capabilities, as opposed to how we might *imagine* they will respond. Truly professional airmen bent on serious leadership roles should make these understandings their lifetime passions and pursue them beyond the required reading lists of their respective war colleges and chiefs of staff. They also should develop the credibility to demand similar levels of intelligent and helpful collaboration from their counterparts in other services and agencies.

Notes

1. This account of opening operations is drawn from HQ Sixth Air Army, "Final Report, Exercise Sage Brush," January 25, 1956, 41 and throughout; and HQ Twenty-Ninth Air Force, "Twenty-Ninth Air Force Final Report on Exercise Sage Brush," 4–5; both located in Ninth Air Force, *History of Ninth Air Force 1 July—31 December 1955, Vol. VIII* (Shaw AFB, NC: HQ Ninth AF, 1955). Also see US Continental Army Command, "Report of Army Tests: Exercise Sage Brush," 1, pt. 2, (November 28, 1955), III-1, and John D. Stevenson, "Exercise Sagebrush," *Air University Quarterly Review* VIII, no. 4 (Fall 1956), 31–32.

2. Within the relevant records the name of this exercise in generally rendered as "Sagebrush" but sometimes as "Sage Brush." In either case, the name has relevance since initial plans were to hold it in the sagebrush prairie of central Texas. But, when local

ranchers refused to lease maneuver access to their land, exercise planners shifted it to Louisiana too quickly to change it to something more relevant, like "Swamp Gas" or "Rotting Trees."

3. Tactical Air Command, *History of the Tactical Air Command 1 July 1955–31 December 1955*, vol. 8, 64 and 76, unpublished report, Tactical Air Command Headquarters, 1955, author's files and in Ninth Air Force Office of History archives, Shaw AFB, South Carolina.

4. US Congress, House Subcommittee on Department of the Army Appropriations, *Department of the Army Appropriations for 1957, Exercise Sagebrush*, sudoc Y4.Ap6/1:Ar5/2/957 (Washington DC: GPO, 1956), 662.

5. Lawrence E. Wheeler, Assistant Adjutant, Tactical Air Command, to Major General D. W. Hutchison, Deputy Maneuver Director, Exercise Sage Brush; and "Evaluation of Exercise Sage Brush," April 11, 1955, in *History of Ninth Air Force 1 July—31 December 1955 Vol. VII* (Shaw AFB, NC: HQ Ninth AF, 1955), n.p., 198. NOTE: many of the reports of this exercise were not paginated by their authors, even though some were quite long. In those cases, the author uses the page numbers in the consolidated electronic files provided to him by the Ninth AF History Office in March 2020. The author would also like to take this moment to thank the Ninth AF historian, Kathy Jones, and her staff for their above-and-beyond support of the research for this study.

6. Robert F. Futrell, *Ideas, Concepts, Doctrine: Basic Thinking in the United States Air Force 1907–1960* (Maxwell AFB, AL: Air University Press, 1989), 448–50.

7. US Congress, House Subcommittee on Department of Defense Appropriations, Department of the Army Appropriations for 1956, Y4.Ap6/1:Ar5/2/956, 561–3; and John B. Wilson, *Maneuver and Firepower: The Evolution of Divisions and Separate Brigades* (Washington, DC: Center of Military History, 1998), 264–69.

8. Stevenson, "Exercise Sagebrush," 25. General Stevenson was the TAC Director of Plans and the principal Air Force planner of Exercise Sagebrush.

9. Tactical Air Command, *History*, 74.

10. Ninth AF, *History*, 393; and Stevenson, "Exercise Sagebrush," 33–34.

11. Tactical Air Command, *History*, 39–40. Apparently, 254 weapons were actually used during the exercise; 149 in the air war and 105 against ground targets; see Jean R. Moenk, *A History of Large-Scale Army Maneuvers in the United States, 1935–1964* (Ft. Monroe, VA: Continental Army Command, 1969), 212.

12. John J. Midgley, *Deadly Illusion: Army Policies for the Nuclear Battlefield* (Boulder, CO: Westview Press, 1986), 51.

13. Stevenson, "Exercise Sagebrush," 22–23.

14. House Subcommittee on Department of the Army Appropriations, *Army Appropriations for 1957*, 662.

15. TAC, *History*, 72.

16. Ninth AF, *History*, 126, 137–38.

17. Brigadier General Gerald J. Higgins, "Comments," included in Lieutenant General Lauris Norstad, "Critique: Exercise Swarmer," May 1950, in Military Air Transport Service. History Branch. *History of MATS, January to June 1950*, 5 and 7–8.

18. Moenk, *Large-Scale Army Maneuvers*, 216.

19. House, Subcommittee on Army Appropriations, *Army Appropriations for 1957*, 662; and Wilson, *Maneuver and Firepower*, 264–69.

20. Futrell, *Ideas Concepts and Doctrine*, 228–31.

21. Ninth Air Force, "Evaluation of Exercise Sage Brush 1955," in *History of the Ninth Air Force 1 July—31 December 1955, Vol. VII* (Shaw AFB, SC: Headquarters Ninth AF, 1955), 86–90.

22. USAF, *United States Air Force Statistical Digest Fiscal Year 1956, Eleventh Edition* (Washington, DC: USAF, 1956), 7–13, 545.

23. Midgley, *Deadly Illusions*, 51.

24. Hanson Baldwin, "The New Face of War," *Bulletin of Atomic Scientists* XII, no. 5 (May 1956), 154 and 157.

25. Stevenson, "Exercise Sagebrush," 28.

26. Ninth Air Force, "Evaluation of Exercise Sage Brush 1955," 272.

27. Twenty-Ninth Air Force, "Final Report," 7 and 12.

28. Sixth Air Army, "Final Report: Exercise Sagebrush," 23.

29. Ninth Air Force, "Evaluation of Exercise Sage Brush," 82.

30. Sixth Air Army, "Final Report, Exercise Sage Brush," 28–29; and Stevenson, "Exercise Sagebrush," 25.

31. Twenty-Ninth Air Force, "Final Report," Enclosure 6, Tab A, 4.

32. Tactical Air Command, "Exercise Sagebrush," 82.

33. Ninth Air Force, "Evaluation of Exercise Sage Brush," 269.

34. Tactical Air Command, *History of the Tactical Air Command Vol. VIII*, 78–79; Stevenson, "Exercise Sagebrush," 78.

35. Moenk, *A History of Large-Scale Army Maneuvers*, 217.

36. Continental Army Command, *Exercise Sage Brush*, III-1; and HQ Sixth Air Army, "Final Report, Exercise SAGE BRUSH," 20.

37. Tactical Air Command, "Exercise Sagebrush," 56–63.

38. Stevenson, "Exercise Sagebrush," 16 and 35. For a general discussion of the inadequacy of joint nuclear doctrines at the time, see David O. Smith, "The Past as Prologue: A Cautionary Tale of the U. S. Experience with Tactical Nuclear Weapons," (Naval Post Graduate School, 2011), 7–9.

39. William H. Tunner, *Over the Hump* (New York: Duell, Sloan, and Pearce, 1968; reprint Washington, DC: Office of Air Force History, 1985), 229–31; Futrell, *Ideas, Concepts and Doctrine*, 556–61; William T. Y'Blood, ed., *The Three Wars of Lt. Gen. George E. Stratemeyer: His Korean War Diary* (Washington, DC: AF History and Museums, 1999), 135.

40. Ninth Air Force, "Evaluation of Exercise Sagebrush," 96–97, and Sage Brush, "25 January 1956, 9th Air Force History Office," 25–27.

41. HQ Sixth Air Army, "Final Report, Exercise Sage Brush," 14.

42. Major General Edward Timberlake, "Tactical Air Doctrine," *Air Force Magazine*, July 1955, 45.

43. General O. P. Weyland, "Tactical Air Power—Worldwide," *Air Force Magazine*, July 1955, 39.

44. John Foster Dulles, "Speech of Secretary of State John Foster Dulles before the Council on Foreign Relations January 12, 1954"; retrieved, https://babel.hathitrust.org/cgi/pt?id=umn.31951d024881358&view=1up&seq=1, November 20, 2020.

45. Futrell, *Ideas, Concepts, Doctrine*, 422 and 433–34.

46. Futrell, *Ideas, Concepts, Doctrine*, 441.

47. "We Must Avoid the First Blow," interview with General Curtis E. LeMay, chief, Strategic Air Command, *U. S. News and World Report,* December 9, 1955, 44.

48. Among numerous examples of these studies are William W. Kaufmann, *The Requirements of Deterrence* (Princeton, NJ: Princeton University, 1954), Bernard Brodie, "Unlimited Weapons and Limited War," *The Reporter* 11, no. 9, (November 18, 1954), and Robert E. Osgood, *Limited War: The Challenge to American Security* (Chicago: University of Chicago Press, 1957).

49. Futrell, *Ideas, Concepts, Doctrine,* 462–67.

50. Twenty-Ninth Air Force, "Final Report," Enclosure 1 Tab A, 8.

51. Robert P. Grathwol and Donita M. Moorhus, *Building for Peace: U. S. Army Engineers in Europe 1945–1991* (Washington, DC: US Army Center of Military History, 2005), 160–61; and Alan J. Vick, *Air Base Attacks and Defensive Counters: Historical Lessons and Future Challenges* (Los Angeles: RAND, 2015), 48. "TAB VEE" stood for Theater Air Base Vulnerability Evaluation Exercise.

52. General Maxwell D. Taylor, "The Army Needs Mobility," *National Defense Transportation Journal* 11, no. 6 (November–December, 1955), 52.

53. "The Status Quo on Airlift," unattributed editorial, *Army Magazine,* 7, no. 1 (August 1956), 16 and 55–57.

54. Futrell, *Ideas, Concepts, Doctrine,* 441.

55. Benjamin F. Bradlee, *Conversations With Kennedy* (New York: Norton, 1975), 122.

56. Thomas D. White, Chief of Staff, United States Air Force, "We Must Give Top Priority to Survival," *Air Force Magazine* 40, no. 9, (September 1957), 54–55.

57. House Subcommittee on Department of the Army Appropriations, *Army Appropriations for 1957, Exercise Sagebrush,* 1493–1504.

58. *US Congress,* House Subcommittee on Department of Defense Appropriations, *Department of Defense Appropriations for 1958,* 2070–2088.

3

The Yom Kippur War 1973

Lazar Berman

Introduction

This chapter examines air warfare escalation and escalation management during the 1973 Yom Kippur War, mainly from the Israeli perspective. This war is remembered mostly for its dramatic battles on land; the brazen Egyptian crossing of the Suez Canal, the desperate effort by small Israel Defense Forces (IDF) armored formations to hold back the Syrian tide washing over the southern half of the Golan Heights, the massive tank battle of October 14 that shattered the Egyptian offensive, and the Israeli crossing into "Africa" (IDF shorthand for crossing the Suez) that trapped the Egyptian Third Army and gave the IDF victory on the battlefield. Less commonly understood: The war also included several milestone decisions by Israel to employ the Israeli Air Force (IAF) in ways that could have or did escalate or deescalate the conflict.

Six years after the 1967 Six-Day War that was effectively decided on the first day by a surprise Israeli aerial attack, and less than three years after the War of Attrition that was largely fought in the air, the story of airpower for both sides of the Yom Kippur War was characterized in contrast by the nonuse and misuse of airpower. Despite possessing state-of-the-art Soviet jets, for example, Arab pilots were unable to conduct successful strategic attacks, nor were they able to affect Israeli ground advances in any meaningful fashion. Little more than a week into the war, Israeli commanders understood that Egyptian and Syrian warplanes had little impact on the outcome of the war. Despite possessing arguably the finest pilots in the world, Israel's aerial campaign also left much to be desired. It was marked first of all by the glaring decision not to use airpower to decide the war at the very outset. Israeli pilots had knocked out Egypt's and Syria's air forces in Operation *Moked* (Focus) in 1967, but Israel chose not to attempt a repeat in 1973. When Israel did attempt a concerted and concentrated use of its air force in major operations, the result was a demoralizing failure.

In many ways, the Yom Kippur War was a war characterized by decisions on both sides to reduce the possibility of intentional or accidental escalations. Despite the ability of both sides to strike deep against cities, bases, and other strategic targets, Israel and Egypt spared each other's civilian home front. Likewise, Syrian tanks stopped on the Golan Heights when nothing stood between them and the heavily settled Galilee. Days later, Israeli armored forces halted their advance deep inside Syrian territory but did not attempt to push on to Damascus. King Hussein of Jordan chose to stay out of the war to the extent circumstances permitted, reluctantly deploying his 40th Armored Brigade to Syria and posing no threat to Israel from his own territory. Despite rising tensions and misunderstanding, the Americans and Soviets avoided conflict in the eastern Mediterranean. Critically, Israeli leaders refrained from seriously considering using their own nuclear arsenal, despite overblown accounts to the contrary.[1]

Within this context of operational restraint, this chapter focuses on the Israeli Air Force (IAF) during the 1973 war. It looks back at the doctrinal and technological developments that took place between the War of Attrition—when the SAM threat reared its head—and the Yom Kippur War to help understand why the IAF was employed as it was early in the conflict. It will also examine the subject of strategic attacks by air during the war. The goal is to come to an understanding of how the employment—and non-employment—or airpower influenced the course of the Yom Kippur War, and what that tells us about escalation management in an air war between what at first appeared to be peer opponents.

Israel before the War

On June 5, 1967, the first day of the Six-Day War, Israeli jets took off from Israeli air bases just before 0700 in complete radio silence, flying low to avoid enemy radar. Forty-five minutes later, the morning stillness was rent apart by Israeli planes rising up to release their bombs on Egyptian runways, hangars, and aircraft arrayed in rows on the ground. They then came back around for another pass, bombing and strafing whatever targets they could find. Just after noon, the IAF turned to the Syrian, Jordanian, and Iraqi air forces. The result was an unqualified success—389 enemy aircraft were destroyed on the ground, and the Egyptian air force was effectively knocked out in the first minutes of the war. By the end of the day, Israel enjoyed air supremacy, paving the way for the IDF's rapid victory over the next five days.

Six years later, the much-improved IAF would not be ordered to carry out a dramatic strike to open the war, which could have given it command of the skies and a major advantage in the conflict's first act. Why was the IAF used in such a drastically different fashion in the first week of the Yom Kippur War?

The core IAF doctrine hadn't changed since 1967. The IAF understood that its ultimate mission was to support the ground forces as they maneuvered quickly into enemy territory, moving to the offensive in keeping with Israel's classic approach to employing the IDF in war. In order to provide close air support, the IAF needed freedom of action, and therefore the first act in a war—a stage expected to last ninety-six hours—had to be gaining air supremacy by knocking out enemy air forces and ground-based air defenses. Of course, once Israel ordered such a strike, war could no longer be avoided, as no Arab leader would accept a last-minute arrangement mediated by outside powers once their air forces had been struck.

Under General Motti Hod, the IAF changed and improved significantly in its matériel makeup after the Six-Day War. While it was busy playing a central role in the War of Attrition against Egypt then Syria and Lebanon, the IAF went through a number of important changes. It finished the move from French fighter aircraft to more technologically advanced American fighter-bombers, purchasing several versions of the A-4 Skyhawk and the F-4E Phantom. The IAF nearly doubled its number of warplanes, going from 203 French planes in 1967 to 380 total in 1973, 310 of which were new American models.[2] In order to service this new force, the IAF itself nearly doubled in size to 20,000 men overall, while tripling the number of personnel in its ground and air crews.

At the same time, the successes in 1967 presented new challenges. With the capture of the Sinai and the Golan, Israel now had to defend the skies over a far larger area. It purchased seven new Hawk surface-to-air missile (SAM) batteries from the United States, moved its antiaircraft force from the Artillery Corps to the IAF, and spread a new radar array along the Suez

This F-4 Phantom II is a veteran of the 1973 War and bears three kill markings on its nose. (Oren Rozen. https://commons.wikimedia.org/wiki/File:F-4E_Tel_Noft_160413_02.jpg)

Canal.³ To fund this massive upgrade, the IAF accounted for more than 48 percent of the total IDF budget between the two wars.⁴

In 1967, Israeli pilots proved far superior to their adversaries, and that remained the case over the ensuing years. In general, Egyptian pilots were extremely conservative and stayed in formation, while Syrians were seen by some as bolder.⁵ Right up to the war the dominance of Israeli pilots over their Egyptian and Syrian counterparts was readily apparent. On September 13, 1973, in the last major air encounter before conflict broke out, thirteen Syrian MiG-21s were shot down against the loss of one Israeli Mirage over the Mediterranean Sea.⁶ From the end of the 1967 Six-Day War until the Yom Kippur War, Israel downed sixty Syrian planes while losing only three to Syrian fire.⁷

But Israel's adversaries learned their lessons. A new, formidable challenge to the IAF's freedom of action appeared overnight between June 23–24, 1970, as the Egyptians deployed Soviet-made SA-2C and SA-3 antiaircraft missile batteries along the Suez Canal. The threat became even stronger in 1972 with

Along with other missiles and gun systems, SA-6s drastically increased the lethality of Egyptian ground-based air defenses. (Srđan Popović. https://upload.wikimedia.org/wikipedia/commons/a/a2/2P25_VS_2.jpg)

the arrival of the SA-6, about which the IAF still knew little. It was unfamiliar with its technological specifications, and because of its mobility, Israel could not know where all the batteries were at any given time. On the eve of the war, Egypt had fifty SAM batteries deployed along the canal, and almost 146 batteries in total. Its SAM batteries were tightly integrated with ZSU-23-4 Shilka antiaircraft guns, which could hit aircraft flying low to avoid the SAMs.

IAF leadership understood it had a serious problem on its hands. In the summer of 1970, the IAF developed its initial tactic for countering the new threat. It first settled on standoff fire, at a range of at least thirty to forty kilometers, according to former IAF Chief Motti Hod decades after the war.[8] But the options for carrying out this idea disappointed IAF leaders. US-made AGM-45 Shrike missiles were purchased for this purpose, but they failed badly in their first operational use.[9] The alternative, a domestic long-range cruise missile developed at Rafael, was held up by budgetary problems.

Without long-range precision weapons to deal with the SAM threat, the IAF had to develop another solution. It settled on toss bombing, a technique that allows pilots to fly just above the ground before rising up several miles from their targets to release their bombs in an upward "toss" and then execute a diving turn to avoid SAMs. Generally, toss bombing was very accurate in terms of lateral displacement, but it lacked the range accuracy to hit entrenched targets reliably.

With that tactic chosen, and working on intelligence gleaned from a series of Egyptian exercises in the years leading up to the 1973 war, the IAF developed a number of operational plans for an upcoming conflict. To deal with the Egyptian and Syrian SAM batteries, the IAF developed a plan based on massive tightly scripted operations to knock them out. It drew up the *Taggar* (Challenge) plan against Egypt beginning in 1970, and the *Dugman* (Model) plan against Syria in 1973 (by the time the war broke out, the IAF was using *Taggar 4* and *Dugman 5)*. These plans bear some similarity to Operation *Moked* in 1967, in that multiple air and missile bases were to be hit at the same time to prevent them from coming to the assistance of other bases under attack.

Both plans rested on a number of preconditions in order to succeed. They had to be carried out at the outset of the conflict, needed updated intelligence on the location of at least 80 percent of the SAM batteries, demanded the full power of the IAF during which no other significant air missions could be carried out for twenty-four hours, and had to be done during the day in decent weather conditions.[10]

In the case of a surprise invasion by Arab armies, the IAF developed the *Srita* (Scratch) Plan, in which its planes would attack concentrations of Egyptian and Syrian ground forces in support of IDF armored divisions. *Srita* was first published in the IAF in February 1971. The plan itself was bare-bones, only seven pages long, without specific targets. In addition, a crucial target during an Egyptian crossing would be enemy bridges. Though the IDF leadership expected a nighttime crossing of the Suez Canal by Egypt, IAF pilots did not focus their training on nighttime toss bombing and would have had great difficulty striking narrow targets like bridges at night. Furthermore, the forward air control system for close air support in the IDF was outdated and incapable of supporting a maneuver war like that envisioned in *Srita*.

Still, the IAF was meant to hold off any surprise incursion until the reserves could be called up. During the "Blue and White" Exercise in May 1973, Chief of Staff David Elazar said, "In any event, we see the IAF as the first responsible body—on defense and on offense . . . this is the time in which the air force must pay its dividends for the fact that such significant means were invested in it, more than 50 percent of the defense budget, they are paying for that in this situation."[11]

But what the IAF truly wanted to do was to strike enemy airfields and knock Egyptian and Syrian planes out of the war before they even got into the fight, as it did in 1967. Since the early 1950s, IAF doctrine called for quickly gaining air supremacy over numerically superior foes by striking first and knocking out enemy air forces on the ground, to keep them from interdicting reserve forces as they streamed toward the battlefield.[12] The plan for this course of action against Egypt, developed from 1971–1973, was called *Ngicha* (Gore). It envisioned forty to sixty planes, led by Phantoms, attacking each airfield in a massive strike meant to destroy it.

General Hod, who was IAF chief until 1973, pushed for the IAF to begin a war by knocking out the SAMs, but his replacement, Benny Peled, was of a different mind. "In the three forums in which the IAF presented its plans," writes IDF military historian Shimon Golan, "it came up that according to [Peled] it was preferable to attack first enemy airfields, and from the presentation to the defense minister, it came up that only if the situation among the ground forces demands it, will attacking the missiles come before attacking the airfields."[13]

The Arab air forces that were caught on the ground in 1967 were determined not to make the same mistake again. The Soviet Union was quick to make up the losses of aircraft, replacing them with more advanced models. Both Egypt and Syria built reinforced underground hangars to protect planes on the ground. Bases were outfitted with multiple runways. Specialized teams were created to rapidly return bombed runways to service, and air defenses around bases were enhanced. Most importantly, Egypt arrayed a dense multi-layered network of SAM batteries to protect its airfields.[14] Many of these batteries were mobile, making it far more challenging for Israel to strike in a surprise attack.

In a presentation of IAF plans to Elazar in April 1973, it was clear the IAF was under the expectation that it would be asked to carry out a surprise strike on airports and enemy SAM arrays at the outset of the next conflict. The IAF understood the importance of surprise opening air strikes and improved its capabilities to make large-scale and coordinated attacks in the six years between the Six-Day War and the Yom Kippur War. IAF planes were able to carry an average of only two bombs in 1967; by 1973 that number had tripled, with some planes capable of carrying ten bombs. Navigation and targeting technology were both improved as well.[15]

But Israel's leadership didn't expect that war to come as early as it did. Their overarching strategic *conceptzia* (concept) was that the Egyptians would not attack until they had deep-strike capabilities necessary to deter strategic attacks from Israel, and that the Syrians would not attack without the Egyptians. Thus, since the Egyptian's would not have the necessary long-range aircraft and missiles until 1975, Israeli leaders downplayed or overlooked political and order-of-battle information that pointed to a likely start of the war in the nearer future.[16]

War Breaks Out

There had been growing indications that Syria and Egypt were preparing for war throughout the year, but Israeli leaders mostly dismissed them. By the night of October 4–5, 1973, there was a drastic change in how Israel interpreted the signs pointing toward war. IDF and Mossad leadership for the first time considered the possibility that Egypt and Syria were about to attack. Israeli intelligence reported the evacuation of the families of Soviet advisors from both countries, as five Aeroflot flights landed in Cairo and three in Syria. Later in the day, Israel discovered that Soviet naval forces sailed out of Egyptian ports. In addition, an extremely well-placed intelligence source sent a message to Mossad Chief Zvi Zamir's bureau chief, using the code word for the outbreak of war. According to the Agranat Commission Report after the war, Zamir passed the warning along to IDF MI chief Eli Zeira, telling him, "This is war. We don't have a date . . . but it is imminent."[17] These assessments were corroborated by newly interpreted aerial photographs—the first since September 23—indicating that Egypt had significantly reinforced its forces on the canal. There were 308 more artillery pieces and additional tank units gathered along the canal.[18]

Israel's leadership waited for another indication that war was imminent. Zamir went to meet with the intelligence source in person, and his bureau chief sent a message out in the early hours of October 6 that "the Egyptians are going to attack today just before evening . . . . According to the source . . . the likelihood is 99.9 percent."[19] War would break out within hours, the IDF leadership believed, meaning there was not enough time to call up the reserves and deploy them to the front. The air force would have to hold back the invasion.

Chief of Staff David Elazar called Peled at 0440 to discuss a preemptive strike. They decided to concentrate on the Syrian front, which posed a greater danger to Israel. There was no natural barrier on the Golan front like the

Suez Canal in the south, and the IDF had only 175 tanks, eleven artillery batteries, and seven infantry companies stationed on the Heights. In addition, unlike the vast Sinai desert, Israeli civilians lived close to the Syrian border, and the Israeli-controlled Golan Heights did not offer the strategic depth that the Sinai did. The dense Syrian SAM array, fully deployed by August 1973, was a major problem for the IAF. It consisted of thirty-six batteries, including fifteen SA-6 batteries whose ranges reached into the Galilee.[20] In net, Egypt and Syria enjoyed a 3.6:1 advantage in fighter planes, but only a 1.1:1 advantage in pilots. Their antiaircraft missile edge was much more significant, a 15.2:1 advantage.[21] With these quantitative imbalances in mind Elazar and Peled agreed on an opening strike against the Syrian missile array (*Dugman*) and then the airfields (*Ngicha*) in order to give them air superiority to stop the ground advance.[22] The attack—which would have meant that war would not be staved off—was meant to take place around midday. Then, at 0645 they changed the attack plan to target only the airfields because of low cloud cover. But, even then, the government continued to deliberate over the wisdom of a preemptive strike, which could endanger critical US support. Ultimately, the Israeli government's knowledge that American support would be critical to its ability to prosecute the war militarily and diplomatically determined the outcome of the discussion about preemption. By midday Prime Minister Golda Meir's government, already under pressure from the US, decided it would not strike the first blow.[23] Once he understood that there would be no opening strike, Peled feared that he did not have enough planes ready to defend Israel's skies from the Arab assaults he knew were coming. Accordingly, he ordered the F-4s to be rearmed for air-to-air combat instead of bombing airfields, in anticipation of enemy aerial raids at 1800 that evening. There were still 185 planes ready to carry out *Ngicha* and *Dugman*.

For IAF commanders, the initial Arab attacks were the last time that the war went according to their prewar doctrines and expectations. Instead of the systematic destruction of enemy air defenses followed by massive close support of the Army for which it had rehearsed, the IAF was employed in a piecemeal fashion to deal with a sequence of crises and conflicting priorities consequent to letting the enemy strike first. IAF radars identified Syrian and Egyptian warplanes taking off at 1355 on October 6. Though most of his planes were loaded for air strikes, General Peled hastily ordered all of them into the air to defend the skies. Many dumped munitions into the sea to lighten their loads. Only minutes later, shortly after 1400, Elazar asked whether the IAF could still attack Syrian airfields. Peled informed him that his planes had been preparing for defensive missions since the preemptive strike had been called off. Elazar ordered him to arm the planes once again for *Ngicha* against Syrian air force facilities. Thereafter, missions were maddeningly and repeatedly changed, and the IAF found itself on the defensive, with the initiative in the hands of the enemy. In the chaotic first hour of the war, Defense Minister Moshe Dayan did approve limited raids into Syria. But it appears he wanted to avoid unnecessary escalation—which could invite missile or air attacks on Israeli civilian targets—and conditioned his approval on the raids being limited to military targets and to avoid striking any targets in Damascus.[24] In keeping with that old military truism, Israel's carefully crafted plans had not survived first contact with the enemy.

The confusion over missions and priorities persisted. By late afternoon on the first day of the war, the ferocity and speed of the Egyptian crossing of the Suez worried IDF commanders enough for them to send the bulk of the air force to the south to help plug the Egyptian advance. Instead of first achieving aerial superiority by knocking out the SAMS, they called on the IAF to provide close air support and interdiction in the face of a dense and intact air defense network.[25] Despite Israel having the *Srita* plan ready, it was never used. Israel's planes were instead used in an ad hoc fashion. There were other complications as well. The reservist forward air controllers had not yet reached their bases, and planes already aloft did not have targets to strike. On the first day of the war, the air force did not contribute meaningfully to the Israeli ground support effort to stop the Egyptians crossing the Suez or the Syrians moving into the Golan.

Still, both sides of the air war did achieve meaningful success in the first day of war. Israeli pilots achieved unqualified success in defending Israel's skies. On the first day of the war, both Egyptian and Syrian planes tried to invade Israeli airspace. They suffered heavy casualties. A major air battle took place at the Israeli base Ofir at the southern tip of the Sinai Peninsula. Twenty MiG-17s and eight MiG-21 escorts attacked the base, which had only two F-4 Phantoms for protection. The relatively inexperienced Israeli pilots split up to protect opposite ends of the base, and in the ensuing battle downed seven Egyptian planes. On its part, Egypt's air force did achieve some early success attacking IDF positions across the Sinai, including a raid by Sukhoi-7s on the main forward air base in the Sinai, Refidim. In this latter attack, all Egyptian planes escaped unscathed after knocking the runways out of service for several hours.

Despite having the initiative, the overall Egyptian performance in the air war's first day was poor. For example, they experienced a disastrous failure when they sent a significant number of helicopters to land commandos in the Sinai to disrupt the ability of IDF reserves to reach the front. Of the 1700 or so commandos taking part in the air assault, 750 were killed and 330 were captured. The survivors were more interested in finding their way back to Egyptian lines than attacking IDF positions.[26] In all, 25 percent of the Arab planes that flew into Israeli airspace on the first day were shot down, and Syria and Egypt gave up on any concerted attempts to strike beyond the front lines. The Arab air forces would not play a meaningful role in the war's outcome from that point.

Still, there is no hiding from the fact that the IAF had not been used effectively on October 6. Far from controlling the war's escalation, it was not given the opportunity to win the war and played a shockingly minor role in the way the first day turned out. "They did not have the initiative," wrote Eliezer Cohen and Zvi Lavi in *The Sky Is Not the Limit*. "Both fronts were broken through, and the invasion had not been stopped. The plan for destroying the missile array was not carried out. Enemy air forces were not yet defeated. The skies over the fronts were not totally clean, and the IAF planes were still asked to be the saviors—sometimes the final lifesavers—in the places the ground forces had failed."[27]

The Air Force's Day

For Israel, October 7 was the most perilous day of the war. On both fronts, the enemy penetrated without Israeli reserves deployed to stop them. For the next day, the IAF was the only force in any conditions to stop the Egyptians and Syrians if they chose to press on to population centers inside Israel.[28] Under these circumstances, the IAF sought to put the chaotic first day behind it and return to operating according to its doctrine in an orderly fashion. It needed to deal with the SAM batteries in order to achieve aerial superiority and support the ground troops holding on in the face of overwhelming numerical inferiority.

But panic over enemy advances on both fronts threatened to derail the operations against the SAMs. Shortly after midnight on October 7, Northern Command GOC Maj. Gen. Yitzhak Hofi reported to Elazar that Syrian tanks had broken through in the southern Golan and that he didn't have enough forces to stop the advance. He asked for air support to stop the Syrian tanks. A similar request came in from Southern Command GOC Shmuel Gonen. Neither received the air support, as Elazar wanted to ensure that the IAF was fully prepared for the operations on the 7th. October 7 would be "the air force's day," predicted Elazar.[29]

In the early hours of the morning, the defense minister tried to convince Elazar to call off the operations against the SAMs and focus on ground support. Dayan was concerned about the number of tanks crossing the Suez and argued that the IAF should operate against them directly, in order to ensure a reasonable force ratio. Elazar also believed that the IAF should support the ground troops against the Egyptian advance but wanted to knock out the Egyptian SAMs before turning his pilots' attention to the crossing, as IAF doctrine dictated. Peled agreed with Elazar. "The moment we finish off the missiles, I will have freedom of action," he told Dayan.[30]

Ultimately, the IDF's commanders settled upon *Taggar 4*, the focused and systematic attack on Egyptian bases and air defenses. The operation was designed in four waves, progressing from north to south along the canal, with four hours in between each one in order to re-arm and refuel. The first wave, 150 planes, was directed at antiaircraft batteries defending the corridors through which the IAF would penetrate, and SAMs located in the far northern edge of the Suez Canal. The second wave was the main attack, with up to 300 planes attacking antiaircraft cannons and radars, then the SAM batteries themselves in the central sector of the canal. The third wave would focus on the batteries in the south, while the fourth, the only wave carried out after dark, would be directed at enemy forces attempting to rehabilitate or move antiaircraft batteries.[31]

But overnight there was a growing understanding that the impending threat was not on the banks of the Suez but was about to pour down off the Golan Heights. At 0320 the order went out to evacuate all civilians from the Golan. Israeli commanders felt that there was nothing left on the southern Golan Heights to stop the Syrian tanks from advancing and descending to the Jordan River. Once they held the bridges there, Israeli efforts to stream reserve forces up to the plateau would become exponentially more complicated.

The situation on the Golan kept the IDF command from carrying out its orchestrated attacks according to plan. At 0530 General Hofi spoke with Elazar and described the deteriorating situation. He needed air support, he stressed. The chief of staff told the IAF to give as much support as they could on the Golan Heights, but in the meantime to let the first waves of *Taggar* move forward. "I knew that the only force that could delay the Syrian forces now was the air force," Dayan explained. "We could not waste a moment. If we operate according to the doctrine, we might ultimately succeed in silencing the missile batteries, but in the meantime—Syrian tanks would already control the Jordan."[32] Even the transfer of the General Staff's reserve force, Division 146, to the Golan did not seem like it would be sufficient in Dayan's eyes. "If there are not foursomes in the air by noon, they will break through to the Jordan Valley.... The air force is the only one that can hold until the armor arrives at noon. On the southern route only the air force can deal with it consistently, otherwise we'll lose not only the Golan, but also the Jordan Valley," he told Peled.

As Dayan and Elazar fretted about the north, the opening wave of *Taggar* 4 started at 0530 as planned, with Israeli planes attacking Egyptian antiaircraft guns in a highly choreographed and complex operation that cost Israel two Skyhawks. The first wave of *Taggar* was wrapping up just before 0700, and the second wave was slated to take off a half hour later. Elazar asked Peled about transferring the IAF to the northern front. The IAF chief didn't like the suggestion for two reasons—it would take till 1200 to prepare the force to carry out *Dugman* and by then it might be too late, and he felt that the opening stage of *Taggar* had gone well and should be followed up. Peled suggested using the Mirages defending Israel's skies to attack Syrian armored columns, but Elazar did not want piecemeal strikes. He wanted the full might of the IAF up north to stop the Syrian advance until the reserve tank formations could reach the plateau.

Recognizing the growing emergency in the Golan, Elazar gave the order to complete the second phase of *Taggar* then carry out an improvised version of *Dugman* (which demanded fewer planes than *Taggar*), while immediately beginning attacks on Syrian armor despite the SAM threat. At 0720, the IAF carried out the second phase of *Taggar* against Egyptian airfields—*Ngicha*—striking, among others, Tanta, Mansoura, Bir Arida, Janaklis, Beni Suef, and antiaircraft division twenty headquarters in Lakana.[33] The IAF suffered no losses but was only able to shut down one airfield entirely. It was able to temporarily knock out runways, but it quickly became clear that Israel had underestimated the depth of the concrete of Egyptian bunkers protecting its planes.

The focus then shifted north to the Golan. *Dugman* was based on a similar concept to *Taggar*, with alterations made for the fact that there were far fewer batteries in Syria, but were mostly mobile SA-6 batteries, and the antiaircraft cannons were more densely arrayed. *Dugman* was designed to maximize surprise, with no preparatory strikes or electronic warfare (EW) support. The first wave was meant to draw fire from the SAM batteries while using Shrike missiles against enemy radar. The second would attack nearby batteries with artillery while attacking deeper batteries that were located in the first wave, and the final wave would target command and control sites, bases, artillery, and antiaircraft guns.[34]

The attack was carried out by fifteen Israeli Phantoms in three formations of five.[35] They flew toward the Syrian SAM array, which was deployed with the SA-6 batteries in the first line and the SA-3 and SA-2 batteries behind them.[36] By 1000, sixty sorties had already been flown against Syrian ground forces. The main *Dugman* attack commenced at 1130, with 113 sorties in total carried out.

Many commanders and scholars support Elazar's decision to move the IAF effort to the north, given the dire situation on the Golan. But it was not executed properly, and the results were rather disappointing. The IAF did not possess up-to-date intelligence of the locations of the SA-6 batteries, which were mobile and could not be tracked if they were shut off. Pilots struggled to locate the batteries and attack them accurately. Six Phantoms were lost in the failed effort. "The Syrian SAM array was not damaged, freedom of action was not achieved, and warplanes continued to suffer losses when they came to the aid of what little Israeli armored forces survived on the Golan Heights," writes Israeli historian Shmuel Gordon.[37]

Israeli scholar Meir Finkel identifies two approaches in the historiography to explain why the IAF's preparation for dealing with the SAMs failed. The first approach argues that the IDF understood the severity of the SAM threat but had not overcome the technological challenges they posed when the war broke out. According to the second approach, the operations were a logical and effective way to deal with the SAMs, and the IAF was fully trained and prepared to carry them out. They failed in practice because they were hastily ordered and not carried out properly during the war.

Finkel sides with the second approach, arguing that IAF commanders had developed a reasonable response and felt superbly confident in it. At a conference two years after the war, the featured speaker reminded the audience that in a January 1973 seminar on missiles, a squadron commander proclaimed, "I think even we will be surprised at how successful [the anti-SAM operations] will be." Another presenter predicted that no planes would be lost during *Taggar*.[38] "The IAF was indeed burned during the War of Attrition," writes Finkel, "but the processes that it undertook until the Yom Kippur War to solve the SAM problem were broad in scope and systematic, and the IAF went into the war with confidence in its abilities that was based on comprehensive experiments and exercises."[39]

Despite the failure of *Dugman*, there was a feeling that the IAF attacks on Syrian armor on October 7 were what stopped them. "We held the entire southern part of the Golan solely from the air. We didn't allow them to descend to Ein Gev. In our sector there was not a single Israeli tank," boasted Hod, who was responsible for coordinating close air support for Northern Command.[40]

But the close air support came at a heavy cost. With Syrian SAMs still in action, Israeli jets suffered major attrition in the early hours of the war. By the end of October 7, the IAF had already lost 10 percent of its planes.[41]

Faced by an equally desperate situation in the Southern (Sinai) Command area, Defense Minister Elazar further divided the IAF's efforts, with predictably disappointing results. Even as *Dugman* was failing, reports from Southern Command told of a rapidly deteriorating reality. Just before 1000, Gonen reported three Egyptian penetrations, and asked Elazar for IAF attacks on bridges and for close air support. At 1245, Elazar made the decision to shift the IAF back to the south to stop the advance of the Egyptian columns, which was not meant to be at the expense of *Dugman*.[42] According to Peled, the General Staff was losing hope, and was considering a retreat from the canal. "I left that depressing basement, from the Pit of the 'greens' (ground forces commanders), slammed the door and threatened the entire senior leadership: If you continue to plan a retreat, I will personally come back here with an Uzi and shoot all of you. To this day there is a crack around that door. I went back to the IAF pit and ordered an attack on the bridges. They were all destroyed at a cost of three Phantoms."[43] Peled was exaggerating the success of the attacks on the bridges on October 7. In the Pit in Tel Aviv, Elazar received reports that seven of the fourteen bridges over the canal had been damaged. In his autobiography, Egyptian Chief of Staff Saad el-Din El-Shazly also wrote that "a great number" of bridges had been destroyed by Israeli planes.[44] In all, the IAF carried out 317 sorties along the canal in the first two days, ninety-eight of them against the bridges. The IAF lost twenty-eight planes on October 6 and 7, thirteen on the Egyptian front and fifteen against Syria.

Elazar's incomplete and even panicked way in which he ordered the IAF to carry out *Taggar* in the south, then *Dugman* in the north, then close air support back in the south, has rightly been under scrutiny since the immediate aftermath of the war. Shmuel Gordon argues that the fact that Elazar was "a ground commander in every part of his body" meant that he did not know how to properly use airpower. Past chiefs of staff would observe operations from the IAF headquarters, he writes, but would not "interfere with a complex, complicated, and professional act like controlling all the IAF's planes in real time." Elazar, however, made the critical command decisions regarding airpower. "His involvement had critical drawbacks at critical junctions of airpower decisions . . . . The decision to move to the attack on the missiles in Syria (*Dugman*) is a decision with severe strategic significance for the IAF and the IDF in the entire war."[45]

Meir Finkel contests this view. The chief of staff, he writes, knew the IAF plans well and understood deeply the concept that held that aerial superiority—achieved by knocking out the SAMs and enemy planes—must be gained before close air support. Finkel points at Elazar's summary of the 1972 "Iron Ram" exercise, in which the chief of staff explains how he views the IAF's job in stopping an Egyptian advance into the Sinai:

"Aerial superiority is a prerequisite for stopping the enemy. All of our movements are conditioned on this. Aerial superiority is a condition in defensive missions too . . . . When the canal crossing begins, we will order the ground forces, the armored brigades, to make contact, to absorb, with less artillery support and without air support in the first stage and we will hold back. At this stage we will carry out the big aerial attack on the missile array with the assumption that it will take several hours. We will wipe out systematically the missile array, then we will enjoy freedom of action that will pay dividends for the rest of the holding effort."

Moreover, Elazar was briefed by Peled on all the IAF's operational plans: *Taggar*, *Dugman*, *Ngicha*, and *Srita*. Finkel argues further that the main problem with IAF plans was that *Srita* against enemy ground forces was incomplete and based on the assumption that the IAF would have aerial superiority.[46] When Israeli planes were asked to carry out close air support in the face of enemy air defenses, losses were high.

On October 8, the Israeli armored counterattack to smash the Egyptian advance in the south failed spectacularly. It was the nadir of the war for Israel. Israel and its American ally had assumed that Israel would win within several days and were ready to make a diplomatic push for a rapid end to the war. But once the counterattack failed, it was clear that Israel needed to prepare for a longer conflict than it wanted. It would take time for Israel to properly build up the necessary reserve force and knock out one of its adversaries before turning the IDF's full might to the other one.

Throughout the first week of the war, Israel had ceded the initiative in the air to the enemy. Israel could have dictated the terms of the war by ordering a preemptive strike, or even a complete *Taggar* or *Dugman*. Instead, the IAF was asked to react to enemy advances and remain on the defensive. Not surprisingly, the losses and disorganized and improvisational way with which the IAF brass was using its force shocked the pilots.

Attacking Civilian Depth

At the start, Israeli leaders misunderstood Egypt's strategy and, in particular, its desire to hit strategic targets. Israel's intelligence concept held that Sadat would not go to war before his planes could strike deep inside the Jewish state. Though they were right that Egypt could not effectively hit strategic targets in Israel in 1973, Sadat had no intention of doing so. He wanted only a limited war. Sadat reportedly told Soviet advisers in March 1971, "I don't want a large war. Help me free even ten centimeters of the Suez Canal's east bank so that the world notices the Middle Eastern issue—which it has abandoned—and helps solve it, as well as make the Americans stop the war and begin peace talks."[47] Sadat was well aware that if Egyptian planes or missiles struck in pre-1967 Israel, Cairo would be the next Israeli target.

However, on the first day of the war, an Egyptian plane did target Tel Aviv. Just as the Arab invasion commenced, an Egyptian Tupolev-16 bomber fired two Kelt cruise missiles at Tel Aviv. One missile malfunctioned and crashed into the sea, while Israeli planes scrambled from the Hazor air base easily destroyed the other over the Mediterranean. Veteran IDF intelligence officer and author Col. (res.) Pesach Melubani argues that the missiles were fired by mistake. According to Melubani, Russian sources concluded that the Egyptian pilot missed his target in northern Sinai and released his missile when he was intercepted by IAF fighters.

For the rest of the war, Egypt did not try to strike strategic targets in Israel, which would have been a major escalation that Sadat preferred to avoid. Israel also sought to avoid an escalation and did not carry out strategic attacks on civilian targets in Egypt. However, senior officials did occasionally push for attacks on civilian targets in Egypt. On the evening of October 10, for example, Dayan expressed his support for bombing economic targets deep inside Egypt.[48] These attacks were not carried out.

In contrast, strategic attacks were elements of the war with Syria from the start. Over the first four days of the war, Syrian forces fired about twenty FROG rockets into the Jezreel and Hula valleys in northern Israel. On the night of October 8 into October 9, a FROG rocket struck the Ramat David air base. In response, Israel decided to carry out attacks on strategic targets in Damascus. The first squadron of eight Phantoms—less one that turned back after a malfunction—targeted the Syrian General Staff building and the Air Force headquarters. The attack was considered a success by Israel, as both buildings suffered damage. The general staff and the air force both had to move to new buildings (along with captured Israeli pilots being held in the General Staff basement), which both disrupted their functioning and sent a clear message about the IAF's capabilities.[49] Syria fired no more FROG missiles at Israel.[50] The attack also killed a number of Russians working at the nearby Soviet cultural center. The two other squadrons slated to attack Damascus that day had to abort because of the weather. The next stage of Israeli strikes targeted Syrian civilian infrastructure. Power stations, oil refineries, bridges, and water infrastructure were all hit. The electricity supply to Syria was severely reduced when the IAF struck two power stations outside of Damascus.[51] In all, the IAF carried out 130 sorties against military and civilian targets deep inside Syria. On its part, Syria occasionally attempted desultory aerial raids inside Israel. On October 20, for instance, a Syrian Sukhoi-20 reached Haifa Bay and exploded—seemingly from a malfunction—without taking any fire from Israeli defenses. Its target was likely oil refineries in Haifa, as Damascus Radio was already reporting that they were on fire.[52]

The IAF invested significantly more effort during the war attacking enemy airfields and control stations. It is somewhat difficult to understand why the IAF persisted in committing its finest aircraft to raids on enemy air bases throughout the war, even when Egypt's and Syria's air forces were clearly no longer a serious threat. One reason might be that it was simply in the IAF's organizational DNA to attack air bases. Another possibility is that the attacks forced enemy aircraft to spend most of their time after the first day of the war defending these sites. Ninety percent of Syrian and Egyptian sorties from October 7 onward were protecting their airfields. On the defensive, enemy air forces were no longer a factor in the outcome of the war.[53] After striking eight Egyptian airfields during the truncated *Taggar* on October 7, Israel started attacking Syrian airfields the next day. Initially, Syrian ground crews were able to get fields up and running again within hours, but with every attack the recovery time increased.[54] Over the course of the war, Israeli pilots destroyed eleven Syrian planes on the ground and twenty-one in dogfights over the airports, losing four Phantoms.[55]

The Tables Turn

Less than a week into the war it seemed to be headed toward a cease fire, not a further escalation. The Arab states were in no rush to call an end to the fighting, though they may well have gotten Israel to agree to a ceasefire in place—with Arab forces holding territory on both fronts—had they pushed for one. The Soviets certainly desired an end to the conflict, especially by October 10, by which time Israel had blunted the Syrian attack and was on the offensive. On the evening of the 10th, Israel's ambassador in Washington informed Jerusalem that the Soviets had offered US Secretary of State Henry Kissinger a joint call for a ceasefire. Kissinger told the Israelis that Nixon was inclined to accept a proposal for a ceasefire on the morning of the 12th.

In the face of possible ceasefire, Elazar adopted a sort of endgame, in which the Israelis sought to definitively defeat the Syrians before the war ended. Accordingly, he decided to move to a defensive posture in the south and focus on knocking Syria out of the war. By October 10, Syrian forces had been pushed out of Israel, and three days later, the IDF held a salient that reached to within forty kilometers from Damascus. In other words, it took eight days for Israel to recover from a massive surprise attack, a major Syrian breakthrough in the southern Golan Heights, and a functioning SAM array and to reach a decision on the Syrian front. Meanwhile, the war seemed to be winding down with Egyptian forces still firmly entrenched on the eastern side of the canal.

The possibility of a ceasefire that left Egyptian forces east of the canal and closer to Israel proper led IAF commander Benny Peled to push Elazar to be more aggressive and order a crossing of the Suez before the impending ceasefire. On the 11th, he began warning Elazar that because of its heavy losses, the IAF would soon drop below its "red line" of 200–220 planes and could only support a ground offensive for the next forty-eight hours, until October 14. Elazar took Peled, who later admitted to exaggerating the problem, at his word, and instead of ordering an immediate crossing of the Suez, decided the least bad course of action was to sue for a ceasefire by the 14th, when the IAF could no longer support a major ground operation.

Attrition of Israeli forces was already a problem given the distinct numerical advantage Egypt and Syria enjoyed. But it became even more acute on October 10, when twenty-one Soviet AN-12 transport planes landed in Syria to mark the start of the Soviet airlift.[56] With Arab forces enjoying resupply, and promised American aid yet to arrive, Israel faced the possibility of adversaries whose numbers remained stable while its own forces steadily declined. "Ultimately," said Elazar on October 12, "I want a ceasefire. We are approaching 250 planes with the air force and reaching the critical line. Two or three more days like the way we operated today will work, but not much more than that, such that I would want a ceasefire in the next two days, and the morning of the day after tomorrow with be ideal."

The looming possibility that Israel might be forced to accept a ceasefire with Arab forces still holding territories on the Golan and east of the Suez forced the American government's hand regarding direct involvement in the war. From the start of the conflict, Secretary of State Henry Kissinger had declared to all interested that the US had confidence that Israeli military capabilities would force a cease fire based on the "status quo ante."[57] For that reason, President Nixon delayed authorizing an airlift of arms and ammunition to replace Israel's losses. At the same time, the Americans were not prepared to see Israel suffer a defeat that might prompt it to brandish its nuclear arsenal or undermine America's credibility in the Middle East.[58] So, struggling to gain control of the war's diplomatic events and to preclude any further escalations of the fighting, the USAF's Military Airlift Command (MAC) began flights to Lod Airport on October 12, with the first aircraft arriving at Lod at 2200 on October 14.

Nickel Grass, the American operational name for the airlift, was a logistical and diplomatic triumph that enabled continued Israeli offensive operations and put Secretary Kissinger in control of the diplomacy to end the war on terms favorable to Israel. Covered by ships of the U.S. Sixth Fleet past Libya and Egypt, and then escorted by the IAF for the last 150 miles of the route to

Tel Aviv, the big C-141s and C-5s of the Military Airlift Command flew 566 sorties into Israel over the next thirty-three days and delivered 22,395 tons of cargo. Given the distances involved, this effort equated to 144 million-ton-miles (MTM), while the best the Soviets could do was to deliver 15,000 tons over the thirty-seven days of their lift, for a total effort of twenty-five MTM. Moreover, as one historian of the operation has assessed, the Soviet lift was poorly managed and delivered much equipment that was of no immediate value to the fighting and was often lost in the Egyptian supply system. Meanwhile, the Americans and Israelis coordinated closely on the Nickel Grass deliveries that consisted of aircraft parts as large as fuselage sections, tanks, artillery pieces, and thousands of tons of ammunition that often went into battle only hours after delivery.[59] USAF units also flew dozens of A-4, F-4, and C-130 aircraft over the Atlantic and dropped them off at IAF bases. After inspecting these aircraft and painting the Star of David roundel over the USAF star, the IAF often had them flying combat only hours after arriving.

Three things changed Israel's desire for a quick cease fire. First, Nickel Grass was reversing its most desperate supply concerns and restocking its magazines. Second, intelligence arrived from the Mossad that the Egyptians were preparing to move their armored divisions across the Suez, beyond the SAM umbrella. Finally, Israeli forces stabilized the Northern Front by October 13 through its bombing of strategic targets and destroying much of the combined Syrian and Iraqi forces between them and Damascus.[60] Although the Israeli forces engaged in those harrowing battles required rest and refurbishment, their victories freed the rest of the IDF to focus on the Southern Front.

In the south, the IDF focus moved to prepare to smash the Egyptian advance then shift quickly to the offensive across the canal, where there would be far less resistance waiting for them. The Egyptian armored attack indeed took place on October 14 and was utterly routed by Israeli forces. IDF tanks destroyed around 250 Egyptian tanks while only losing ten to fifteen of their own. The Egyptian air force seemed spent as well. It only flew thirty sorties to support the attack and was unable to affect IDF ground operations.[61]

With the war finally going its way, Israel's government approved the crossing of the Suez on the night of October 14–15, and Elazar decided to carry out the operation the next night. Despite trouble getting the bridges to the canal and stubborn Egyptian resistance on the eastern side of the canal, tanks from Division 162 crossed into Africa, the western side of the canal, on

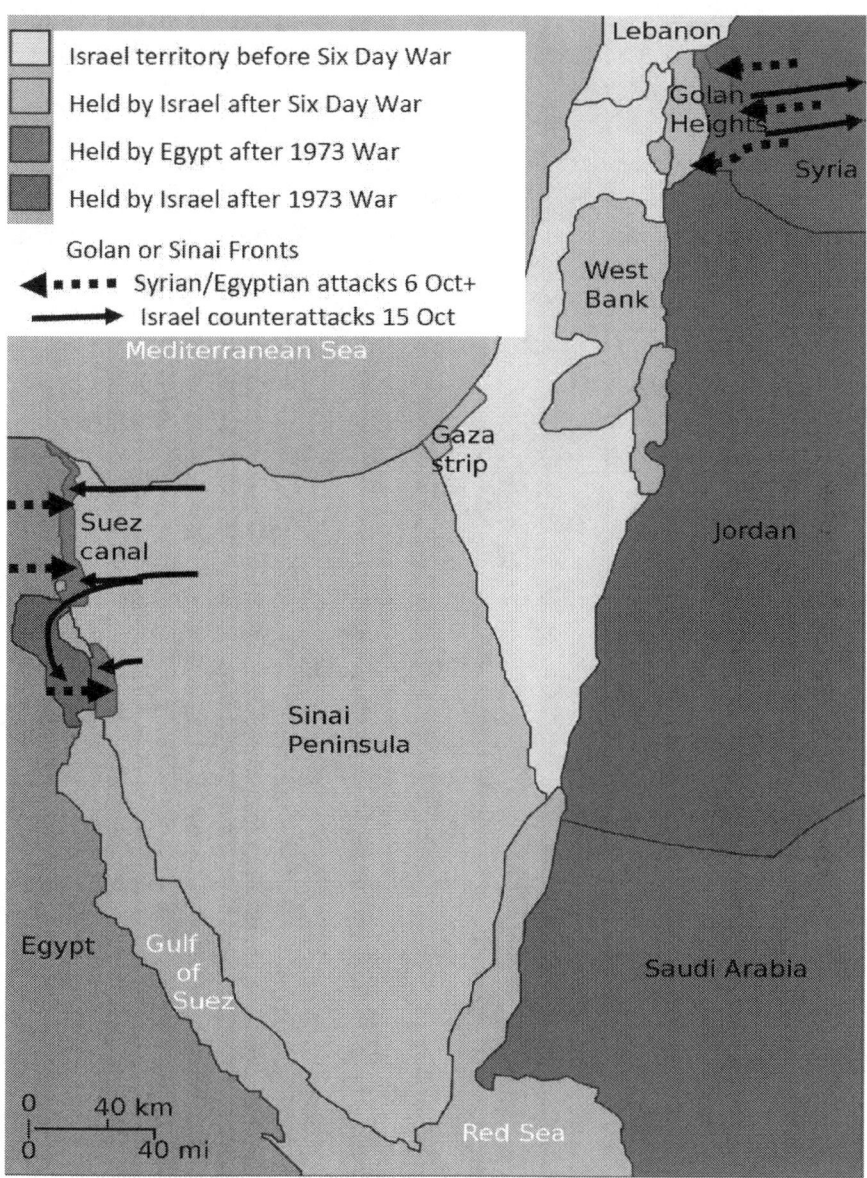

1973 War Zone (https://en.wikipedia.org/wiki/Yom_Kippur_War#/media/File:Yom_Kippur_War_map.svg. Map adapted by Robert Owen)

October 17–18. Once the bridge was erected, the Israeli bridgehead stabilized, and the main Israeli force moved south to clear out Egyptian forces and SAM batteries along the western bank of the canal. The air force's priority was providing support for the advancing Israeli armor.

As Israeli forces moved south, the diplomatic process advanced rapidly. On October 19, the Soviets invited Kissinger for talks on a ceasefire, and Israel understood its time was limited. Indeed, with Israel winning but dependent on the US airlift, and with the Soviet airlift a failure and the performance of its military allies an embarrassment, Kissinger had the leverages he needed to push all parties into accepting a cease fire based on prewar boundaries. As Kissinger's energetic shuttle diplomacy pushed negotiations through the 20th and 21st, the IDF kept up military pressure, capturing Syrian bases on Mount Hermon but failed to complete the encirclement of the Egyptian Third Army on the east bank of the canal. The ceasefire finally went into effect on October 22 at 18:52.[62]

Fighting continued after the ceasefire. Israel wanted to ensure Syria remained out of the war, and Elazar ordered the IAF to strike Syrian fuel depots. Israeli forces finally cut the Third Army off on the night of October 23–24. As the fighting continued, and Egyptian forces were in danger of dying of thirst, tensions rose dangerously between the superpowers. On the night of October 24–25 international pressures came to a head, when Soviet Premier Leonid Brezhnev told the Americans that he was prepared to take "unilateral actions" to force a cease fire. This vague threat prompted the Americans to increase their nuclear alert status which, in turn, startled the Soviets and reinforced Secretary of State Kissinger's actions to force a cease fire on both sides. Finally, on October 27, Egypt agreed to a meeting between Israeli and Egyptian officials, and the war came to an end.

Summary

The failures of the Israeli Air Force during the Yom Kippur War—perhaps justifiably—have stuck with Israelis over the decades. Six years after the IAF's finest performance, it suffered tremendous losses and failed to influence the war for several tense days.

The IAF suffered half its losses—fifty-four out of 103—in the first four days,[63] as it attacked enemy ground formations without having gained aerial supremacy first. It developed intricate operations for knocking out enemy

SAMs and trained hard. But the IAF managed to destroy only three to five Syrian SAMs and damaged five more.[64] The Syrian SAM array remained operational through the last day of the war. It knocked out forty-two batteries in Egypt, but many of these were repaired or replaced quickly.[65]

In total, the IAF carried out 11,223 sorties, and 117 dogfights. It lost around 109 planes to antiaircraft fire—mostly guns and not SAM missiles—but lost six in aerial battles.[66] The U.S. airlift brought eighty-three Phantoms and Skyhawks to replace the losses. Arab forces, on the other hand, started the war with 1040 planes, and lost 450.

Despite the favorable kill ratio, and the battlefield victory, the war ended with an overall feeling of failure. "The IAF did not overcome the Egyptian and Syrian missile arrays in the necessary time . . .," reflected former IAF chief Ezer Weizman. "And it also was unable to participate with the appropriate force to stopping the enemy on both fronts . . . . In this war, the missile bent the wing of the airplane—this a fact that must be studied closely and from which lessons must be learned."[67]

At the same time, the IAF displayed stunning flexibility as it moved quickly from mission to mission and theater to theater. When ground forces were either not present or were under pressure, the IAF was called on to stop the enemy from advancing. Its pilots showed skill and bravery, and the force as a whole coolly adapted even after a terrible opening round.

Used differently, the IAF could have influenced the war far more profoundly, perhaps winning it in its first days. But when it was used defensively, against its doctrine and ethos, it played a far smaller role than it could have, and both Israeli ground forces and pilots paid the price.

The first instance where the IAF could have exerted a decisive influence on the war was before it even started. The IAF was not ordered to carry out *Ngicha* or *Taggar/Dugman*, thus missing an opportunity to gain control of the skies before the Arab armies attacked. The decision not to do so had nothing to do with professional military considerations. Instead, it was for purely diplomatic reasons that Israel avoided that escalation, prioritizing maintaining the support of its most important ally over operational advantage. Indeed, Israel's leaders knew they'd be starting the wat at a disadvantage because of the decision not to strike.

The second instance was on October 7, when the IAF tried to carry out its rehearsed operations against the SAMs. Both *Taggar* and *Dugman* were carried out only in part, and largely unsuccessfully. The failure had little to do with enemy airpower. Instead, it was the success of Egyptian and Syrian ground offensives that forced the IAF into piecemeal tactical attacks rather than more consequential operations to wipe out the SAM arrays.

The IDF crossing of the Suez was the beginning of the end for Egypt, as IDF armor found its way across in growing numbers, then broke out to the south to eventually encircle the Third Army. It wasn't the application of air power that enabled the crossing. Instead, the Egyptian decision to attempt to break out of its well-defended bridgeheads both brought about the destruction of hundreds of its tanks and removed the preponderance of forces from the western side of the canal. In many ways, it was ground attacks on SAM sites that helped opened the skies for the IAF to carry out CAS missions for Israeli tank formations.

Israel's decisions about escalation and de-escalation were ultimately not taken based on what advantages they would offer Israel on the battlefield. The absolute need to preserve American diplomatic and logistical support loomed large at the beginning of the war, when Israel opted to forgo the opening strike, and at its close, when Israel chose not to destroy the Third Army. Veterans and historians will continue to debate whether these decisions were prudent. But their ultimate logic is defensible—without the American airlift, Israel could not have prosecuted a multi-week campaign with the losses it suffered on the ground and in the air. Even had Israel won, it would need American support to replace its tanks, planes, and other losses planes at least as would its adversaries. It is simply a reality of Israel's conflicts that American interests and concerns must form an important part of its considerations. Further, though it is not the core focus of this study, it is important to realize that inadvertent actions, Brezhnev's blustering, and deliberate actions, the airlifts and U.S. nuclear alert, largely set the boundaries of escalation and de-escalation in the regional conflict.

Israel was also deterred from escalating against Egypt, at the same time that it deterred Cairo. Both sides feared attacks on strategic infrastructure and refrained from targeting them during the war. This mutual deterrence kept the conflict from escalating out of control, and possibly bringing the superpowers into the fight.

Many of the decisions to escalate or not escalate in this war were less about capabilities than political considerations and the strategic risks involved. Conflicts do not naturally spiral into increased violence just because the opponents have the means to do so. A range of factors plays into the decision: Some are military considerations, and many have to do with what the country's leadership wants, but some come from the desires of allies and patrons.

Notes

1. Adam Raz, "The Significant of the Reputed Yom Kippur War Nuclear Affair," *INSS Strategic Assessment* 16, no. 4 (January 2014). https://www.inss.org.il/he/wp-content/uploads/sites/2/systemfiles/The%20Significance%20of%20the%20Reputed%20Yom%20Kippur%20War%20Nuclear%20Affair.pdf.

2. Meir Finkel, "The Development of the Response to Surface-to-Air Missiles and of Attacking Airfields from the War of Attrition to the Yom Kippur War, 1970–1973," *Yesodot* 3 (IDF History Department, 2021), 2. (Hebrew). https://www.idf.il/media/81837/%D7%9E%D7%A2%D7%A0%D7%94-%D7%9C%D7%98%D7%A7%D7%90-%D7%95%D7%AA%D7%A7%D7%99%D7%A4%D7%95%D7%AA-%D7%A9%D7%93%D7%AA.pdf.

3. Finkel, "Development," 2.

4. Shmuel Gordon, *Thirty Hours in October* (Tel Aviv: Maariv, 2008), 474.

5. Eliezer Cohen and Zvi Lavi, *The Sky Is Not the Limit* (Tel Aviv: Maariv, 1990), 515.

6. "Israeli and Syrian Planes in Major Fight Off Coast; Tel Aviv Claiming 13 MIG's," *The New York Times*, September 14, 1973.

7. "13 Syrian mig-21s Downed, 1 Israeli Plane Downed in Biggest Air Clash Since the Six-day War," *Jewish Telegraphic Agency*, September 14, 1973.

8. Gordon, *Thirty Hours*, 483; General Motti Hod, in Benny Michaelson, Effi Meltzer, "The Yom Kippur War—Seminar.

9. Michaelson and Meltzer, "The Yom Kippur War."

10. Finkel, "Development," 19.

11. LTG David Elazar, " 'Blue and White' presentation of program to the prime minister," War Room Agam/Operations, May 9, 1973, 15, IDF Archives 41/264/2016. The Blue and White exercises were annual training events for the IAF.

12. John R. Carter, *Israeli Air Force, 1967–73* (Air University Press, 1998), 52–65, *Airpower and the Cult of the Offensive*, www.jstor.org/stable/resrep13771.10. Accessed March 30, 2021.

13. Shimon Golan, *War on Yom Kippur: Decision-making in the Supreme Command during the Yom Kippur War* (Tel Aviv, Maarachot, 2013), 89.

14. BG Eitan Ben Eliyahu, "Aerial Combat," *Maarachot* 332, (October 1993), 15.

15. Ben Eliyahu, "Aerial Combat," 15.

16. Shimon Golan, "The Yom Kippur War," in *A Never-Ending Conflict: A Guide to Israeli Military History*, ed. Mordechai Bar-On (Westport: Praeger), 159.

17. Agranat Commission Report, 2, 51–54. The Agranat Commission conducted the official investigation of IDF performance and mistakes during the war. The Israelis kept the U. S. government apprised of these developments as they happened. See, Deputy Assistant to the President for National Security, Brent Scowcroft, to Kissinger, October 5, 1973, "Message from Israeli Prime Minister Golda Meir." This and all other US Department of State documents referenced in this chapter were retrieved from the George

Washington University national security archive, retrieved https://nsarchive2.gwu.edu/NSAEBB/NSAEBB98/#docs, on June 19, 2021.

18. Golan, *War on Yom Kippur*, 224.
19. Golan, *War on Yom Kippur*, 249.
20. Gordon, *Thirty Hours*, 483.
21. Gordon, *Thirty Hours*, 484.
22. Cohen and Lavi, *The Sky Is Not the Limit*, 443.
23. American Embassy (Ambassador Kenneth Keating) to Secretary of State, "Subject GOI Concern About Possible Syrian and Egyptian Attack Today," October 6, 1973, GWU National Security Archive, document 9, and David Rodman, "The Israel Air Force in the 1967 and 1973 Wars: Revisiting the Historical Record," *Israel Affairs* 16, no. 2, 224.
24. Golan, *War on Yom Kippur*, 307.
25. Golan, *War on Yom Kippur*, 374–75.
26. Cohen, *The Sky Is Not the Limit*, 463.
27. Cohen, *The Sky Is Not the Limit*, 468.
28. Shmuel Gordon, "The Paradox of October 7," *Maarachot* 361, 57.
29. Golan, *War on Yom Kippur*, 356.
30. Golan, *War on Yom Kippur*, 345.
31. Finkel, "Development," 18.
32. Moshe Dayan, *Milestones* (Jerusalem: Idanim, 1976), 596.
33. Golan, *War on Yom Kippur*, 375.
34. Finkel, "Development," 18.
35. Cohen and Lavi, *The Sky Is Not the Limit*, 475.
36. Cohen and Lavi, *The Sky Is Not the Limit*, 474.
37. Gordon, "Paradox," 45.
38. Gordon, "Paradox," 5.
39. Gordon, "Paradox," 6.
40. Hanoch Bartov, *Dado: 48 Years and Another 20 Days*, vol. 2 (Tel Aviv: Maariv, 1978), 94.
41. Gordon, "Paradox," 46.
42. Golan, *War on Yom Kippur*, 382.
43. Binyamin Peled, "If You Continue to Plan a Retreat, I Threatened, I Will Return with an Uzi and Shoot All of You," *IAF Journal* (Ramot: Tel Aviv, 1998), 37–38. (Hebrew).
44. Saad a-Din a-Shazly, *Crossing the Canal (Hebrew translation)* (Tel Aviv: Maarachot, 1987), 168–69.
45. Gordon, *Thirty Hours*, 443–45.
46. Meir Finkel, *The Chief of Staff* (Modan, 2018), 70–75.
47. Hadas Levav and Eitam Almadon, "The Closest Call," *Israeli Air Force website*.
48. Discussion at PM office, 10.10.73, 21.10
49. Cohen, *The Sky Is Not the Limit*, 483
50. Abraham Rabinovich, *The Yom Kippur War: The Epic Encounter that Transformed the Middle East* (New York: Schocken Books, 2004), 266.
51. Rabinovich, *The Yom Kippur War*, 267.
52. Golan, *War on Yom Kippur*, 1099
53. Gordon, "Paradox," 49.

54. Cohen and Lavi, *The Sky Is Not the Limit*, 484
55. Cohen and Lavi, *The Sky Is Not the Limit*, 485
56. William B. Quandt, "Soviet Policy in the October 1973 War," *Rand Corporation* (May 1976), 19.
57. Henry A. Kissinger, 0emorandum of Conversation with Ambassador Huang Chen, Peoples Republic of China Liaison Office, October 6
58. Department of State, "Secretary's Staff Meeting, Tuesday, October 23, 1973–4:35 P.M.," GWU National Security Archives; and "Black October: Old Enemies at War Again," *Time Magazine* 102, no. 16, 32.
59. Walter J. Boyne, *The Two O'clock War: The 1973 Yom Kippur Conflict and the Airlift That Saved Israel* (New York: St Martins, 2002), 168.
60. Golan, *War on Yom Kippur,* 900
61. Golan, *War on Yom Kippur,* 911
62. Department of State, "Secretary's Staff Meeting, Tuesday, October 23, 1973."
63. Gordon, *Thirty Hours,* 493.
64. Cohen, *The Sky Is Not the Limit,* 477.
65. Cohen, *The Sky Is Not the Limit,* 513
66. Cohen, *The Sky Is Not the Limit,* 512
67. Ezer Weizmman, *For You the Sky, For You the Land* (Tel Aviv: Maariv, 1975), 329.

4

The Angolan War 1975–1988

ROBERT C. OWEN

This chapter examines whether the escalatory decisions of the major combatants during the air war over southern Angola from 1975 to 1988 were driven by factors internal or external to the nature of air warfare. This study broadens the standard definition of the term *escalatory* to include any decision to increase, decrease, or let stand the scope, intensity, and targeting of air operations. "Internal" in this case refers to doctrines, force structures, or other characteristics of the air "weapon" itself. "External" considerations include such things as broader strategic circumstances, constraints imposed by sponsor governments, domestic politics, and other factors not inherent to the nature of air warfare, but nevertheless that shaped escalation decisions. Given the thirteen-year ebb and flow of this complex war, it is not surprising that internal and external considerations shaped combatant decisions regarding the application of their air forces. But the mix of considerations varied substantially from decision to decision, so the conflict overall provides a valuable window on the controllability of escalation in air warfare.

At the outset, it is important to understand that the air operations under discussion here were components of the three interconnected conflicts that made up the broader Angolan War. The first conflict was a civil war between the three movements that had fought since the early 1960s to liberate Angola from Portuguese colonialism. When the Portuguese left in November 1975, the People's Movement for the Liberation of Angola (MPLA) forcibly established itself in Luanda, the capital, and declared itself the new national government. This arrogation was contested by the other two important liberation movements: the National Union for the Total Independence of Angola (UNITA) and the National Liberation Front of Angola (FNLA). The second conflict was an insurgency-counterinsurgency between the South West African People's Organization (SWAPO) and the Republic of South Africa over the political destiny of South West Africa/Namibia, hereinafter referred to only as Namibia.[1] Finally, the Angolan conflict became at times predominantly one between South Africa and the MPLA government and its Cuban allies. South Arica's objectives were to disrupt the MPLA's ability to govern southern Angola and make it a launching pad for further communist operations against the "White Redoubt" countries of Rhodesia, Namibia, and South Africa. This objective transcended all others for South Africa and put it in large-scale, direct combat with Angolan, Cuban, and SWAPO forces. Because most of these combat operations occurred in the transborder region between Namibia and Angola, what Namibians called their "Struggle for Independence," has been called "The Border War" by most South African combatants and scholars.

Overlaying these three local conflicts was the identity of the Angolan War as a Cold War confrontation between the Communist bloc of states, led by Cuba and the Soviet Union, and the United States and its allies. Beginning in the early 1960s, as one former colony after the other became independent, these outside powers vied with their governments and dissidents for ideological influence and economic advantage. This competition manifested in a welter of covert activities, insurgencies, wars, and other interactions in many new African states, including in the Portuguese colony of Angola. Hardly established as a communist state itself, Cuba initiated active involvements in African affairs in the mid-1960s, which eventually included providing moral, advisory, and limited material support to the MPLA by the early 1970s.[2] As Cuba's financier during these decades, the Soviet Union indirectly underwrote its client's activities in Angola and itself provided small-scale funding to the MPLA. But the Soviet strategy for Africa was more pacific than the one preferred by Fidel Castro, Cuba's President. Castro favored aggressive military actions, while Soviet leaders saw Africa as a long-term investment in influence-building through foreign aid and diplomacy.[3] Concerned by the potential spread of communism in Southern Africa, the U.S. government orchestrated and modestly funded the activities of the right-pandering FNLA and, after its formation in 1966, UNITA. By the mid-1970s the objectives of all of the outside intruders in Angolan affairs were aimed at securing some influence over the ideology and policies of whatever African government succeed the Portuguese colonial government. American leaders, particularly

Secretary of State Henry Kissinger, also worried that failure in Angola would undermine American prestige and ability to hold the loyalties of other allies and client states.[4]

Air Forces

The course of the air war over Angola was shaped by the cultural and matériel characteristics of the three air forces involved. These air forces were the People's Air Force of Angola / Air and Antiaircraft Defense (FAPA), the Cuban Revolutionary Air and Air Defense Force (DAAFAR), and the South African Air Force (SAAF). The DAAFAR operated some of its own regiments in Angola, but pilots of Cuba and other communist air forces also staffed and maintained all FAPA combat aircraft early in the war. Since the interactions of the military spirits, air warfare skills, and equipage of these combatants influenced decisions to escalate or not escalate operations, they are worth exploring at the outset.

The Angolan Air Force

Culturally, the FAPA was defensive-minded and comfortable only when its pilots were operating under the direct guidance of radar ground controllers. This defensive-mindedness reflected the air combat doctrines of their Soviet Bloc trainers and the limited training FAPA pilots received from them. Formed in late 1975, the FAPA did not become an *Angolan* air force until around 1978 into 1979, after its first cadres of pilots returned from their flight training assignments in Russia and other Soviet Bloc countries and had some time to season in the skies above their own country. From their record and the rare inside accounts of their operations available in the literature, however, it does not seem that their seasoning progressed very far. During the entire war, no FAPA fighter, whether Angolan- or Cuban-piloted, successfully destroyed a SAAF fighter. They launched often in response to SAAF operations and, beginning in 1982, began air attacks on SADF ground units. But, throughout the war, their standard tactics were to stay near their own heavily defended airfields and to run with afterburners blazing when SAAF fighters turned on them.[5]

Undoubtedly the FAPA had brave and patriotic pilots willing to fight. But there also is some evidence of a wholesale unwillingness to take risks. One Cuban pilot recounts that an entire FAPA MiG-17 squadron "had suddenly

Soviet AF MiG-23 similar to those flown in Angola (https://commons.wikimedia.org/wiki/File:Mig-23-DNST8908431_JPG.jpg)

taken sick" when ordered to accompany the Cubans in an attack on a particularly dangerous objective.[6] While this squadron's actions could be dismissed as an isolated incident, the FAPA's poor performance during the major battles in the latter 1980s cannot. FAPA tactics, designed more for survival than actually hitting targets, produced thousands of "spectacularly unsuccessful" strike sorties that killed a grand total of four SADF and two UNITA soldiers.[7]

Only in its equipage was the FAPA in good shape. In December of 1975 Cuba and possibly Nigeria donated the equivalent of a squadron of MiG-17s to Angola and ordered another squadron of MiG-21s from Russia, all to be flown by Cuban pilots and maintained by Cuban mechanics.[8] The Soviets also delivered large numbers of air defense weapons to Angola, initially SA-7 shoulder-launched missiles and light antiaircraft cannon; while Soviet Bloc states, such as East Germany, provided the technicians needed to operate and maintain the beginnings of a radar net and more sophisticated missile systems. By the latter 1980s, the FAPA's integrated air defense system (IADS) in southern Angola included a ground radar net that covered most of the region, large numbers of ZSU-23–4 Shilka mobile guns, and a layered defense of surface-to-air missiles (SAMs). Meanwhile, the fighter force had grown to over 200 combat aircraft, including about twenty-five MiG-17s, seventy-five MiG-21s, fifty MiG-23s, ten Su-22s, and twenty-five attack helicopters. The FAPA also possessed eighty light and medium transport helicopters, forty-five to fifty light and medium transport aircraft, and a squadron of An-12 transports probably flown by Soviet pilots.[9]

The Cuban Air Force

Regarding military culture, available sources suggest that the DAAFAR did not have the leadership or level of training needed to conduct effective operations in the face of competent resistance. Indeed, outside observers at the time recognized that Cuba sent many senior officers to Angola not because they were effective leaders, but rather to give them opportunities to prove their loyalty to Castro or to redeem themselves from earlier failures.[10] Two high-ranking Cuban defectors, Brigadier General Rafael del Pino and Colonel Orestes Lorenzo, have written books that reinforce this perception of political hacks focused on ingratiating themselves to Castro and otherwise just surviving their tours of duty in Angola.[11] These two officers described corruption and self-indulgence as endemic among senior air officers in Angola. Lorenzo complained that DAAFAR senior officers lived in confiscated Portuguese villas, pampered themselves with servants and good food, and were often reluctant to fight.[12] Indeed, the U.S. Central Intelligence Agency assessed early in the civil war that the Angolans recognized and resented "Cuban and Soviet monopolization of the few remaining luxuries in the country."[13] Del Pino reported that many of those same leaders stayed well clear of combat themselves and kept their children and the children of their friends either out of Angola or at least assigned to safe postings.[14] Lorenzo, who flew MiG-21s in Angola, describes two cases of outright cowardice. In the first, the colonel leading a formation exaggerated weather visibility limitations to break off an attack on a target expected to be heavily defended by UNITA. In the other case, another colonel led a formation to attack an empty field, rather than the primary target a few miles away, which had been reported to be protected by shoulder-launched SA-7 missiles.[15]

Below such officers was a generally brave and enthusiastic pilot corps, but also one that was incompletely trained. General Del Pino tells of a junior pilot sent out on a solo night mission, despite having no training or experience in such operations.[16] The pilot crashed and died. Drawing on official Cuban documents, Del Pino also describes the outcome of the engagement of two underprepared DAAFAR MiG-21 pilots by SAAF F1 pilots on November 6, 1981. Neither of the DAAFAR lieutenants saw the F1s maneuvering in behind them. Only when cannon shells began hitting the MiG wingman did they begin maneuvering to escape. In the space of a few seconds, the wingman's plane exploded and he ejected successfully while the lead MiG escaped, largely because the air-to-air missiles on the pursuing Mirage would not fire. The official report on the incident laid the blame squarely on the shoulders of the MiG squadron leaders who, it charged, were negligent in their planning, control, and support of the operation. The report also blamed the inadequate training of the two Cuban pilots. The lead pilot had only 337 total flying hours, while his unfortunate wingman had not completed the basic MiG-21 "assimilation" course, received no training in air-to-air combat, and had flown only 162 hours in the previous two years.[17] Describing another engagement between MiG-21s and Mirage F1s on October 5, 1982, Del Pino reported that one aircraft was shot down and the other returned to base looking like a "colander" from a near miss from a South African air-air-missile.[18] Then, when the MiG-21 unit began remedial training to avoid a repeat of that disaster, it immediately lost two pilots who lost control of their aircraft while trying to fly basic combat maneuvers. From the beginning, Lorenzo recounts, he and his fellow pilots were "troubled by our lack of training for warfare."[19]

As might be expected from such an inferior leadership environment, the logistics of DAAFAR units were often inadequate. Lorenzo reported that his unit was grounded at the beginning of his time in Angola for a persistent radar problem. Given the maturity of the MiG-21 design at that time, it would seem likely that the source of the problem lay more in poor logistical planning and discipline than in a matériel failure. Del Pino touched on the problem when he blamed improper maintenance of a compass system for a DAAFAR AN-26 transport crew getting lost and crashing. Worse, Del Pino discovered that Cuban technical officers had covered up the problem by falsifying the aircraft's records.[20] He intimated the consequences of systemically poor maintenance, and perhaps the operational incompetence of the DAAFAR leadership in Angola, by recounting that a single commander had been responsible for the loss of three MiG-23s in one day in September 1984, and of innumerable helicopters and planes over a period of time.[21] Since late 1984 was a quiet period in the air war, and because no MiG-23s were lost in air-to-air combat, one can reasonably assume that the MiG-23 losses and most of the others were due to some combination of poor maintenance and training accidents—both of which were condemnations of DAAFAR unit leaders and their superiors. Personalizing the impact of these logistical and leadership shortfalls, Colonel Lorenzo related that his unit committed to battle only at desperate moments, obliging him to sit out most of his tour "like a parasite . . . while others died."[22]

The South African Air Force

Drawing on a long operational history and a salting with aviators who had served with the Royal Navy and U.S. Navy, and others who had gained operational experience with both the Portuguese and the Rhodesian Air Forces, the SAAF was an "offensive-minded" organization emphasizing excellence of planning and execution of its operations.[23] Following Operation Savannah, SAAF leaders initiated a program of aggressive training and operational innovations in preparation for the expanded war they expected would come. Drawn exclusively from the privileged white population of the Republic, SAAF pilots and other personnel came into the service well-educated, motivated to defend their country, and receptive to high quality training. SAAF pilots entered combat fully qualified in all the operational capabilities of their aircraft. SAAF operational leaders lived in the field with their subordinates and regularly flew combat missions. They came to their positions through a series of technical and professional education schools and colleges that were on or near par with those of western air forces. Throughout the Angolan War, consequently, the SAAF was ready and capable of fighting a sustained and offensive air war, at least against the likes of the FAPA and DAAFAR. Certainly, the SAAF and its personnel were not perfect, but their professional and operational superiority over their enemies was profound and obvious throughout the war.

In terms of equipage, the SAAF was in good shape at the start of the war. Its fighting line included twenty-three Mirage III fighters in various configurations, thirty-two Mirage F1AZ strike fighters, and fourteen F1CZ all-weather interceptors. The SAAF also possessed a small long-range strike element of six Canberra and six Buccaneer light bombers, and a growing number of MB-326K light attack aircraft produced in South Africa. The SAAF's core transport fleet comprised seven C-130B Hercules, and nine C-160Z Transall medium lifters, plus several C-54s and around two dozen C-47 transports. The SAAF also owned around a hundred light and medium helicopters.[24]

SAAF Mirage F-1AZ (clipperarctic. https://commons.wikimedia.org/wiki/File:SAAF_Mirage_F1CZ_1979.jpg)

Logistically, the South Africans enjoyed a capable but limited technical and manufacturing base of their own. From this base, they produced most of their air munitions, many aircraft parts, and much of their testing and support equipment. As the war progressed, they also developed air-bursting and pre-fragmented "ball-bearing bombs," television-guided glide bombs, low-altitude-released guided bombs, delayed action fuses, and an air-to-air missile, the V3B Kukri, based on the American AIM-9 Sidewinder.[25] As the war progressed, South Africa's Atlas Aviation produced the Cheetah fighter by upgrading the structures, engines, electronics, and radars of the Mirage III fleet. The early versions of the aircraft were in service at the end of the Angolan conflict in 1988, but had yet to be deployed for combat. The definitive Cheetah C version of the aircraft, which had further improvements in engine power, missiles, and radar, did not reach squadron service until 1993.[26]

South Africa received a great deal of assistance from friendly states throughout the war. In a diplomatic marriage of necessity between two states surrounded by enemies, Israel and South Africa signed several secret agreements in the mid-1970s that facilitated professional exchanges and matériel trades. For the SAAF, this relationship brought aircraft engines, spare parts, and exchange visits by Israeli experts on air combat tactics and advanced air maneuvering.[27] Israel also provided indispensable technical assistance in the development of the Cheetah, the V-3, and the Seeker remotely-piloted-aircraft.[28] Israel, in return, benefited from some South African technical exchanges and a lot of South African public and private loans and investments. Indeed, private remittance donations by Jewish South Africans comprised a major source of funding for the Israeli government and private organizations.[29] There also was a nuclear content to these agreements, but more on that later.[30] Other covert sources of weaponry were Taiwan, Singapore, Chile, Zaire, France, and other arms suppliers.[31] At least one Taiwanese exchange pilot served with a SAAF squadron. Chilean Air Force officers translated Cuban radio transmissions at forward command posts in Namibia.[32] These and other forms of outside assistance were absolutely vital to keeping the SAAF and, therefore, South Africa engaged in the Angolan conflict.

The War

Angolan AF MiG-21 (Chris Lofting. Wikimedia Commons https://en.wikipedia.org/wiki/File:Angolan_Air_Force_Mikoyan-Gurevich_MiG-21bis_Lofting-1.jpg)

Opening Moves and Motives

As discussed earlier, outsiders involved themselves in the military affairs of Angola even while it was still a colony of Portugal. Moved by communist internationalist sentiments and seeking influence, Cuba, Russia, and allied states began providing money and weapons to the Marxist-leaning MPLA in the early 1960s.[33] Late in the anti-colonial struggle South Africa covertly reinforced the Portuguese with some infantry units, helicopters, light surveillance/attack aircraft, and pilots. Seizing the opportunity provided by the looming collapse of the Portuguese colonial government, the United States, Russia, and Cuba expanded their covert interaction with their favored liberation movements—interaction that included significant increases in arms shipments and military advisory support.[34] As the Portuguese Army withdrew from southern Angola, SWAPO began establishing camps at locations across the border from Namibia's populous north-central region. Faced by the threat of expanded SWAPO operations and determined to prevent the MPLA from replacing the outgoing Portuguese government, South Africa launched Operation Savannah on October 14, 1975, an invasion of Angola by about 3,000 troops. Anticipating adverse diplomatic repercussions from the invasion, the South Africans took great pains to shield their actions from the global press. Meanwhile, a US-supported hodgepodge "army" of Zairian, FNLA, and mercenary "soldiers" struck south from Zaire toward Luanda, the capital of Angola. With shiploads of military supplies and troops already arrived or underway toward Angola, Cuban President Fidel Castro responded to the South African invasion with Operation Carlota, a sea- and airlift of some 11,000 Cuban troops rushing to the aid of the MPLA.[35] Simultaneously, the Soviet Union stepped up its shipments of arms and technical advisors to Angola and committed to keep the logistics flow going as long as needed.[36] Thus, in a matter of weeks, as one scholar of the conflict has noted, "a minor conflict . . . suddenly came to be seen as a test of wills for different political blocs and their visions of the world's future."[37]

Winning the mobility and logistical competition resulted in victory for the Angolan-Cuban-Soviet alliance. Literally rushed from pierside to their battlefields, Cuban combat troops destroyed the advancing FNLA "army" and impeded the SADF advance in late November 1975.[38] Poorly trained and equipped FAPLA units also fought—but with a lack of skill and reliability that often hindered more than helped their Cuban comrades. Once their presence in Angola was exposed by the capture of several SADF soldiers, the South Africans came under severe international criticism and were obliged to begin withdrawing to the south. Since world opinion was less outraged by the intervention of the two communist states in support of a government that had been elected by no one, Cuba stayed, and the Soviet Union continued to funnel personnel and supplies into Angola. As the South Africans withdrew southward, Cuban and what passed for Angolan military forces followed at a distance. But Castro authorized no operations against the retreating SADF units, partly because he did not want the war or Cuba's role in it to expand, and likely because he feared counterattacks by the SAAF against which he would have no defenses.[39] Poorly led and militarily incompetent, the FNLA suffered a series of defeats at the hands of Angolan/Cuban forces and quickly faded as a significant participant in the Angolan civil war.[40] Also pressed by the Angolan/Cuban alliance, UNITA retreated into stronghold areas in Angola's east-central and south-eastern regions.

Cuba's continuing willingness to escalate its involvement in southern Africa bears some explanation before continuing this narrative of the war. With no significant economic or immediate strategic interests in Angola, the Cuban intervention was largely a product of President Fidel Castro's personal vision of himself as the leader of Communism's advance in the Third World.[41] Supporting other communist revolutions, he believed, was an obligation and a matter of paying Cuba's debt to humanity for its own liberation from capitalist rule. Speaking to President Erich Honecker of East Germany early in the war, Castro said that "the liberation struggle is the most moral thing in existence."[42] Moreover, Angola was politically important to Castro, as an indication of his validity as a socialist leader and as a way to mobilize and focus the Cuban population on revolutionary ideals, rather than the strained economic and social realities of Cuba under his authoritarian rule.[43] In pursuit of those ideals, Castro had initiated or reinforced liberation movements in numerous African countries already, including Algeria, Zaire, Guinea-Bissau, Ethiopia, Zimbabwe, and others. Most failed or produced only limited results. Angola offered the hope of finally achieving a major success.[44] Thus, Cuba's endurance in a long war, the costs of which far exceeded Castro's initial expectations, can best be understood as a product of his ideological commitments and also of his ego and domestic political vulnerabilities.

For South Africa, the war was more a matter of cultural and national survival. The rise of a Marxist Angola carried the threat of it becoming a springboard for further Soviet expansion into the region, starting with Namibia but aiming ultimately at South Africa itself. Also, the presence of SWAPO base camps in southern Angola threatened South Africa's ability to shape Namibia's political destiny. Prior to 1974, South Africa's objective was to retain control of Namibia, either as a protectorate under a 1922 League of Nations mandate or through outright annexation. After 1974, South Africa recognized the inevitable and began a series of political reforms aimed at converting the country into an independent, multi-party democracy that would keep the communists out and not become a threat on South Africa's northern border. South Africa's "Border War" consequently had several objectives. The first was to destroy SWAPO's military capabilities even while allowing the movement to participate in Namibian internal political processes. The second was to prevent a Marxist takeover of Angola or, having failed that, to weaken the Angolan government and to prevent it from becoming a base of further communist advances to the south.[45] Both of these objectives pushed South Africa and UNITA together in a de facto and unnatural alliance between an African liberation movement and Apartheid South Africa.

The War: Steps along the Path of Escalation

If the first phase of the Angolan War was a feeding frenzy by internal and external interests snapping at the ideological, political, and economic remains of decolonized Angola, the second phase was about consolidation and preparations for bigger battles to come. When it became clear that the MPLA government was in danger of losing ground to UNITA, the Cubans reversed a planned withdrawal from Angola and sent in reinforcements. By mid-1976, contemporary and later estimates of the number of Cuban troops in the country ranged from 20,000 to 36,000, along with thousands of civilians backing up government operations, providing medical care, setting up schools, and so on.[46] The Cubans, along with much smaller contingents from the Soviet Union and its client states, also worked to transform the FAPLA into an effective army, and to organize and train the new Angolan Air Force. But, the incompetence of FAPLA leaders and lack of motivation and divided loyalties of FAPLA soldiers, many of whom had been shanghaied into service off the streets and from market places, hindered Cuban efforts to hand over more of the war effort to them.[47] Indeed, Cuban air and ground combat units provided security in most Angolan provinces, and Fidel Castro complained in 1977 that FAPLA was leaving the Cubans to do most of the fighting against the "bandits" of the FNLA and UNITA.[48]

To the extent that its occupational deployments allowed, the Cubans garrisoned most of their forces around Luanda or along the so-called ATS (*Agrupacion de Tropas Del Sur*—Southern Grouping of Forces) main line of defense, which corresponded to the railroad running from the port of Namibe to Menongue. Some Cuban units went still further south, but they generally encamped separately from SWAPO and FAPLA units and avoided any contact with South African forces moving in the area.[49] Moreover, the DAAF-AR squadrons showed no interest in directly engaging SAAF aircraft operating over southern Angola in pursuit of SWAPO. Having gotten themselves into Angola, the Cubans were avoiding actions or assuming obligations that might escalate their part of the war.

During the first two years following Savannah, roughly 1976 through mid-1978, the South Africans also were not interested in picking a fight with the MPLA, let alone the Cubans. The severe criticisms and strengthened arms and economic sanctions they had suffered as a consequence of invading Angola had made them chary of further such operations. During this period SAAF leaders and airmen focused on preparing for the big air battles they expected to come. Tactically, they focused on improving their ability to conduct extreme low-level day and night flying, precision low-altitude navigation, toss-bombing, and testing new weapons.[50] The SADF did conduct reconnaissance and harassing activities in the "near" border area of southern Angola, which often required helicopter and light aircraft support from the SAAF. Otherwise, the SADF and SAAF helicopter and light strike units focused on counterinsurgency operations inside Namibia.

In late 1977 and into 1978, the South African's intentionally escalated the war. Operating from base camps often located just across the border, SWAPO had steadily increased the size and effectiveness of its military wing, the Peoples Liberation Army of Namibia (PLAN), and of its incursions into Namibia. Responding to the urgings of senior military commanders, the South African president, John Vorster, and his cabinet met and endorsed the use of large cross-border raids to break up SWAPO camps and troop concentrations before they could penetrate into Namibia.[51]

Operation Reindeer was the first major result of this new policy. Taking advantage of the start of the winter dry season, the SADF and SAAF attacked two SWAPO camps on May 4, 1978. The first was located about twenty kilometers north of the border and the other was a major SWAPO base at Cassinga, about 240 kilometers further north. The South African's believed that Cassinga housed an operational headquarters, logistics and training units, and some refugees from Namibia. For the first time in the war, the SAAF opened the assault with attacks by a combined force of fast jets. Canberra and Buccaneer light bombers opened the battle with preparatory strikes on the camp, while Mirage III fighters provided air cover and close air support, should Angolan air or ground forces counterattack. These strikes were followed by a battalion-size parachute assault against the camp. The location of the camp so deep into Angolan territory, and the use of modern combat aircraft, carried a clear risk of starting an air war with the Cubans or at least picking a fight with one of their field units located near the objective.

Cassinga resulted in a hard-fought tactical success for the South Africans. The bombing attacks and subsequent ground fighting killed hundreds of PLAN soldiers and a still-uncertain number of civilian supporters and refugees sheltering in the camp. The SAAF also struck a Cuban relief column advancing from the nearby garrison, ultimately killing as many as 150 soldiers and destroying dozens of vehicles. Despite several errors of execution while under determined attacks by the Cubans, the South Africans successfully withdrew by helicopter to Namibia, having lost only three soldiers killed, one missing and presumed dead, and suffering only a handful of wounded.[52] As a result of these attacks, the Cassinga operation greatly disrupted the PLAN's ability to infiltrate insurgents into Namibia for the rest of the dry season. Once the rains came around November, further operations would go on hold until the ground dried.

Strategically, the Cassinga raid was not a success. Essentially a hit-and-withdraw raid, it caused no long-term damage to SWAPO, since the movement could replace its losses from the steady flow of angry young men and women coming out of Namibia and the supplies pouring out of Soviet ships and planes. Even more damaging for the long run, Angolan and SWAPO accusations that the raid had killed hundreds of civilians proved to be a global public image disaster for South Africa. Although later UN and other assessments indicated that the camp housed a mixture of civilian and armed military units, SWAPO exploited some blurry photos of a mass grave and friendly press reports to create a global perception of the raid as an example of the callousness and brutality of the Apartheid regime. South Africa's counter claims then, and in later academic studies, changed few minds.[53] The raid's bad press immediately disrupted ongoing peace negotiations by a five-nation "Contact Group" and the warring states. A few months later, in September 1978, the UN Security Council issued Resolution 435, which reiterated its demand for "the withdrawal of South Africa's illegal administration from Namibia and the transfer of power to the people of Namibia"[54] The attack also led SWAPO to locate many of its camps in close proximity to FAPLA and Cuban installations for mutual defense, particularly from SAAF air strikes.[55] This action guaranteed that direct South African engagements with FAPLA and Cuban field units would be a matter of routine during future operations against SWAPO, a major and unanticipated step down the escalatory road.

Indeed, over the next couple of years, fighting between South Africa and the Angolans and Cubans became the main theme of the war. Through 1980 the two sides did try to avoid each other when possible. During Operation Sceptic in June of that year, for example, SADF commanders ordered their units to avoid any contact with FAPLA, and warned FAPLA commanders not to interfere with attacks on SWAPO camps. Most FAPLA commanders complied, though there was an accidental meeting engagement between a withdrawing SADF unit and a large FAPLA patrol at the end of the operation.[56] Still, during this period some Soviet advisors felt confident enough in the SADF's restraint that they brought out their wives to live with them in camps that were only a few kilometers north of the border.[57] But when SAAF flights into Angola began to meet stiffening resistance from FAPA ground-based air defenses, South Africa took "another step up the escalation ladder" in August 1981 by opening Operation Protea with air attacks on Cuban and East German-manned radar sites and Russian-occupied command centers.[58] Protea involved around 5,000 SADF troops and the largest concentration of SAAF aircraft in a single operation since World War II. The SADF's operations broke up several SWAPO camps, devastated some FAPLA field units, captured a Russian officer, and killed a Russian wife.[59]

The Air War Follows Suit

As the war escalated in general, the air war followed suit. Prior to Operation Reindeer, FAPA and DAAFAR MiG-21 pilots patrolled south of the ATS line but stayed well clear of the border and generally close to their bases.[60] Their primary role, when they flew, was ground attack against UNITA forces: a task they performed with little skill. Once SAAF fast jets appeared over Cassinga, however, the Cubans often made attempts or at least gestures toward intercepting intruding Mirages.[61] But, when their ground radar controllers warned them that the SAAF fighters were turning to fight, the Cubans followed their defensive doctrines and ran for home. Under no circumstances were they willing to engage F1s in maneuvering fights. Nevertheless, their presence was a nuisance that sometimes forced SAAF strike aircraft to jettison their bombs early and turn into the attack. So, the SAAF went on the hunt and, once again, escalated the air war. In November 1981, two F1CZs used ambush tactics to zoom from low level into attack positions behind two MiG-21s, shooting one down with guns after their Matra 550 missiles failed. Similarly, in October 1982, two F1CZs escorting a photo reconnaissance aircraft were able to reverse turn on two MiG-21s stalking from behind and, after some brief maneuvers and more Matra 550 failures, shoot one of them down and send the other one home with severe damage.[62] Technically, the MiG-21 and the F1 were roughly equivalent in speed, maneuverability, and weaponry, apart from the Matra's poor performance. But, in the hands of a skilled South African pilot, the F1 and its 30mm cannon outclassed whatever the Cubans and Angolans could do with their MiGs.

Determined to prosecute the air war however possible, the South Africans also sent air defense artillery teams deep into the battle zone to ambush FAPA and DAAFAR aircraft. Exploiting the great gaps between the spots of southern Angola actually occupied by enemy forces, the SADF frequently attached these teams to special operations and other patrol groups operating near enemy air bases or along flight paths from those bases to forward combat areas. Operation Agony (November 1980–October 1982), for example, involved the attachment of SADF teams to UNITA units to shoot down attacking aircraft with captured SA-7 missiles. Ultimately, Agony resulted in shootdowns of at least three FAPA transport aircraft and two helicopters. Operations Catamaran 2 (June 1985) and Cerberus (October 1985) also resulted in several shootdowns. Between April and June 1986, the South Africans kept antiaircraft teams deployed between the major Cuban air base at Menongue and the ongoing battle zone around Cuito Cuanavale. In the latter years of the war, the SADF maintained special operations teams near Menongue to report on the aircraft numbers and weapon loads of departing aircraft. On one occasion during the battle of Cuito Cuanavale, a SADF artillery unit armed with multiple-rocket launchers (MRLs) covertly approached close enough to Menongue to launch a shoot-and-scoot raid, though with only limited results.[63]

By 1983, the gloves were off. In December of that year, the SAAF participated in Operation Askari with devastating attacks on FAPLA and Cuban forces. After unexpectedly hard fighting the SADF cleared the battlefield and gathered up dozens of abandoned vehicles, air defense missile sets, and convoy-loads of munitions. Global public and diplomatic pressure then obliged the South African government to terminate the operation early and pull back into Namibia.[64] As was now their habit, FAPLA/Cuban forces flowed right back into the contested areas and started over. Thus, although they had once again demonstrated their tactical superiority, the South Africans also showed that they did not have the depth of forces and political stamina needed to deal their enemies a decisive blow. The structure of the war had escalated from a low-intensity counterinsurgency focused on SWAPO to become a high-intensity conventional war with Angola, Cuba, and Russia, a war that South Africa had limited prospects of winning.[65]

The Period of Shared Freedom of the Air

Frustrated by the back-and-forth stalemate of the preceding several years, the Russians took their turn in 1984 to escalate the war. Pressing for a decisive battle, they abandoned the careful counterinsurgency and casualty-avoidance strategy favored by the Cubans and began preparing FAPLA for the kind of large, combined-arms, strategic offensive featured in their doctrines and preparations for major wars in Europe.[66] Over the next two years, Russia provided FAPLA with over $4 billion in material aid in the form of aircraft, air defense weapons, armored fighting vehicles, tube and rocket artillery, and thousands of logistics vehicles. They focused this largess and intensive training on a number of select FAPLA brigades, which would lead the offensives to come. By this time, the Soviets and outside intelligence organizations also recognized that checkmating South African air power was key to sustaining any offensives in and beyond the borders of Angola. According to the U.S. Central Intelligence Agency, the Russians strengthened the FAPA's air defense capabilities by sending out "every SAM [surface-to-air missile—au] model which the Soviets have exported to the Third World except the SA-5." In 1984 the Soviets also donated MiG-23s to the war effort.[67] These MiG-23s had the potential of shifting the character and balance of the air war. Armed with the advanced Vympel R-23 (NATO reporting name AA-7 *Apex*) missile, the new MiGs represented a serious air-to-air threat, and they also had the range to bomb SAAF bases in northern Namibia.[68]

When FAPA and its Soviet advisors did put their new strategy to the test, the South Africans and UNITA handed them a resounding defeat. In July 1985, FAPLA launched Operation Congresso II, an ambitious advance from their logistics base at Cuito Cuanavale toward the vital UNITA-held town of Mavinga about 150 kilometers to the southeast. The advance involved some eighteen "brigades" (reinforced battalions) and perhaps eighty Cuban-piloted MiGs and the rest of the FAPA, and hundreds of Soviet advisers attached down to the battalion level.[69] Recognizing that UNITA could not stop this advance alone, South Africa intervened with artillery, airlift, and combat air support. Forced to operate at extreme low levels to avoid FAPA SAMs, the SAAF employed a variation of toss bombing that they dubbed *Vergooi* (throw-away) tactics. When combined with their newly developed, pre-fragmented, "ball-bearing" bombs, these tactics allowed tosses of seven to eight kilometers with excellent lateral accuracy and good longitudinal (distance) accuracy. By "walking" these unguided bombs through general target areas, the SAAF could inflict heavy casualties against FAPLA equipment and soldiers in the open or sheltering in field entrenchments and bunkers.[70] As a consequence, combined *Vergooi* and artillery strikes devastated the lead FAPLA brigades and subsequently shattered other units retreating back to Cuito Cuanavale. In their precipitous rush back to safety, FAPLA units once again left behind large quantities of supplies and serviceable equipment for use by the SADF and UNITA.

Despite the devastating effectiveness of the SAAF strike operations, the FAPA made no significant efforts to contest air control through air-to-air combat.[71] Ground-based missiles were their weapons in the battle for air control. The Angolan Air Force, including the MiG-21 and MiG-23 squadrons piloted by the supposedly expert Cubans, remained focused on air-to-ground strikes.[72] Exploiting the cover they had from the FAPA IADS, they generally went into the operational area at medium altitudes of 15,000 to 25,000 feet to avoid the US-supplied Stinger and captured SA-7 missiles protecting UNITA and SADF ground units. At these altitudes, their aircraft were operating miles above the SAAF Mirages conducting their low-level penetrations to *their* targets.[73] During the course of Congresso II, the FAPA sent in hundreds of strikes against South African and UNITA ground units, mainly by MiG-21s piloted by Angolans.[74] The Cuban's did send in attacks, but their determination is indicated by the fact that only one DAAFAR-piloted MiG 21 was lost during the campaign—either they were suddenly very good or still remembered how to avoid dangerous targets.⁷⁵ These attacks, consequently, enjoyed a remarkable lack of success in terms of destroying equipment or causing casualties. But their threat obliged South African and UNITA ground units to exercise camouflage discipline and to make major movements only at night.

The DAAFAR's continued ineffectiveness and reluctant showing in Congresso II had several probable explanations. For one, Fidel Castro wanted no longer to dance to the Soviet fiddle. His vision of the proper prosecution of the war was of a slow and careful advance, relying on the Angolan forces to do most of the fighting and taking most of the casualties, while Cuban forces provided firepower and defensive back up. He and his commanders were not confident or enthusiastic about the Soviet Blitzkrieg-like operational concepts, which he felt were unnecessary or even harmful to success in the war and would be beyond the capabilities of the FAPLA to perform. But so long as most of his own troops remained in garrison, he yielded to the move by his benefactors to take over the planning and operational direction of the war.⁷⁶ Further, despite the infusion of some better-qualified pilots into the MiG-23 squadrons, the DAAFAR also largely sat out Congresso II. FAPA and the DAAFAR conducted air-to-ground strikes but made no significant effort to take on SAAF fighters. The DAAFAR, after all, was still mainly a MiG-21 force and no more ready for air-to-air combat than it had ever been.

Even with the Soviets and Angolans carrying most of the load, contemporary observers recognized that the war in Angola was straining the Cuban economy and Castro's political credibility. Writing in *Foreign Affairs* in the summer of 1987, one scholar stated that "the economic drain, loss of life, and domestic discontent in Cuba . . . suggest that Castro might re-evaluate his African agenda, particularly in Angola, where Cuban soldiers are now being called into frontline combat." Despite the Soviet Union's largess in providing vast quantities of material support gratis, the author estimated that involvement in seventeen African conflict zones, of which Angola was by far the largest, were consuming 11 percent of Cuba's national economy and had "crippled Cuba's domestic development plans." Meanwhile, declining prices for Angola's oil production in Cabinda Province sharply reduced Angola's ability to reimburse Cuba for its involvement. Domestic unrest was growing, particularly among Cuba's youth facing induction into the military and deployments far from home.⁷⁷ Given these concerns, escalation of the war, particularly an unproductive escalation, carried serious dangers for the Cuban dictator's hold on power.

Apparently not overly concerned by Fidel Castro's political vulnerabilities or dismayed by the failure of their initial effort to train an African army to fight in their style, the Russians prepared throughout 1986 and early 1987 to do it again with an even more lavishly equipped FAPLA. This second big offensive, Operation *Saludando Octubre* (October Salute) began in early June 1987 with four elite FAPLA brigades, fielding about 6,000 soldiers, leading the advance on Mavinga, under cover of an even more powerful IADS.[78] In a couple of weeks, South Africa was obliged again to come to UNITA's assistance. Its initial commitment consisted of artillery, some light infantry, and support from SAAF transport and strike forces.[79] By early October the South African ground force had grown to a full mechanized brigade, which received further reinforcement as the battle progressed.[80] In close integration, the combined SADF/UNITA force halted the FAPLA advance once again about halfway to Mavinga. In subsequent fighting their coordinated ground, artillery, and air strikes destroyed FAPLA's lead brigade and mauled the other three. Once again, the whole FAPLA force broke and fled back to Cuito-Cuanavale and left much of its supplies and equipment on the battlefield.[81]

Seeking an even greater victory, the South Africans and UNITA initiated a series of follow-on attacks that became known as the Battle of Cuito Cuanavale. Initially, these attacks inflicted heavy casualties on FAPLA brigades dug in on the eastern side of the Cuito River, just across from the town. Surrounded and under constant artillery attack, and with its one supply route being interdicted almost daily by F1s and SADF artillery, Cuito Cuanavale seemed in danger of falling. Even the Russian officers in the area received instructions to evacuate, though they were at a loss to identify a secure route of escape.[82] Indeed, upon learning that the Soviets planned to fly out of the battle zone, the SAAF ambushed and shot down several helicopters that might be carrying them.[83]

THE SHORT FIGHT FOR AIR CONTROL

The Angolans were saved from defeat by the Cubans. Most important, Castro reinforced the Cuito Cuanavale garrison with more Cuban troops, which put some backbone into FAPLA defensive operations.[84] Second, the DAAFAR finally began to use its MiG-23s in an offensive air-to-air role against SAAF Mirage fighters and other aircraft. Although the Cubans flew the aircraft with their usual mediocrity, their presence did present the SAAF leaders with the danger of losing precious aircraft that, given the international arms embargo imposed on them, they could not replace. After a MiG damaged an F1 with a missile hit, the SAAF decided to avoid further air-to-air combat while assessing and adjusting to the situation.[85] So, for the first time in the war, the South Africans relinquished a degree of air control to the Cubans. Then, after the failure of a final assault to push FAPLA west across the Cuito River in April 1988, the exhausted South Africans began a stealthy but orderly withdrawal back to Namibia.

South Africa's withdrawal reflected its rapidly changing strategic circumstances. Above all else, Fidel Castro had reasserted his role as the strategic leader of the communist side of the war. Openly critical of the Soviet concept of massive offensives, he convinced Soviet and Angolan leaders to keep defending Cuito Cuanavale while positioning forces for a second front in the southwest.[86] Castro began building the second front in November 1987, by deploying his best division, the 50th, and supporting forces, about 15,000 to 20,000 Cuban and Angolan soldiers, into southwestern Angola. They moved under an air defense umbrella that included about eighty MiG-21s and 23s operating from new bases located nearer the Namibian border.[87] As these forces methodically expanded their zone of control eastward from the coast, they posed real threats of invasion into Namibia and of cutting off the retreat of SADF units still around Cuito Cuanavale. Castro also played his diplomatic cards by agreeing to pull Cuban forces out of Angola if South Africa first pulled out of Namibia. This linkage between the Cuban and South African pull-outs had been a major thrust of the American-led peace negotiations since 1981 under Assistant Secretary of State for Africa, Chester Crocker.[88] With it now unequivocally on the table, South African leaders recognized that a peace settlement was in the offing. So, with their forces worn down and with a weakening economy and declining political support at home, they simultaneously began to cooperate with the peace process and to prepare for battle, if the Cubans did in fact invade. They had lost the strategic initiative to their enemies in the Angolan conflict for the first and only time in the war.[89]

In retrospect, Castro probably had no near-term intentions to prosecute the war into Namibia. More likely, he intended the advance of the 50th Division as a way to preserve his image as a competent military leader and to put pressure on the South Africans and outside peace negotiators. American diplomats and outside analysts echoed this view that Castro probably did not plan to go into Namibia, but also acknowledged that the approach of such a large force created a strategic dilemma.[90] Under those circumstances, Castro had incentives to wait and see how negotiations went, while avoiding the "negative consequences on the international stage" that he always suspected would result from a Soviet-supported Cuban advance into Namibia.[91] Finally, pushing into the SADF's home ground and closer to the SAAF's main bases would have asked the Angolan/Cuban forces to do what they had already failed to do in Congresso II and October Salute—conduct and supply an organized offensive in the face of resistance. An advance deeper into the SAAF's radar net and nearer its operating bases also would have returned some of the advantage in the air war back to the South Africans. Finally, there is evidence that Castro had already promised his Russian sponsors that he would not invade Namibia—at least not right away.[92]

Hedging their bets, however, the South Africans began preparing for a bold interdiction of the Cuban supply line into southwestern Angola. In early June 1988, the SADF began organizing a division-sized force (its first since World War II) of about 10,000 troops, artillery, and tanks for deployment into northern Namibia and possible offensive operations. This offensive likely would have aimed at destroying the DAAFAR MiG bases at Cahama and Xangongo, as well as destroying the Cuban logistical infrastructure from the Port of Namibe into the interior.[93] In conjunction with general offensive planning for the 10th Division, South African paratroop and marine officers began planning a risky attack on Namibe, Operation KWÊVOËL.[94] In the absence of SAAF air cover or supporting strikes, KWÊVOËL planning called for a night airborne drop of a small battalion of paratroops with light vehicle support about thirty kilometers outside of the target objective, simultaneous with a marine commando landing in the Port of Namibe itself. Against superior defending forces and DAAFAR air superiority, this small force was to destroy a key bridge, fuel storage tanks, ship unloading cranes, and other installations during the day and then withdraw by sea the next night.[95] The plan, in short, contained many points of possible failure and significant risk of ending in a bloody debacle. Such desperate risks were unavoidable in the absence of South African control of the air.

As it turned out, the war ended after a little more fighting and without a call for further large-scale South African offensives. In May and June 1988, SADF units protecting the strategically important Calueque reservoir and Ruacana power station on the Angolan-Namibian border probed SWAPO and FAPLA positions just to the north. The fighting included small-scale infantry, artillery, and armor exchanges. From a strategic perspective, the most important event was an attack on the Calueque dam by two flights of DAAF-AR MiG-23s. The MiGs penetrated to their targets with little opposition from SADF light antiaircraft artillery and bombed their target with better-than-usual accuracy, killing eleven SADF soldiers in the process.[96] Once again, the SAAF's failure to take on the DAAFAR was painfully obvious. The Calueque air attack proved to be a "psychological watershed" because it proved that the war could still expand into something far more dangerous than it had been thus far.[97] With South Africa's intensifying racial conflict at home, popular resistance to the war, and a stressed economy, and with Russia waffling on the continued costs of the Angolan war, such a prospect was unacceptable for South Africa and Cuba. So, before either side could organize follow-up or revenge strikes in response to the Calueque attack, the peace negotiators agreed to the outlines of a settlement, and the combatants ceased active operations on June 27, 1988.

Concluding Thoughts

As it promised in the beginning, this report will conclude with a summary answer to the question of whether the escalatory decisions of the major combatants during the air war over southern Angola from 1975 through 1988 were driven by internal or external factors. By now it should be obvious that the complex answer to this simple question is something like, "yes, in different ways at different times." The internal dynamics of air warfare, mainly military culture and technology, and external forces, mainly international politics, strategy, and resources, clearly impacted the escalatory decisions of the Cubans and South Africans. These decisions—whether to escalate, back off, or stand pat—confronted the leaders of all three air forces frequently, though sometimes with a subtlety that later analysts could miss. But, before discussing these, it will be useful to pause for a moment and discuss two of the persistent mythologies of the Angolan Conflict; that South Africa's possession of nuclear weapons shaped the war's outcome and that Cubans in MiG-23s took air control away from the SAAF.

The Bomb

Over the past three decades many details of South Africa's covert nuclear programs have become known—but by no means all of them. The country's nuclear research program began in the 1950s with direct technical and logistical support from the United States, Britain, and France, including provisions of reactors, equipment, and enriched uranium.[98] By 1967 South Africa was operating a research reactor (SAFARI-1) and a feeder reactor (SAFARI-2). Despite gaps in the public record, several researchers have concluded that South African leaders authorized a covert weapons program in the mid-1970s, likely in response to the country's growing estrangement from traditional allies as a consequence of its violent suppressions of anti-Apartheid protests.[99] Public revelation of the beginning of South Africa's weapons test program in 1977, along with its invasion of Angola in the previous year, prompted the UN Security Council to impose a general embargo on any arms sales to the country and specifically directed that "all States shall refrain from any co-operation with South Africa in the manufacture and development of nuclear weapons."[100] By that time, however, South Africa was collaborating with Israel and Pakistan to share technologies and trade in nuclear materials, namely tons of uranium to Israel in return for refined products like tritium. South Africa's development program continued with test of a device in September 1979, prototyping a deliverable bomb in 1982, and production of a small magazine of six Hiroshima-scale weapons by 1987, with another undergoing assembly.

South Africa's nuclear capabilities hovered as a poorly kept secret in the background of the Angolan War, but they were never an escalatory element in the war's conduct. The intelligence services of the United States, Britain, Russia, and France remained current on the program's status and milestones through satellite surveillance, intentional hints by South African leaders, and spies.[101] Perhaps the closest South Africa came to brandishing its nuclear capabilities was to reopen an access tunnel to a known weapon test site in 1988, probably to influence peace negotiations with Cuba, Angola, and the United States.[102] Otherwise, the South African's never threatened to use their atomic bombs, and apart from guesses by various historians, there is no smoking-gun evidence that Fidel Castro held back for fear that they might be used against his forces in Angola. Former South African State President F.W. deKlerk much later asserted that the bombs had been built as a deterrent to Soviet-sponsored aggression, not as weapons that government leaders ever expected to use. DeKlerk and others hoped that, in an emergency, South Africa would only have to reveal the existence of the weapons to raise the stakes of a conflict and force western countries to get involved to force the

Soviets to back off. One could argue that a Cuban advance into Namibia could have been the tripwire for such a sequence of events. Fortunately, the war ended before Castro found himself in a position to test South African resolve presuming, of course, that he saw the need to take such a risk. Believing that the weapons were ultimately immoral and a diplomatic "noose" around South Africa's neck, DeKlerk publicly announced their existence in 1990 and began the process of disassembling them.[103]

THE MiG-23

There is no doubt that the MiG-23 and particularly the AA-7 missile influenced the operational conduct of the war. Writers sympathetic to the Cuban cause in the war usually credit the aircraft with decisive influence. One dripping bit of propaganda argued that Cuban and Angolan MiG-23 pilots operating under the control of ground radar positions "proved equal and even superior to their counterparts in the South African Air Force," who "were . . . trounced with the Angolan pilots in firm control of Angolan airspace."[104] More dispassionately and accurately, a former SAAF chief of operations, Brigadier Jan Steyn, reported that the SAAF recognized that the technical lag of the F1 and its unsuccessful missiles made it "useless to confront the enemy in air-to-air combat and reveal one of our weaknesses. We therefore . . . avoid[ed] direct combat with enemy fighter planes as far as possible."[105]

Beyond immediate operations, the MiG-23's strategic effects were limited. While Angolan air-to-ground attacks caused almost no physical damage to South African and UNITA forces, they did make *daytime* unit movements above company level too dangerous to attempt except in emergencies, and FAPA air attacks often disrupted SADF and UNITA ground operations.[106] De-escalating its air-to-air confrontation with the DAAFAR, however, did not equate to the SAAF leaving the battle. Throughout the battle of Cuito Cuanavale and until the last days of the war, the SAAF continued to operate transport aircraft, helicopters, light strike fighters, and ground-attacking Mirages everywhere in the operational area.[107] Indeed, during Cuito Cuanavale the SAAF flew some 794 strike sorties into the area, dropped almost 4,000 bombs, struck a key bridge with guided bombs, stopped a major advance in its tracks, and killed thousands of enemy soldiers. So, while it is fair to say that the MiG-23 obliged the SAAF to cut its losses in the air-to-air battle, it is completely inaccurate to assert that it became ineffective in other operational realms. Until the very end of the war, the SAAF and the ground forces it supported stayed on the battlefield and did most of the killing.

The reality was that the MiG-23's capabilities did not live up to its propaganda. When it entered the Soviet inventory in the early 1970s, the "Flogger" was a formidable aircraft. In afterburner, it had thrust-to-weight ratio of about .9/1.0 which enabled it to accelerate faster than older-design aircraft, such as the F-4 Phantom II, British Lightening, and the F1, which had thrust-to-weight ratios of around .7/1.0. It also had a pulse-doppler radar that allowed it to identify moving targets against a background of ground clutter. Most important, the MiG-23s sent to Angola were armed with the AA-7, a radar beam-rider that could engage aircraft from the frontal aspect and from beyond visual range. But the Flogger was not designed for maneuvering in air-to-air combat. When RAND fighter expert Benjamin Lambeth flew the aircraft, he found it to be optimized for ground-controlled intercepts, not dogfighting. The pilot's seat was low, making it difficult to see out of the aircraft. Its aileron roll and turning rates were no faster than earlier fighter aircraft and no match for the next generation of western fighters coming on line in the latter 1970s. It also had a prodigious fuel consumption, which sharply limited the use of its afterburner in takeoffs and sustained high-g-force dogfights.[108] The South Africans themselves learned that the F1 had a tighter initial turn radius, though its lower thrust-to-weight ratio could not sustain the advantage. In short, the MiG-23 was a threat to the SAAF, but not an overwhelming one.

Under the defense-minded and inexpert direction of senior DAAFAR commanders in Angola, therefore, and benefiting from only the most rudimentary training, Cuban pilots racked up a profoundly unimpressive operational record. On September 10, 1987, two Mirage F1s jumped two MiG-23s and quickly got on their tails and fired Matra missiles, which exploded prematurely. The MiG-23s were saved from cannon fire by their ability to out-accelerate the Mirages and escape the fight. Interestingly, Cuban reports of this air battle indicate that the two engaged MiGs were escorting eight others carrying bombs. Revealing the combat doctrine of the DAAFAR, or lack thereof, these MiGs ran for home, rather than dump their bombs and engage the outnumbered South Africans.[109] Two weeks later, on September 27, two Floggers and F1s maneuvered into a head-on-engagement, which allowed the DAAFAR pilots to employ their AA-7s, two of which missed and one of which exploded close enough to an F1 to damage its hydraulic system and cause it to make a crash landing, which left the pilot severely injured.[110] On February 25, 1988, there were two further engagements between F1s and MiG-23s. In the first, the DAAFAR pilots refused combat and fled. In the second, the Mirages again got into position to fire their V3B missiles and cannons, but the MiGs outran them and did not turn to fight.[111] Thus, from 1984, in thousands of sorties, DAAFAR MiG-23 pilots were only once able to successfully engage another fighter aircraft of generally inferior operational characteristics. Meanwhile, from 1984 through 1988 the DAAFAR lost perhaps sixteen or more MiG-23s to accidents and ground fire.[112] Consequently, it never achieved air superiority in any meaningful sense, as it never managed to prevent the SAAF from supporting SADF and UNITA ground forces.

The lackluster performance of the DAAFAR raises the counter-factual question of what would have happened had the air war continued beyond 1988. The question has no definitive answer, of course. But a reasonable conjecture is that the SAAF would have fought hard and likely inflicted serious losses on the DAAFAR, including the MiG-23 force. Even when they were operating near their bases and under the protection of a comprehensive IADS of overlapping radar control and surface-to-air missiles, the DAAFAR and FAPLA inflicted few material losses on their enemies. Had they pushed their air operations southward, these IADS components would have gone forward, in accordance with Soviet doctrines. But in the advance, the ability of the communist forces to maintain the cohesion and control of the IADS would have suffered, creating shifting gaps in its coverage and coordination. The South Africans could have exploited those gaps. Moreover, the SAAF pilots would have been operating closer to their bases and with greater assistance from *their* ground radar controllers. The resulting increases in their on-scene flight endurance and situational awareness would have allowed them to employ tactics that they were not able to use when the air fight was hundreds of kilometers to the north near Cuito Cuanavale or in southwestern Angola. For examples, they could have used classic fighter tactics such as operational feints to separate enemy formations, high-low teaming to draw MiGs into ambushes, or soak offs to force them to burn fuel chasing one threat and lose their ability to turn and fight another. Such tactics would have allowed the SAAF to exploit its superior planning, coordination, and pilot skills to get back into the air fight, this time with Cheetahs and V3C missiles.[113] Of course, the Soviets could have escalated again by sending in more advanced fighters and missiles, and even their own pilots. But such actions would have taken the war further down a path from which they badly wanted to get off. Given the looming collapse of the Soviet Union in 1989, they likely couldn't have gone much further in Angola anyway.

Escalate, De-escalate, or Stand Pat

A discussion of escalation for the Cuban Air Force in Angola is somewhat strained, since the DARFAAR maintained a defensive posture throughout the conflict. Ground attacks were its primary mode of employment. Prior to the arrival of the MiG-23 in 1984, Cuban MiG-21 pilots frequently flew air-interception profiles when SAAF planes came across the border, but they made sure that those flights did not end in actual combat. In the cases where Cuban radar controllers failed to keep DAAFAR pilots clear of SAAF F1s, they ran a high risk seeing them shot down, as was the case in 1981 and 1982. Even when the MiG-23s came on line, the Cubans operated them like they did the MiG-21, in occasional ground strikes that they quickly broke off when Mirages appeared on their radar scopes. When finally forced to go after the SAAF's Mirages, the Cuban's still avoided the risk of maneuvering combat with the more agile and better flown F1s. In the one case where Cuban pilots damaged an F1 with a missile in 1987, their maneuvering to get into a face-to-face position was a result of natural reactions to keep the SAAF planes off their tails in the first seconds of a meeting engagement. For a few seconds, the Cuban pilots had an opportunity to fire their AA-7s before they passed the SAAF aircraft and then followed their usual tactic of making an afterburner departure from the battle.[114] Importantly, after the SAAF restricted its F1s to air base defense only, the DAAFAR made no effort to go after those bases to force a fight or withdrawal.

So, the main explanation of Cuba's reluctance throughout the war to escalate its operations against the SAAF were both internal and external. Most obviously, the DAAFAR was not capable of conducting sustained air combat. It had the pieces of a useful regional air force—modern aircraft, an IADS, command and control centers, air bases, nearly unlimited supply, etc.—but it lacked the quality of leadership, doctrines, and pilot training to make itself effective. From the start, Castro and his minions probably understood that the DAAFAR's role was to conduct limited air strikes and otherwise exist as a fleet-in-being, representing the image, if not the reality, of strength and risk to its enemies.

The South Africans represented an entirely different concept of air war from that of the Cubans, one that was *necessarily* offensive in its structure, doctrines, and training because of its traditions and minimal resources in relationship to its security challenges. Southern Africa below the Congo and Tanzania is nearly the size of the continental United States. With its limited force structure, the SAAF could not conduct a general defense, waiting for the enemy to come to it. Instead, its basic operational concept was to move forward and strike enemy forces and strategic targets where they were. Moreover, it had to be a high-quality air arm with first-class aircraft, skilled personnel, and excellent intelligence and planning organizations to make sure it fought with maximum economy of force and minimal casualties. As arms embargos and financial sanctions increased in the 1970s and thereafter, the aspect of minimizing losses became acutely important, as the SAAF had no sources of new combat aircraft, radars, air defense equipment, and so on.

Despite the SAAF's offensive mindset, the South African government tempered its employment with a desire to keep the scale and the costs of the war as low as possible and to not precipitate further embargos and sanctions from western countries and what few allies it had left in the war. Despite limiting Operation Savannah to just 3,000 troops, for example, the South Africans launched the invasion of Angola on the naïve belief that they enjoyed reliable political support from the United States and other countries, and the hope that it could keep the scale and even the origins of the advance secret.[115] The South African government's subsequent withdrawal from Angola in turn reflected its sensitivity and almost shock at the level of international criticism heaped on it, particularly from the United States. This escalation of international opprobrium was an early example of the numerous inadvertent military and diplomatic escalations that happened during the long war. The Reindeer Operation in 1978 was another example of inadvertent escalation, since the SADF launched it to restrict SWAPO movements into Namibia but wound up putting South African forces in routine combat with the Angolans and Cubans, and indirectly the Soviet Union. After Askari in 1983, and under strong encouragement from the United States and other western countries to negotiate, South Africa agreed to a cease fire while it participated in peace talks. Even after these talks proved abortive, South Africa restricted the SADF and SAAF to surveillance and small-scale raids against SWAPO until the Angolans launched Operation Congresso II in 1985. Thereafter, fighting was more-or-less continual between all combatants through the end of the war. South Africa's major de-escalatory decision during this period was withdrawal from the air-to-air battle, when the AA-7 threatened to impose irreplaceable losses on the SAAF.

Ultimately, then, getting at the question of whether internal and external factors drove the escalatory decisions of the South Africans and Cubans begins with an assessment of whether they would have escalated if they had the means to do so. Both countries were constrained by outside pressures. The Cubans depended absolutely on Soviet support and, when that began to wane in the latter 1980s, Castro had to take the gamble of deploying the 50th Division to try to force a quick end to the war. The South Africans were far less dependent on outside sponsorship than the Cubans, but they were materially and emotionally sensitive to their political and economic ostracism from most of the outside world. More specifically, the South Africans probably ran out of resources before they ran out of willingness to hit the Cubans and Angolans harder and across a wider range of targets. At several points in the war—Operations Reindeer, Protea, and Askari were important milestones—they did just that. They did not back off until the Battle of Cuito Cuanavale, when the AA-7 missile made life untenable for SAAF F1 pilots trying to defend airspace. But, had the SAAF had better missiles and a longer-range fighter, they likely would have stood their ground and, at least possibly, they would have gone after FAPA air bases. In the case of the Cubans, they had an ultimate vision of crushing Apartheid South Africa, but were forced to move cautiously by material, ideological, and quality-of-force issues. While the Angolan and Cuban air forces had superior equipment relative to the SAAF, they lacked the leaders, trained pilots, and doctrines needed to conduct offensive air warfare. Moreover, Fidel Castro's vision of how to go about a revolutionary war and his increasing political sensitivity to casualties and costs as the war progressed held back the DAAFAR for years, even as the SAAF patrolled the skies and bombed almost at will. The final evidence of his almost purely defensive understanding of air warfare was the failure (inability?) of the DAAFAR to exploit its MiG-23s to bomb the SAAF's bases in northern Namibia and force it to fight. If there is an aphorism to summarize each side's simultaneous decision to stop escalating and to end the war, it would be that "the South Africans would have but could not, while the Cubans could have but would not."

Notes

1. South Africa referred to the territory as "South West Africa," and that name appears in many of the military histories written by South Africans. However, UN General Assembly resolution 2372, June 12, 1968, established its name as "Namibia" and most of the rest of the world followed.

2. Government of Cuba, Memorandum, "Report about my visit to Angola," from Major Raúl Diaz Arguelles to Major Raúl Castro Ruz., August 11, 1975, Document from the Centro de Informacion de la Defensa de las Fuerzas Armadas Revolucionarias, CIDFAR, (Center of Information of the Armed Forces). Retrieved https://nsarchive2.gwu.edu/NSAEBB/NSAEBB67/, June 23, 2021. Also see Edward George, *The Cuban Intervention in Angola, 1965-1991: From Che Guevara to Cuito Cuanavale* (London: Frank Cass, 2005), 100-101, 105, 138, 191, 197.

3. U. S. Central Intelligence Agency, "Special Memorandum—Bolsheviks and Heroes: The USSR and Cuba," November 21, 1967; retrieved https://nsarchive2.gwu.edu/NSAEBB/NSAEBB67/, June 23, 2021.

4. U. S. Office of the President, "Minutes of Washington Special Actions Group Meeting: Subject—Cuba," March 24, 1976; retrieved https://nsarchive2.gwu.edu/NSAEBB/NSAEBB487/, June 23, 2021.

5. Dick Lord, *Vlamgat: The Story of the Mirage F1 in the South African Air Force* (Johannesburg, South Africa: 30° South Publishers, 2000), 120-21.

6. Orestes Lorenzo, *Wings of the Morning: The Flights of Orestes Lorenzo* (New York: St. Martins, 1994), 123-24.

7. Fred Bridgland, *The War for Africa: Twelve Months that Transformed a Continent* (Gibraltar: Ashanti Publishing, 1990), 102, 276.

8. U. S. Department of State, "Message: Subject—Cuban Military Intervention in Angola," January 19, 1976, retrieved https://nsarchive2.gwu.edu/NSAEBB/NSAEBB487/, June 23, 2021. Also see Rubén Urribarres and Mike Little, "The Cuban MiGs," unnumbered article, (Latin American Aviation Historical Society, April 15, 2018), 4; retrieved https://www.laahs.com/the-cuban-MiGs, April 28, 2019.

9. The International Institute for Strategic Studies, *The Military Balance 1989-1990* (London: Brassey's, 1989), 120-21.

10. Pamela Falk, "Cuba in Africa," *Foreign Affairs*, (summer 1987), 1084.

11. Rafael del Pino, *General del Pino Speaks: An Insight into Elite Corruption and Military Dissension in Castro's Cuba* (Miami, FL: Cuban-American National Foundation, 1987); and Orestes Lorenzo, *Wings of the Morning: The Flights of Orestes Lorenzo* (New York: St. Martins, 1994).

12. Lorenzo, *Wings*, 113.

13. U. S. Central Intelligence Agency, "Memorandum for Director of Central Intelligence, SUBJECT Cuban Involvement in Angola," June 23, 1977, 5.

14. Del Pino, *Speaks*, 14.

15. Lorenzo, *Wings*, 120-24.

16. Del Pino, *Speaks*, 6.

17. Rafael del Pino, *Los anos de la Guerra* (self-published, 2013), 143-48.

18. Lorenzo, *Wings*, 114. NOTE: Lorenzo's account is confusing, since he relates that two aircraft came back, while SAAF gun camera film in this appears to show one aircraft exploding from cannon hits.

19. Lorenzo, *Wings*, 113 and 116–17. See also Lord, *Eagle*, 354.

20. Del Pino, *Speaks*, 18–19.

21. Del Pino, *Speaks*, 13.

22. Lorenzo, *Wings*, 126.

23. Scholtz, *SADF*, 57.

24. The International Institute for Strategic Studies, *The Military Balance 1979–1980* (London: Brassey's, 1989), 53–54.

25. Lord, *Eagle*, 380, 403, and 410, and *Vlamgat*, 65. Also, the website, *SAAF: The Unofficial Website on the South African Air Force*, presents a comprehensive list of Border War era aircraft and weaponry, including production dates, numbers, and general capabilities, at http://www.saairforce.co.za/the-airforce/weapons/out-of-service.

26. "Cheetah Multirole Fighter Aircraft," *Air Force Technology*, webpage, https://www.airforce-technology.com/projects/cheetah-fighter

27. Lord, *Eagle*, 158.

28. Bridgland, *The War for Africa*, 116–17.

29. Helen E. Purkitt and Stephen F. Burgess, *South Africa's Weapons of Mass Destruction* (Bloomington, IN: Indiana University Press, 2005), 50.

30. Chris McGreal, "Brothers in Arms—Israel's secret pact with Pretoria," *The Guardian*, February 7, 2006.

31. Jeremy Leudi, "Apartheid's Surprising Asian Connections," Asia by Africa (blog), n.d., retrieved https://www.asiabyafrica.com/point-a-to-a/apartheid-asia-connection, May 1, 2019.

32. Lord, *Vlamgat*, 198, 206.

33. U. S. Central Intelligence Agency, memorandum, "Cuban Involvement in Angola," June 22, 1977, 1. Original classified SECRET, approved for public release, January 01, 2006

34. Piero Gleijeses, *Conflicting Missions: Havana, Washington, and Africa 1959–1976* (Chapel Hill, NC: Univ. of North Carolina, 2002), 246–48; Vladimir Shubin, *The USSR and Southern African during the Cold War* (Bologna, Italy: University of Bologna, 2008), 6.

35. Gleijeses, *Conflicting Missions*, 261.

36. Shubin, *USSR*, 7; Fidel Castro, "1977 Southern Africa Tour: A Report to Honecker (excerpt)," Wilson Center Digital Archive, retrieved https://digitalarchive.wilsoncenter.org/document/112142.pdf?v=e825d0601fd775132a5b5926ef190d7c, May 1, 2019.

37. Jamie Miller, "Castro in Africa: The contradictions of exporting revolution," *The Atlantic*, December 3, 2016; retrieved https://www.theatlantic.com/international/archive/2016/12/castro-south-africa-angola/509243/, March 9, 2019.

38. George, *Cuban Intervention*, 86–98.

39. Sholtz, *SADF*, 21.

40. George, *Cuban Intervention*, 106–8.

41. George, *Cuban Intervention*, 16–19, 78, 113–14, 201.

42. Fidel Castro, "1977 Southern Africa Tour: A Report to Honecker (excerpt)," Wilson Center Digital Archive, retrieved https://digitalarchive.wilsoncenter.org/

document/112142.pdf?v=e825d0601fd775132a5b5926ef190d7c, May 1, 2019. U. S. recognition of Castro's sense of revolutionary moral obligation was recognized in U. S. Central Intelligence Agency, Memorandum for Director of Central Intelligence, SUBJECT Cuban Involvement in Angola," June 23, 1977, 3.

43. Jacob Key, "Ulterior Motives: Understanding Castro's Intervention in Angola, 1975–1989," *The Catalyst* 2, no. 1 (2012), 16, presents a largely inferential case that Castro also may have seen access to Angola's oil as a path to reducing his dependence on Soviet financial support and its impact on his independence of action. Though this case has no smoking-gun evidence behind it, it is consistent with the Cuban government's policies of supporting revolutionary movements while simultaneously advancing the interests of the Cuban nation.

44. No source discusses the complex history of Cuba's early incursions into African conflicts better than Gleijeses, 30–229.

45. Robert C. Owen "Counterrevolution in Namibia." *Airpower Journal* (winter 1987/88), 52–62.

46. U. S. Central Intelligence Agency, "Cuban Involvement," 5–7; Edward George, *The Cuban Intervention in Angola, 1965-1991* (London: Frank Cass, 2005), 116–20.

47. George, *Cuban Intervention*, 155.

48. Castro, "Report to Honecker."

49. George, *Cuban Intervention*, 120–21.

50. Dick Lord, *From Fledgling to Eagle: The South African Air Force during the Border War* (Johannesburg, South Africa: 30° South Publishers, 2008), 66–67; Leopold Scholtz, *The SADF in the Border War 1966-1989* (Cape Town, South Africa: Tafelberg, 2013), 33–49.

51. Scholtz, *SADF*, 57; and Lord, *Eagle*, 78.

52. Edward George McGill Alexander, *The Cassinga Raid* (thesis, University of South Africa, July 2003), 113–58.

53. A useful summary of the Cassinga operation and an excellent discussion of the efforts by both sides of the raid to gain control of the historical narrative about this battle is Gary Baines, "Conflicting memories, competing narratives and complicating histories: Revisiting the Cassinga controversy," *Journal of Namibian Studies*, vol. 6 (2009), 7–26.

54. Alexander, *Cassinga*, 80–95; George, *Cuban Intervention*, 135–7; and R. Dreyer, *Namibia and Southern Africa: Regional Dynamics of Decolonization, 1945-1990* (New York, Kegan Paul International, 1994), 122–37.

55. Scholtz, *SADF*, 120–21.

56. Scholtz, *SADF*, 103 and 114.

57. Tatiana Khodoyerko, *Angola Diary of the Wife of a Russian Advisor*, 1985, retrieved from webpage, Russian Veterans, http://www.veteranangola.ru/main/english/diary, March 30, 2019.

58. Lord, *Fledgling to Eagle*, 111; and Dick Lord, *Vlamgat: The Story of the Mirage F1 in the South African Air Force* (Johannesburg, South Africa: 30° South Publishers, 2000), 108–12.

59. Lord, *Eagle*, 167–87; Joseph Lelyveld, "South Africans Display the Spoils of Angola Raid," *New York Times*, September 16, 1981, 2.

60. Lord, *Eagle*, 69–72.

61. Lord, *Eagle*, 92; and *Vlamgat*, 120–1, 134.

62. Lord, *Vlamgat*, 122–24 and 139–42.

63. Helmoed Romer Heitman, emails to Robert C. Owen, June 5 and 6, 2019, author's files.
64. Lord, *Fledgling to Eagle,* 306.
65. Lord, *Fledgling to Eagle,* 321–22.
66. Scholtz, *SADF,* 238; and U. S. Government, Central Intelligence Agency, Directorate of Intelligence, "The Nature of Soviet Military Doctrine," research report, April 1989, 1–2.
67. The Soviet S-200 (NATO code name SA-5) was a large missile designed for area defense against high-flying bombers. It was not suited to the demands of the war or movement in the heat and sandy terrain conditions of southern Angola—author.
68. U. S. Government, Central Intelligence Agency, Directorate of Intelligence, "Soviet Military Options for Neutralizing South African Air Power in Angola," May 2, 1986, 12; and Lord, *Fledgling to Eagle,* 327.
69. George, *Cuban Intervention,* 192–95.
70. Lord, *Vlamgat,* 169.
71. U. S. Government, Central Intelligence Agency, "Soviet Military Options," 3.
72. Urribarres and Little, "The Cuban MiGs."
73. Bridgland, *War for Africa,* 250
74. Bridgland, *War for Africa,* 15.
75. Cuba has never reported officially on DAAFAR losses. But a reasonably credible private compilation of Cuban pilots lost during the war is "Angolan Conflict 1975/89: Pilots," located in the webpage "Soldiers of Fortune: Mercenary Wars," retrieved from https://www.mercenary-wars.net/angola/angola-86-89/russian-downed-pilots.html, May 10, 2019.
76. George, *Cuban Intervention,* 193.
77. Pamela S. Falk, "Cuba in Africa," *Foreign Affairs* (Summer 1987), 1077–1078 and 1095.
78. Scholtz, *SADF,* 263–65.
79. Lord, *Eagle,* 184.
80. Bridgland, *War for Africa,* 56; Lord, *Vlamgat,* 184.
81. Bridgland, *War,* 87–100.
82. Shubin, *USSR and Southern Africa,* 13; and Piero Gleijeses, "The Battle of Cuito Cuanavale," Interview, Royal Institute of African Affairs, March 23, 2018, index 4:10–5:20, https://www.chathamhouse.org/file/battle-cuito-cuanavale-professor-piero-gleijeses#.
83. Lord, *Vlamgat,* 168–69.
84. Campbell, *Cuban Intervention,* 210–13.
85. Lord, *Eagle,* 406.
86. Joseph B. Treaster, "Castro Faults Soviet Tactics in War in Angola," *New York Times,* July 28, 1988, 13.
87. Scholtz, *SADF,* 372–74; and U. S. Government, Department of State, "Summary minutes of meeting held at the United States Embassy in Cairo," June 24, 1988, between the South African and United States delegations to the Cairo Talks, retrieved https://www.aluka.org/stable/10.5555/AL.SFF.DOCUMENT.min19880624.035.017.d1.18a, May 5, 2019.
88. Chester A. Crocker, *High Noon in Southern Africa: Making Peace in a Rough Neighborhood* (New York: W. W. Norton, 1992), 63–67, 368–69, 373–75, and throughout.

89. Bernard E. Trainor, "South Africa's Strategy on Angola Falls Short," *New York Times*, July 12, 1988, 6.

90. Trainor, "South Africa's Strategy on Angola Falls Short," 6; and Department of State, "Summary minutes of meeting."

91. "March 11, 1976, Minutes of the Meeting between Todor Zhivkov and Fidel Castro in Sofia," Wilson Center Digital Archive, retrieved https://digitalarchive.wilsoncenter.org/document/112241, May 1, 2019.

92. Shubin, *USSR*, 15.

93. Scholtz, *SADF*, 387–89.

94. KWÊVOËL is the word Afrikaans word for the grey lourie, a bird known for its raucous "go-away, go-away" call when threatened.

95. McGill Alexander, "Operation KWÊVOËL: The End of the War in Angola," excerpt from PhD dissertation, 2008, 10–14, provided to author via email from General Alexander. While in the SADF, Brigadier General Alexander (retired) directed the training of South African airborne forces, ran doctrine development projects, and commanded several paratroop units in several operations.

96. Helmoed-Romer Heitman, *War in Angola: The Final South African Phase* (Gibraltar: Ashanti Publishing, 1990), 298–309.

97. Crocker, *High Noon in Southern Africa*, 372.

98. For a detailed discussion of the origins, motivations, technologies, and key events of the South African nuclear program see Helen E. Purkitt and Stephen F. Burgess, *South Africa's Weapons of Mass Destruction* (Bloomington, IN: Indiana University Press, 2005), 27–57.

99. Former South African president F. W. deKlerk suggested that the program started in 1972, see F. W. de Klerk, *The Last Trek—A New Beginning: The Autobiography* (London: Macmillan, 1998), 272.

100. UNSCR 418, November 4, 1977.

101. Recent research gives strong evidence that the U. S. government and probably the Soviets chose to not to reveal what they knew about the 1979 test and South African nuclear developments in deference to broader Cold War concerns and to protect allies from scrutiny and sanctions by the UN and, in the case of the US, their own government and legal imperatives. See William Burr, Avner Cohen, et al, "Blast from the Past," *Foreign Policy*, September 22, 2019, retrieved https://foreignpolicy.com/2019/09/22/blast-from-the-past-vela-satellite-israel-nuclear-double-flash-1979-ptbt-south-atlantic-south-africa/, June 22, 2020.

102. Frank V. Pabian. "South Africa's Nuclear Weapon Program: Lessons for U. S. Non Proliferation Policy," *James Martin Center for Nonproliferation Studies*, 8.

103. Uri Friedman, "Why One President Gave up His Country's Nukes," *The Atlantic*, September 9, 2017, retrieved https://www.theatlantic.com/international/archive/2017/09/north-korea-south-africa/539265/, March 8, 2020.

104. Horace Campbell, "Cuito Cuanavale: A Tribute to Fidel Castro and the African Revolution," *Pambazuka News*, June 3, 2008, https://www.pambazuka.org/governance/cuito-cuanavale-tribute-fidel-castro-and-african-revolution.

105. Bridgland, *War for Africa*, 102.

106. Bridgland, *War for Africa*, 102.

107. Heitman, *War in Angola,* 310–11.
108. Benjamin S. Lambeth, "Flying the Flogger: Reflections on an Early Post-Cold War MiG-23 Experience, *Daedalus Flyer* (spring, 2016), 26–29.
109. Lord, *Eagle,* 403; and Urribarres and Little, "Cuban MiGs."
110. Lord, *Eagle,* 405–6.
111. Lord, *Eagle,* 439–40 and 513; and Urribarres and Little, "Cuban MiGs."
112. "Angolan Conflict 1975/89—Pilots," Soldiers of Fortune Mercenary Wars (blog), retrieved https://www.mercenary-wars.net/angola/angola-86-89/russian-downed-pilots.html, April 28, 2019
113. "V3C Darter," from *SAAF: The Unofficial Website on the South African Air Force,* retrieved http://www.saairforce.co.za/the-airforce/weapons/67/v3c-darter, May 20, 2019.
114. Lord, *Vlamgat,* 185–86.
115. *Scholtz,* SADF, 19–21.

5

The South Atlantic War 1982

ROBERT C. OWEN AND STEVEN PAGET

In 1982 an objective observer likely would have not seen the Falkland Islands as a prize over which two formerly friendly powers, Britain and Argentina, would fight a war.[1] Indeed, the Falklands Conflict was famously described by Jorge Luis Borge as "a fight between two bald men over a comb."[2] Consisting of East and West Falkland Islands and about 700 smaller points of land, the archipelago encompasses 4,700 square miles of territory. From Stanley, the capital and only real town on the islands, the British Governor General also administered South Georgia Island (1,360 square miles) and the chain of tiny South Sandwich Islands. The geographic center of the Falklands is about 350 nautical miles east of the nearest point on the Argentine coast and about 1,050 nautical miles SSE of Buenos Aires. South Georgia is over 750 nautical miles further to the east of Stanley. About 3,000 people live on the Falklands, and there are no permanent residents on the other islands. The weather in the region ranges from uncomfortably cold, wet, and windy to really bad. About 80 percent of the Falklanders, or "Kelpers" as they call themselves, live in the metropolitan bustle of Stanley's hundred or so square blocks, and the rest are scattered widely in tiny settlements and farmsteads. Mostly these hardy folk raise sheep and some cattle, fish, or work for the government. To date, the islands have no other resources, apart from rumored oil deposits and occasional adventure cruise ships stopping by. Crop farming outside of greenhouses is out of the question in this treeless, rain sodden landscape given to months of sub-freezing temperatures. In 1982 and today the great majority of Falkland Islanders are of British extraction and cultural loyalties. Therein, lay the basis of the South Atlantic War—the islanders did not wish to become citizens of Argentina, ever, and generations

Daggers were capable dogfighters and strike aircraft but were handicapped by limited radar capabilities and range. (Jorge Alberto Leonardi, https://upload.wikimedia.org/wikipedia/commons/d/de/IAI_Finger_2010.jpg)

of Argentines have been raised to believe that the islands had been stolen from them by Britain.[3]

The two countries did indeed go to war over this island group of no particular strategic importance, because the military Junta ruling Argentina in 1982 felt obliged to take the islands by force, and the British government was not prepared to abandon fellow Britons to the clutches of a dictatorship with a brutal record of domestic repression. After a decade of unsuccessful but continuing negotiations over the islands, the Junta sent forces into Stanley on April 2, 1982, and South Georgia the next day. Predictably to anyone familiar with British character—a group that apparently did not include the Argentine dictators—Britain responded by organizing an expedition, supported by a 7,000-nautical mile-long logistics network to retake the islands. Following a preliminary and essentially bloodless retaking of South Georgia on April 25, the British began operations to reoccupy the Falklands on May 1. These first-day operations featured an attack by a Royal Air Force (RAF) Vulcan bomber launched from Ascension Island, further attacks by Royal Navy (RN) Sea Harrier strike aircraft launched from HMS *Hermes*, and naval shore bombardments. The Vulcan attack, shore bombardments, and most of the

Harrier attack sorties concentrated on the area around Stanley on East Falkland to deceive the Argentines into thinking that the British intended to land nearby, rather than at San Carlos, their favored site across the island.[4] In response, the Argentines launched fifty-six defensive sorties from the mainland, losing three fighters and a light bomber for their efforts, with no kills of defending Harriers. HMS Ships *Arrow* and *Glamorgan* were attacked and damaged by Mirages on May 1 and, thereafter, the Fuerza Aérea Argentina (FAA) and Comando de la Aviación Naval Argentina (COAN) conducted sporadic anti-shipping operations and continued to lose aircraft to British defenders. The aircraft losses prompted the Argentinians to exercise caution and conserve resources for the coming moment when the British attempted to land.[5] Nevertheless, the sinking of HMS *Sheffield* by a Super Etendard on May 4 emphasized the threat posed by Argentine air power.[6] HMS *Glasgow* was subsequently damaged by an A-4 attack on May 12, but it was after the British invasion that ships came under intensified attack, with the escorts bearing the brunt of the Argentine air effort during the landings at San Carlos.

The fighting intensified again on May 21, when Royal Marines and British Army units landed at San Carlos. In the air, the FAA launched dozens of aircraft against invasion shipping in San Carlos water, and by the end of the day lost twelve fighters and three helicopters, having shot down no Harriers.[7] Argentine air attacks sank several ships and damaged others, but not enough to force the Royal Navy into retreat or to prevent the amphibious landing. HMS *Ardent* was sunk and HM Ships *Antrim*, *Argonaut*, *Brilliant* and *Broadsword* were all damaged on May 21, but the offloading proceeded with limited impediment.[8] The British Secretary of State for Defence, John Knott, asserted, "Argentinian forces did not interfere to any significant extent with the landing itself. The amphibious ships involved in the first stages of the operation were able to withdraw without incident to safer waters."[9]

While the amphibious landing succeeded, Major General Jeremy Moore, the Landing Force Commander, ruefully observed that the conflict revealed the "appalling shipping losses that can be suffered from even unsophisticated aircraft and weapons systems."[10] The threat was further demonstrated in the wake of the amphibious landings. HMS *Antelope* was attacked on May 23 and subsequently lost, before Royal Fleet Auxiliaries *Sir Bedivere*, *Sir Galahad*, *Sir Tristram* and *Stromness* were damaged on May 24. HMS *Coventry* and *Atlantic Conveyor* were then sunk on May 25, leading to the loss of ten helicopters;

six Wessex, three Chinooks, and a Lynx. Argentine air attacks on June 8 led to *Sir Galahad* and *Sir Tristram* being abandoned—with the damage to the former being fatal—and the loss of one of HMS *Fearless*' larger landing craft. *Plymouth* and the tanker, *British Wye*, were also damaged on the same day.[11] Notably, pre-conflict planning was based on the expectation that six destroyers/frigates could be lost, but the First Sea Lord, Sir Henry Leach, anticipated that twice that number might have to be accepted.[12] Though damaging, the actual effects of Argentine air power were not decisive and, crucially, the two carriers remained unscathed.

Both sides also flew air-to-ground attacks in support of or in resistance to the advance of British ground troops across the island to retake Stanley. A reduction in sortie rates during the land battle, combined with an increase in weapons not being released, has prompted John Shields to evaluate that "Argentine air power was unable or unwilling to support the critical land battles."[13] In the end, estimates of Argentine air losses to combat and accident run as high as 102 aircraft to all causes, while British losses were thirty-four to ground fire and operational accidents.[14] After three weeks of hard fighting across East Falkland, British ground forces took Stanley on June 14, with the Argentine garrison on Thule in the South Sandwich Islands surrendering six days later[15]

In ways that might not seem obvious at first glance, this small, short, and out-of-the-way war has contemporary relevance to anyone seeking to understand military escalation and escalation management. The peculiar mix of its historical, cultural, diplomatic, and military elements makes the South Atlantic War a useful case study of how nations come to that most important escalatory decision of all—going to war in the first place. The dispute over the Falkland/Malvinas islands had been simmering for nearly 150 years when it suddenly roiled into open warfare. The chain of events that convinced the Argentine rulers that the time had come to fight will illuminate the importance of diplomatic signaling, military posturing, chance, and personalities in the outbreaks of wars. Thereafter, the shifting fortunes of the war, relative qualities of the opposing military forces, incomplete and sometimes misinterpreted elements of intelligence, and other happenstances shaped decisions to escalate or not escalate air operations in scope, intensity, and targeting. In the end, the South Atlantic War provides an indispensable case study in the management of escalation between two air forces that started out as peers in their apparent abilities to project force into these isolated islands. If there is an aphorism for the fundamental lesson of this case study, it would be that, if a sufficiently aggrieved side thinks it might get away with escalation, it will give it a try, even if the odds are slender. In other words, escalatory decisions are often as much about perceptions of opportunities or necessities as they are about rational calculations of force balances.

Air Power in the Mix

British Air Forces

Reflecting Britain's overarching concern with the Soviet threat looming to the east, the RAF and the Fleet Air Arm were structured as high-quality regional forces with limited capabilities or expectations of fighting outside of the NATO region. For its part, the RAF's combat capabilities were based on several types of fighter aircraft and a few squadrons of Buccaneer light bombers. The RAF had just taken its Vulcan B.2 heavy bombers off line but, for South Atlantic operations, five would be brought back into service with modifications to their air refueling, navigation, and weapon-carriage systems. Even then, their approximately 1,500 nautical miles unrefueled combat radius reflected the RAF's focus on operations over Europe. The RAF was also limited in its support capabilities for long-distance force projection. Its airlift capabilities resided in medium-range C-130 transports and converted VC-10 airliners. Its air refueling capabilities were based on converted Victor bombers, which were markedly limited in their ability to transfer fuel over transoceanic distances, such as the roughly 3,600 nautical miles between the Falklands and Ascension Island, the latter of which became the RAF's staging base for South Atlantic operations.

Again, in reflection of the overarching importance of countering the Soviet threat, the Fleet Air Arm was focused on control of the Baltic and eastern North Atlantic sea lanes. Force projection against distant land targets was no longer part of its portfolio. In 1978, budget pressures and strategic priorities had obliged the navy to retire HMS *Ark Royal*, its last large-deck aircraft carrier able to embark a balanced wing of high-performance fighters, strike aircraft, and radar-equipped airborne early warning (AEW) planes. Consequently, the Fleet Air Arm in 1982 was based on three light carriers limited to embarking anti-submarine warfare (ASW) helicopters and a handful of Sea Harrier fighters for air defense. Since their main threats in northern waters would be high-flying Soviet maritime patrol aircraft and bombers, the embarked air groups of these ships did not include AEW aircraft to detect low-flying strike fighters. During the South Atlantic War, consequently, the RN was able to dispatch only twenty-four Sea Harriers to the battle zone, augmented by ten RAF GR3 Harriers quickly modified for operations at sea.[16] Even so, the maximum number of Harriers available on scene would never be more than twenty-five.[17] Moreover, these aircraft generally fought without radar support against Argentine fighters flying at extreme low altitudes to strike British shipping.

Given their limited force projection capabilities, the British air arms were exceedingly fortunate in having the support of a first-class aviation industry and military logistics system. Britain had been building, maintaining, and modifying some of the best combat aircraft in the world for almost seven decades, and that showed in the existence of hundreds of large and small aviation technical companies and extensive military maintenance and modification shops. They were ready and able to provide and integrate new systems and capabilities into the RAF and Royal Navy's aircraft to meet the requirements that emerged in the new war.[18] Although too numerous to list completely here, discussing some of the salient accomplishments of the British air logistics system helps to understand the country's approach to escalation and its ultimate success in the war. The installation or reinstallation of aerial refueling capabilities in Vulcan bombers, Hercules transports, and Nimrod surveillance aircraft were the key enablers of long-range bombing, surveillance, and transport operations from Ascension into the South Atlantic. Modification of RAF Harrier GR3s for operations at sea and employment of laser-guided bombs allowed quantitative and qualitative reinforcement of the Royal Navy's very limited Sea Harrier force. All Harriers were adjusted in the field to employ the new American-supplied AIM-9L *Sidewinder* missiles, which were markedly superior to the AIM-9Gs already in the Harrier force. The rapid design, testing, and installation of Blue Eric radar jammers in some Harriers improved their survivability against Argentine air defenses. Other Harriers and Vulcans were modified to carry Shrike anti-radar missiles, also provided by the United States. Nimrods expeditiously equipped with American Harpoon missiles and AIM-9Ls suddenly had long-range punch against ships and planes as they conducted their solitary patrols far beyond the range of any friendly assistance. There were, beyond these, literally dozens of lesser acquisitions, modifications, doctrinal adjustments, and training efforts that enabled British forces to win a war 8,000 miles from

FRS.1 Sea Harrier landing on the U.S. Navy carrier *Eisenhower* shortly after the South Atlantic War. (United States Navy. https://commons.wikimedia.org/wiki/File:DN-SC-87-05770.JPEG)

home against a numerically superior enemy operating only a few hundred miles from its bases.[19]

Because of its importance to later events, it is worth a diversion here to discuss the Sea Harrier in more detail. Its salient military attributes were its ability to make short takeoffs with full payloads from, and vertical landings back on to, small aircraft carriers equipped with sloped launching ramps on their bows. As a fighter, however, it was small, slow (high subsonic), short-ranged, and limited in payload compared to modern first-line fighters of the day. At high altitudes, the FAA's Mirages and Daggers were twice as fast. At medium to low altitudes however, the Sea Harrier was as fast as and more maneuverable than Dagger and Skyhawk strike aircraft, especially when they were loaded with bombs and external fuel tanks. But, as a weapon *system*, the Sea Harrier turned out to be a nightmare for Argentine pilots. Most telling, the super-cooled seeker heads and improved fusing of the AIM-9Ls allowed them to attack aircraft from all angles, not just from behind into their jet plumes, as had been the limitation of earlier versions of the missile.[20] As it turned out during actual fighting, British pilots released most AIM-9Ls as classic "tailpipe" shots after fleeing Argentine aircraft. But, even then, the advanced homing and range capabilities of the missiles exacted a bitter toll; achieving an 80 percent launch/hit ratio that made them the "real enemy" of Argentine pilots.[21] Moreover, the Sea Harriers flew in the hands of aggressive pilots thoroughly trained in aircraft handling and combat and formation tactics.

Argentine Air Forces

As was the case for Britain, the Argentine Junta had strategic interests that transcended any practical importance of the Malvinas Islands. The most important of these interests was a long-standing dispute with Chile over parts of Tierra del Fuego, most specifically control of the Beagle Channel. This territorial dispute almost led to war in December 1978. Argentina only called off an invasion of the area, Operación Soberanía, in response to a diplomatic intervention by Pope John Paul II, poor weather on the planned day of the attack, and perhaps last-minute concerns of army commanders over their ability to maintain a rapid advance through the difficult passes of the southern Andes.[22] Argentina's relationship with its other powerful neighbor, Brazil, was generally friendly. But Brazil was a close ally of Chile and the potential of its intervention in 1978 obliged the Argentine army to withhold brigades from the Chilean front to defend against such an occurrence. Argentina's second strategic concern, at least for the Junta, was to sustain the repression of any form of popular resistance or insurgent actions against its rule. However, in the minds of Junta leaders, these primary missions—Chile and domestic control—had relationships to the Malvinas. In their view, victory there would position Argentina to finally go through with an invasion of Chile. During the South Atlantic war, acting Argentine president General Leopoldo Galtieri was reported to have told his subordinates that "Después de Malvinas, iban a atacar a Chile" (after the Malvinas, would come an attack on Chile).[23] With even more unfounded expectations on their part, Junta leaders viewed the invasion of the Falklands as necessary to make good on their promises to do so, and to placate growing popular resistance to their rule.

In reality, Argentine air force planners recognized from the start that the FAA lacked the structure, doctrines, training, and equipage to take on a first-rate air force. Among numerous shortfalls, they recognized that it lacked autonomous supply sources for sustaining air combat and was deficient in air defense radars, radar detection systems on its aircraft, aircraft drop tanks, night vision equipment, and other critical items. Moreover, the short ranges of its A-4s and Mirages, coupled with limited air-to-air refueling systems and the absence of a suitable runway at Port Stanley, would sharply limit their effectiveness.[24] More specifically, apart from a small squadron of Canberra Bombers, its operational strength included about sixty-eight A-4 Skyhawks, twenty-six Dagger strike fighters, and seventeen Mirage III all-weather interceptors. The rest of the FAA's fleet consisted of transports, trainers, helicopters, and around forty-five Pucará strike aircraft. The turbo-propeller-powered and lightly-armed Pucarás were the Air Force's nod to the internal security mission. But, in the absence of any rural insurgencies in Argentina (organized unrest was in the cities), they had no actual mission to perform, and in the South Atlantic War, they accomplished little in the face of British air defenses and Harriers.[25] Consistent with its focus on short-range warfare against its immediate neighbors and their similarly weak air forces, the FAA possessed only two small C-130 air refueling aircraft, with limited range and fuel transfer capacity.[26] Of great consequence to its performance during the South Atlantic War, the limited availability of tankers and long-range reconnaissance aircraft sharply reduced the FAA's ability to conduct long-range strike and anti-naval operations. Indeed, a 1969 Argentine policy document assigned those roles to the navy. As a result, no FAA aircraft, except the Canberras, were equipped to navigate over water and its squadrons never practiced shipping attacks.

A serious weakness of the FAA was the lack of joint cooperation between its sister services. Indeed, the Army and Navy representatives in the Junta triumvirate, General Galtieri and Admiral Jorge Anaya, thought so little of, and so little desired, the air force's possible involvement in the forthcoming Malvinas operations that they advised its commander, General Basilio Lami Dozo, only of their intent to invade and otherwise left him out of the planning process.[27] Crucially, the British were aware of the lack of jointness between the Argentine services, with planning documents noting: "Each of the armed forces is autonomous and little if any experience of joint operations is available to them. Control of exercises is vested in the individual arm's Commanders in Chief and there has been no apparent co-operation and co-ordination."[28] Reflecting the mutual distrust between the services, Brigadier Ernesto H. Crespo, commander of the FAA's Task Force South, which conducted the air war in support of the Malvinas garrison, complained to the Air Force Chief of

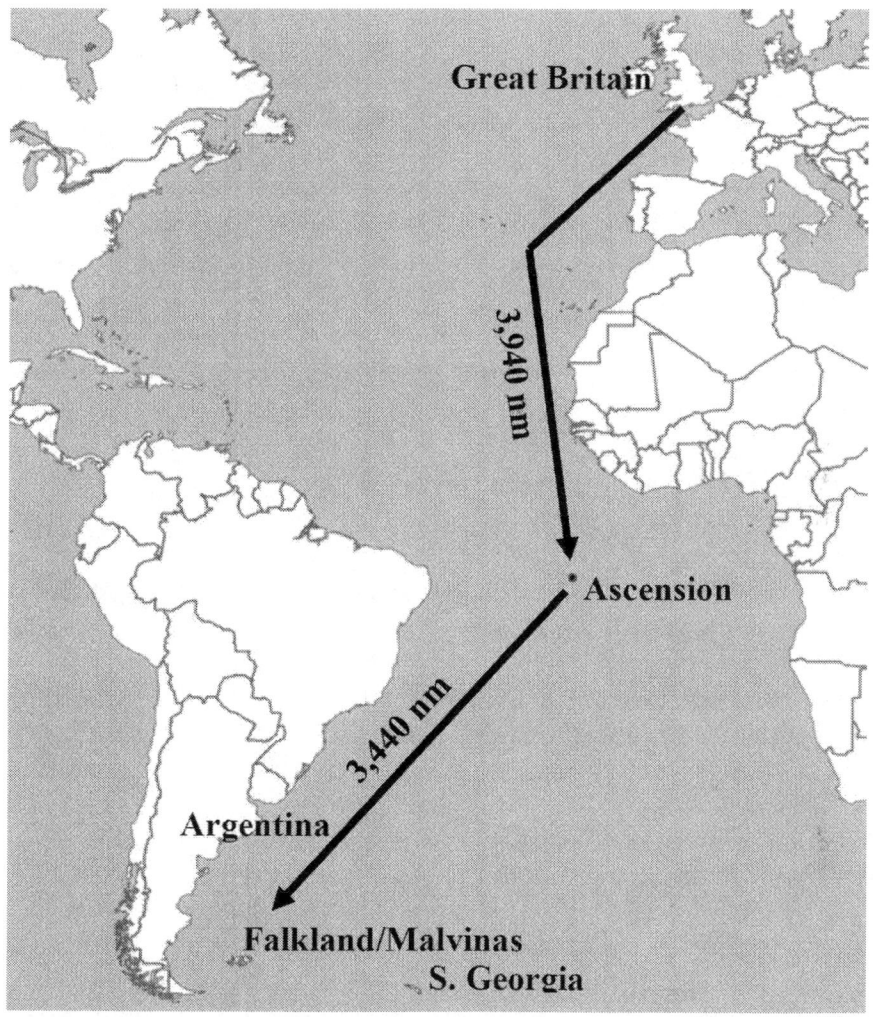

It was a long way from Britain to the Falklands. (Map by Robert Owen, adapted from CIA, World Fact Book, 2015, https://www.cia.gov/library/publications/the-world-factbook/docs/refmaps.html.)

General Staff on July 1, 1982, that "the naval force was dedicated to fighting for national political ends and to conserving its own forces, while devoting a minimum effort to the war.... Although not having a defined war plan, this same force was assigned command of the theatre of operations, but it had neither the capacity nor the will to assume it, despite its own declarations."[29]

Most post-conflict analyses identify Brigadier General Crespo as the most competent of Argentina's operational-level leaders and the individual responsible for getting the Air Force as ready as it could be for the coming fight. Given the task only after the British fleet was underway, Crespo initiated intensive training, logistical, and base-preparation efforts to get ready. A significant challenge was to get his pilots ready for anti-ship operations, missions for which they had neither the training, armament, nor navigation equipment. Training for the maritime mission included overwater flights and pitting FAA Daggers and A-4s against a Royal Navy Type 42 destroyer which the Argentine Navy had purchased from Great Britain in a happier time. From these exercises, the Argentines estimated that they had limited expectations of weapon hits and aircraft survival.[30] Crespo also ensured that tactics were amended throughout the conflict, including ensuring that attack aircraft flew at low altitude and maximum speeds to capitalize on the absence of a British long-range aerial early-warning (AEW) system.[31] Crespo also integrated civilian-owned business jets and turbo propeller aircraft into the FAA's operations. Normally flown by military pilots, these aircraft accompanied A-4 formations to make them appear bigger, provided radio relays, and flew many decoy flights and logistics missions.[32] Under Crespo's leadership, the FAA's small aerial refueling and transport forces, the latter augmented by COAN transports, turned in a credible performance. The FAA carefully coordinated its two KC-130s to provide as much flexibility as possible, though they only enabled the concurrent launch of four strike aircraft.[33] Based on handfuls of C-130s, Fokker F-27s, and COAN Lockheed Electras, the transport force pushed some 8,000 troops and 5,037 tons of supplies and equipment through to Stanley before and during active British operations in the area.[34]

Reviews of the effectiveness of Crespo's efforts are mixed. The writers of the Argentine Defense Ministry's official report on the war, the so-called Rattenbach Report, assessed the Argentine Air Force as being ready to handle the operational demands of this unprecedented war.[35] In contrast to this assessment, John Shields has noted that while "it could be argued that an inexperienced force, flying infrequently, and in basic and aged aircraft delivered beyond what was expected of it," and given the damage inflicted on British ships, he has reasoned: "Practical knowledge and understanding of higher command's intent, operating procedures, local topography and the enemy's capabilities was minimal. As a result, the tactical execution of the operational

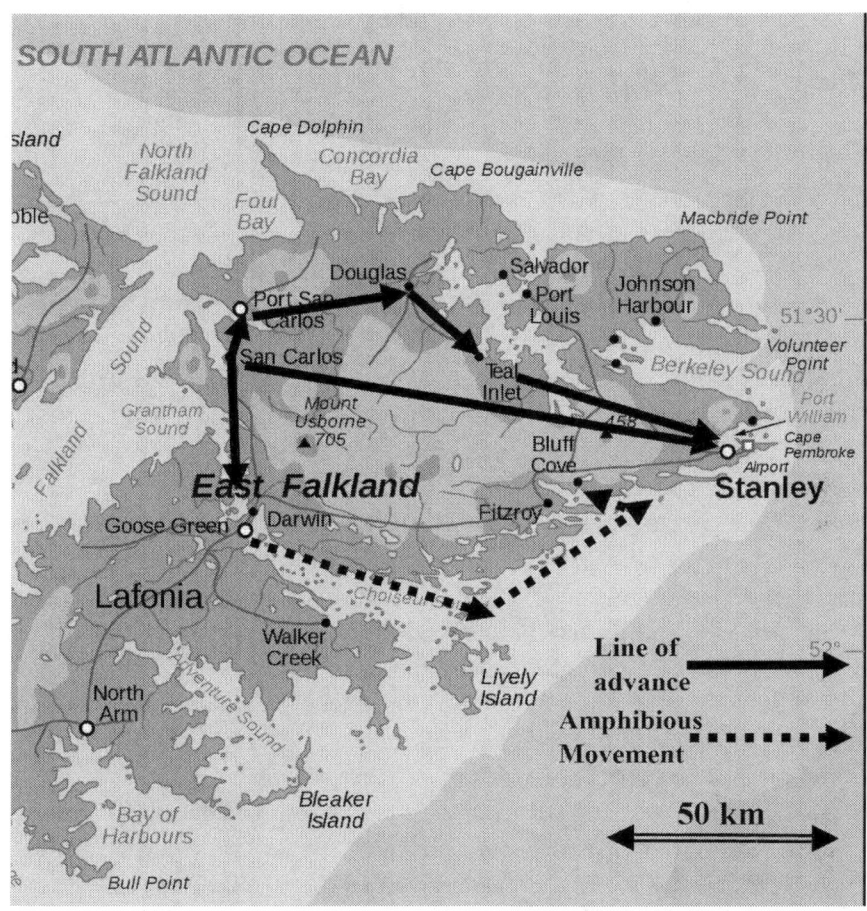

Falkland Islands (Eric Gaba. https://commons.wikimedia.org/wiki/File:Falkland_Islands_map.svg. Composite drawn from Microsoft Encarta atlas [1999 edition] and UK government map 1982 demographic data: CIA map available on the site of the University of Texas at Austin, with additions by Eric Gaba)

plan was flawed."[36] Shield's assessment may have been accurate in general, but there is no denying that the FAA got off many tactically coordinated missions and imposed painful attrition on the British fleet.

The FAA's poor logistical shape also seriously undermined the impact of General Crespo's tactical and operational improvements. Squeezed between the smallest budgets of the three services and the presence of relatively strong air forces on Argentina's borders, the FAA had over the years focused on acquiring as many aircraft as it could and paying for them in part by shortchanging their maintenance. Parts and other supplies were always a problem and, as a consequence, many of the aircraft on strength were in fact little more than sources of spare parts for other aircraft. British intelligence at the time estimated that the FAA had acquired as many as 247 combat aircraft in the years prior to 1982, of which only about 130 were still operational and, of those, only about eighty-two could be available on any one day for operations. Among these operational aircraft were perhaps six Canberra bombers, twenty-four Daggers, eight Mirage IIIs, forty-four A-4s, and five Etendards with five Exocet anti-ship cruise missiles available among them. Moreover, over half of the FAA's personnel were one-year draftees, which equated to a plentitude of people available for unskilled and menial tasks, and shortages of skilled personnel, particularly aircraft mechanics. Consequently, during South Atlantic operations, the FAA managed to get each of its aircraft into the air about once every two days, while Royal Navy and RAF Harriers were flying an average of three sorties *per day*, albeit over shorter distances.[37]

Argentina's aviation technical infrastructure was of little help. In contrast to the numerous modification and modernization programs conducted in Britain to enhance the combat capabilities of ships, fighters, bombers, tankers, and ground forces, the Argentines undertook only a few and generally late efforts to provide better anti-ship bomb fuses, aircraft parts, and electronic components for the FAA. The more than 60 percent failure rate of the FAA bombs that actually struck ships saved numerous Royal Navy ships from sinking or heavy damage and indicated the general incapacity of the Argentine logistical systems. One senior Argentine airman, Brigadier Horacio Mir Gonzalez, identified the failures of the bombs as "our single greatest problem throughout the war."[38] Of course, others had identified the AIM-9L as their greatest challenge.

The FAA did receive some useful help from outside. Although the French were publicly cooperating with the British-American arms embargo and allowing Royal Navy ships to use its West African ports, a technical team contracted to provide support for the Exocet missiles remained in Argentina for a period, though even now the extent of their assistance and whether their continued presence was known in Paris is unclear.[39] In a notably cynical action, Israel ignored U.S. pressure and sold A-4 spare parts and engines to the Argentinians in order to, in its own words, keep its manufacturing workers employed.[40] Other matériel trickled in from several Latin American and other countries, but in a piecemeal manner and never in quantities and nature to sway the war's outcome.

The Argentine Naval Air Arm was even less prepared to fight a sustained campaign than the FAA. In 1982 the COAN was centered on an aging, third-hand light carrier, the ARA *Veinticinco de Mayo*, which had served previously with the Royal Navy and the Royal Netherlands Navy. The ship was in poor mechanical condition, as was much of the Argentine Navy, and not capable of putting to sea for more than a week or so at a time. Its embarked complement included a maximum of eight A-4Q Skyhawks, helicopters, and a couple of decrepit and outdated S-2 Tracker reconnaissance aircraft. The five Etendards and their Exocets were also available for operations, but they and their pilots were not yet certified for carrier operations. None of these strike aircraft had night and bad weather capabilities. Otherwise, the COAN fielded some transport and a few light strike aircraft. The navy made one attempt to launch the A-4s from the carrier on May 2, but the ship's balky engines and low winds prevented it from generating the necessary twenty-five knot over-the-deck wind needed to get the heavily loaded aircraft into the air.[41] From then on, the COAN Skyhawks, like the Etendards, operated from land bases.

Because of its importance to the outcome of the conflict, it is worth another diversion here to consider Argentine leadership during the conflict. In long hindsight, a fair assessment of the three principal leaders; Galtieri, Anaya, and Dozo, is that they were devious and murderous politicians, and posturing and bemedaled buffoons in their military roles. Speaking in regards to the Argentine dictators who planned Operación Soberanía in 1978, Martin Balza, a later chief of the Argentine army, asserted that their incursion into government and politics had totally separated them from their profession.[42] In a thoughtful but scalding critique of Argentine leadership during the Falklands war, René De La Pedraja argued that mediocrity was endemic to a military focused on domestic repression, which allowed "the usual politicking to promote the worst officers to the most important commands [to] continue undisturbed." Galtieri, Anaya, and Dozo were natural products of such politicking, he went on, who filtered the information they chose to receive regarding military issues, and who "displayed a strange detachment from events and . . . difficulty keeping in touch with reality."[43] These men were, in short, political hacks who were unwilling and unable in character to hear advice or think coherently about strategic and military realities that contradicted their political imperatives and jingoistic imaginations. To contradict Brigadier Gonzalez's assessment that unsuitable bomb fuses were Argentina's greatest problem, the root of Argentina's problems was her incompetent leadership.

As is often the case, the personnel serving under the dictators were often better than they were. This was particularly evident in the Argentine pilot corps. Despite the leadership and logistical handicaps of the FAA and COAN, Argentine pilots were motivated and well trained in the basics of their aircraft—an elite selected from large recruitment pools of the country's best and brightest youth. In combat, their British opponents often observed their plane handling skills and their unshakable courage in pressing home attacks in the face of heavy antiaircraft fire and stalking Harriers armed with missiles that seemed to never miss.[44] But, severe budget limitations had restricted their exposure and training in advanced air combat techniques, and those same British pilots assessed that "their combat tactics were often poor and units suffered heavily."[45] Pressed by desperate fuel situations and the absence of timely target intelligence, for example, Argentine pilots generally streaked into the battle zone hugging the earth and flying at near Mach speed. Consequently, they had only seconds to identify and strike whatever targets presented themselves and then to race home "every-man-for-himself," with no time or fuel to exploit their formations and defend one another from Harrier attacks.[46] Throughout the conflict, their commanders dispatched them in series of small formations of usually four aircraft or less, which prevented them from saturating and overwhelming British defenses in the way that mass wave attacks would have done. Put succinctly, Argentine pilots could fly and had no apologies to make for their courage, but their commanders had not had the time and maybe the experience to get them ready to fight a world-class opponent.

Escalation—Why Argentina Went to War

Patriotism and the self-interests of the Junta led Argentina to war in 1982. Argentines were taught in school to always remember that the British had taken the Falklands in 1833, a time when the islands were claimed but temporarily not occupied by Argentina. Accordingly, the first of the so-called "temporary provisions" of the current constitution of Argentina claims "legitimate and non-prescribing sovereignty over the Malvinas, Georgias del Sur [South Georgia], and Sandwich del Sur Islands [South Sandwich Islands]. . . as they are an integral part of the National territory."[47] Always simmering, the dispute between Argentina and Britain heated quickly after the military took over the government in 1976. Having justified their felony in part by promising to settle the Malvinas issue, the first Junta found its popularity and continued legitimacy tied to its resolution. When their unproductive diplomatic efforts to gain sovereignty over the islands joined the list of failed causes fueling popular rejection of their rule, the Junta turned to the tools that had brought them to power in the first place—deceit and force.

The Junta also went to war because they saw no more hope in diplomacy. In rounds of negotiations between 1976 and 1982 British diplomats were stuck on the horns of indecision within their government. Many in government, particularly in the powerful Commonwealth and Foreign Office (CFO), sought an acceptable solution that would transfer sovereignty over the disputed islands to the Argentines, and thereby remove them as impediments to what they saw as more important British economic and political interests in Latin America. Moreover, the CFO and the British military dismissed the possibility of establishing a garrison in the Falklands to defend them against Argentine military action as impractical and unbearably expensive. Reported the Ministry of Defence (MoD) in September 1981, fortifying the islands and retaking them in the event of an Argentine invasion, "would engage a significant portion of the country's naval resources . . .[and] could precipitate the very action it was intended to deter."[48] Opposing the CFO was a strong lobby to retain the islands. This lobby was centered on the Falkland Islands Committee in Parliament, virtually all Falkland islanders and their supporters in Britain, and a standing government guarantee to the islanders "that only solutions they supported would be brought to parliament."[49] On their part, the Falklanders refused to accept any solution that would place them under any version of Argentine sovereignty, particularly an Argentina ruled by anti-democratic dictators who openly repressed their own citizens. They cast their position in concrete with a truculent rejection in 1980 of a "lease-back" proposal by the CFO to recognize Argentine sovereignty over, but retain British control of, the islands for some period of years. Pushed by Admiral Anaya, an ardent "Malvinist," the Galtieri-Anaya-Dozo Junta issued a directive in January 1982 to begin planning for military action in late April or early May as a matter of "national honor."[50] The timing of the invasion was important, since by May the worsening winter weather of the southern latitudes likely would preclude any effective British response to an Argentine invasion of the islands until the antipodean summer.

Perhaps most important, the Junta leaders had reasons by 1982 to think that the British were no longer interested in or capable of protecting the Falklands militarily. Over the past decade, the MoD had systematically drawn down the navy's presence in the South Atlantic. It withdrew from its Simonstown, South Africa base in 1974, and deactivated its West Indies Squadron, based in Bermuda, in 1976. In parallel, the RAF no longer maintained a permanent presence at its mid-Atlantic base on Ascension Island.[51] In 1976 Britain had shown a telling lack of resolve in its acquiescence to the establishment of a small Argentine "scientific" post on South Thule Island in the South Sandwich archipelago. In that case the British government protested and dispatched a few ships, but ultimately backed off and turned a blind eye to the presence of a foreign military force on an island claimed by Britain.[52] Retirement of the *Ark Royal* and the aging state of the Royal Navy's amphibious fleet also signaled rapid deterioration of Britain's force projection capabilities outside the NATO region. Finally, the Secretary of State for Defence, John Nott, made it all official in a white paper in 1981, when he said that the MoD would focus its force structure investments on fulfilling NATO commitments and would "exploit the flexibility of our forces beyond the NATO area so far as our resources permit." In line with those priorities, Secretary Nott announced in that same speech that the two key amphibious ships, HM Ships *Intrepid* and *Fearless*, would be retired earlier than previously scheduled and would not be replaced.[53] In a June 30, 1981, report to the House of Lords, the MoD confirmed that HMS *Endurance*, a lightly armed patrol ship and the only naval presence Britain maintained in the region, would be paid off after the 1982 patrol season also without replacement.[54] Retirement of the *Endurance* left a platoon of Royal Marines as the only force defending British sovereignty over the Falklands and, indeed, the southern Atlantic Ocean. When combined with what they considered as a failure to demonstrate strength in the face of provocations, the Thatcher government was perceived as weak by the Argentines.[55] Collectively, these British actions convinced Argentine leaders that a strong British reaction to an invasion of the Falklands was unlikely: a view that opened the door to military adventure.[56]

Finally, by early 1982, the Junta was under great pressure to do something about the Malvinas. Unelected dictators within a constitutional democracy, their hold on power was undeniably illegal and vulnerable to shifting popular opinion. Their patriotic delusions as the saviors of Argentina from liberalism and communism heightened their emotional sensitivity to popular opinion. Wrote a historian of the Dirty War, the internal repression of Argentine critics of the military's rule, "their self-image as guardians of the nation shrank from the possibility of being hated and opposed by that very nation." They also knew that their tenures in power rested on support from a military system riven with inter- and intraservice political factionalisms and personal fiefdoms. Any shift in the balance of that system could produce the next coup that overthrew them.[57] Also, in the first months of 1982, numerous influential Argentine newspapers and commentators warned that conflict over the Malvinas was becoming increasingly likely and, in some of their editorial opinions, overdue.[58] The Argentine public was also making its dissatisfactions known through peaceful and violent protests over everything from the Junta's political repression, egregious human rights crimes, dismally ineffective economic policies, gender rights, and failure to satisfy the demands of Argentine rights and pride by pushing the British out of the Malvinas and other territories.[59]

The issues of rights and pride were acutely important to the Junta, who justified their power on a cultural vision partly on the restoration of Argentine machismo manhood and national honor in regard to the Malvinas. As the epitomes of those values, failing them in the long-run was unconscionable to these self-appointed "saviors" of Argentine culture.[60] So when the third iteration of the Junta took power in December 1981, resolution of the Falklands was its declared priority for the next year. Admiral Jorge Anaya, the navy chief, was the most zealous and militant "Malvinist" in the Junta, and even General Galtieri acknowledged that his zealotry and force of will cowed other leaders into endorsing the drift toward war.[61] While still willing to let the diplomatic niceties run a little longer, the Junta issued a directive in January that authorized planning for war, since "the prolongation of this situation affects national honor, the full exercise of sovereignty, and the exploration of resource."[62]

Then came one of those small events that, in an atmosphere of mutual distrust and anxiety, can hijack careful plans and precipitate a war. In this case, a small group of Argentine civilians landed on South Georgia on March 19 to salvage metal from an abandoned whaling station. The owner of the scrap company, Constantino Davidoff, had informally coordinated his plans with the United Kingdom ambassador in Bueno Aires as a simple business venture.[63] The agreement apparently did not work up channels to the right people because, in the event, British authorities on South Georgia, Stanley, and London professed surprise that another Argentine group had landed on British territory. Given the South Thule experience, they suspected nefarious intentions, a concern heightened by rumors that the working party had raised an Argentine flag. In a flurry of diplomatic notes and movements of *Endurance*, what everyone wanted to be a minor issue quickly ramped up to a serious confrontation. Suspicious that the British Antarctic supply ship, the RRS *Bransfield*, might be transporting more Royal Marines to Stanley, the Argentines preempted diplomacy by sending their own marines to "protect" the scrap workers and, more to the point, to secure the island.[64] Following hurried planning meetings in Britain, the MoD decided on March 29 to deploy a nuclear attack submarine and to also begin preparing a flotilla of frigates and destroyers to follow.[65] Anticipating the move, the Junta had decided already, on March 26, to take both South Georgia and the Falklands before the Royal Navy got into position to block further access. Argentine suspicions were confirmed on March 30, when blabbering parliamentarians publicly leaked a classified MoD briefing that had just told them about the deployments authorized the day before.[66] Two days later, Argentine marines landed near Stanley and another force took the only inhabited spot on South Georgia, the science station at Grytviken. Thus, in less than two weeks the Argentine leaders had felt driven by events and their political posturing to jump over their deliberate planning to escalate a minor crisis into a war they had not expected to start for at least another month and, consequently, they were not prepared to fight.

The Junta's decision to precipitate a war over the Malvinas when they did was consistent in character with historian Barbara Tuchman's conclusion in *The March of Folly* that rulers are expected to make rational decisions in matters of state, "but more often than not are overpowered by non-rational human frailties—ambition anxiety, status-seeking, face-saving, illusions, self-delusions, and fixed prejudices."[67] In changing the timing of the war's start to early April rather than their previous deadline of mid-May they may have gratified ideological commitments and political aggravations, but they set up their country for a defeat that sacrificed hundreds of Argentine soldiers for naught, put off the country's territorial ambitions indefinitely, cost the members of the Junta their positions, and almost sent them to prison. Going in early April, instead of May, gave the British precious weeks of tolerable weather in which to organize and prosecute a military response before the harsh seas of the antipodean winter precluded operations. Thus, the Junta leaders allowed a minor incident to fan the simmering dispute with Britain into the flames of a military confrontation that could burst into open war. They were allowing events to drive strategy, rather than the other way around—a failure of leadership and situational awareness that earned them sharp criticism in official post-conflict analyses.[68]

At first, things went well. The islands were taken with a few Argentine but no British casualties—painless and not expected by the invaders to spark an emotional reaction from Britain. Anticipating a frolic, hundreds of thousands of Argentines demonstrated their popular support in public gatherings in many Argentine cities, through bellicose news reports, and baking boxes of "Falklands Tarts" for soldiers on the islands to munch; forgetting for the moment all the other reasons they hated the government. An Argentine professor declared, "We are drunken with patriotic feelings, we are standing proud, because we are witnesses and participants of a rescue promised to our forbearers. National joy is as wide as understandable [sic]."[69]

But, almost immediately, evidence began to mount that the Junta had made a profound strategic blunder. On April 2, British Prime Minister Margaret Thatcher vowed to retake the islands. The next day the UN Security Council condemned the invasion and demanded "an immediate withdrawal of all Argentine forces from the Falkland Islands."[70] Two days later the Royal Navy put teeth into Thatcher's vow, when the carriers *Hermes* and *Invincible* and escorts departed Portsmouth with much fanfare and headed south. What should have been most disturbing was the clear message impressed on the Junta and Thatcher by President Ronald Reagan and Secretary of State Alexander Haig: that the British were indispensable allies and that, if war came, America would not be neutral and would tilt toward Britain.[71] The world the Junta had imagined had not turned out to be the world they now faced.

These events gave the Junta leaders their last opportunity to salvage their sensible strategy of waiting until the onset of winter to launch their invasion of the Malvinas. As they knew from the reports of their own services, that delay was essential for them to make the operational, training, and logistical preparations needed to hopefully assure success. Authoritative assessments later argued that, even as *Hermes* and *Invincible* left Britain, the Junta had a chance to defuse the situation by apologizing for their misstep in the heat of the moment, announcing the start of a withdrawal, and calling for a new round of negotiations. Indeed, the U.S. Secretary of State, Alexander Haig, offered them an out only a week after the invasion, by suggesting that

Argentina begin withdrawing their forces and accept a joint government of the Malvinas, leading to eventual Argentine sovereignty. The UN and other outside stakeholders essentially endorsed this position.[72] Doing these things would have been consistent with the original Argentine strategy, or at least hope, of occupying the islands and then negotiating a final settlement. It also might have prompted or even obliged the British to return their fleet back to the strategically vital NATO region to await developments and, thus, opened the way for another and better organized invasion of the Malvinas in May or even the next year. But on April 10, even as Haig was visiting and making his initial offer to help negotiate a settlement, General Galtieri told a large crowd that national dignity and honor did not allow him to negotiate.[73] Thus, by equating intransigence as "dignity and honor," Galtieri pandered to the crowd while letting Argentine strategy drift from holding-and-negotiating to reinforcing the Malvinas garrison to fight at a time when the services had reported that they would not be fully ready to take on the British.[74] Indeed, assessed the Argentine official report, he had created a situation in which the British had begun operations to recover the islands before the Argentines fully understood that they had a fight on their hands.[75]

But the problem for the members of the Junta, besides being autocrats of little imagination, was that their precipitous invasion of Stanley had put them in a political and delusional corner from which their only self-interested escape was to further escalate the conflict. A military withdrawal in early April would have thrown them into the fires of mass patriotism that they themselves had kindled and stoked in the Argentine populace. Their political credibility, maybe even their personal freedom, would have gone up in the resulting inferno of national humiliation, anger, and vengefulness. Additionally, later assessments saw that the "objectivity" of the Junta itself was carried away by the jubilation of popular opinion.[76] In other words, they allowed themselves to believe their own propaganda.

To avoid such a disaster for them personally and for their conservative causes, the Junta leaders and other Argentine leaders chose to cling to their delusional assessments of British intentions. Speaking to a reporter near the end of the war, for example, General Galtieri said "I'll tell you that though an English reaction was considered a possibility, we did not see it as a probability. Personally, I judged it scarcely possible and totally improbable. In any case, I never expected such a disproportionate answer."[77] Likewise, Foreign Minister Nicanor Costa Mendez reflected that he was "truly surprised that the British will go to war for such a small problem as these few rocky islands."[78] Finally, the Junta allowed itself to believe that Britain might see a military takeover of British territory inhabited by British subjects as an opportunity to make an honorable withdrawal from a distant and unwanted burden.[79] Despite warnings from numerous quarters that this was a grossly unfounded apprehension of British character and historically demonstrable reactions to similar aggressions, they plunged ahead, rather than back off for a few weeks and start the war when they might well have won it. Assessing the impact of the Junta's willfully uninformed appreciation of the situation, one scholar later suggested that "some of the most important strategic mistakes made by the Argentines during the war—including the time of the invasion—might have been avoided by the presence of a civilian authority" that, presumably, would have taken a more consultative approach to these decisions.[80]

Escalation—Why the British Went South

In the absence of any tangible, long-term strategic rationale for fighting over the Falklands, the British went to war because they were outraged at the perfidy of a brutal regime's launch of a surprise attack while in the midst of negotiations, and because they were loyal to their fellow Britons on the Falklands. Thatcher commented: "Argentina was the invader, Argentina is occupying British territory, with British people under its heel, who do not wish them to be there... The Falklanders' loyalty to Britain is fantastic. If they wish to stay British we must let them."[81] Gratification of principle was the only possible reward for retaking the islands, and it would be gratification gained only by taking significant military risks. The political motives behind the decision to retake the Falklands have been the subject of some debate. With Thatcher's poll numbers starting to improve in March 1982, it has been reasoned that there was no cause to "gamble for resurrection" because an election victory was more than feasible.[82] It was suggested, retrospectively, that the conflict produced only a three-percentage-point boost to Thatcher's popularity for three months and that macroeconomic considerations resulting from the 1982 budget were responsible for the government's upturn in fortunes.[83] Conversely, other scholars have suggested that the Falklands Conflict was a major factor in Thatcher's re-election and may have contributed a boost of as much as 21 percentage points.[84] Irrespective of the eventual consequences, the Thatcher government's response to the Argentine invasion was inevitably fraught with perceived political risk, including the potential for the Conservative Party to lose their hold on power if they failed to retake the Falklands, or retook them with high casualties. Thatcher's position would also have been precarious if Britain had been compelled by the United States to agree to a compromise peace.[85] The accusations of diplomatic and military intelligence failures roared at the government in Parliament confirmed those expectations. When the conflict arrived, however, most politicians, the press, and the British public settled down and focused on the requirements of going to war.[86] Margaret Thatcher was at the center of Britain's coalescing determination to take back the islands. John Nott retrospectively identified the "determined courage" of Thatcher as "the key to success."[87] Thatcher turned out to be an inspiring wartime leader. It was the Falklands Conflict that crystallized the perception that Thatcher was a leader who "stood up for her principles and could not be deflected from her chosen course."[88]

The decision to retake the island may have been based on principle, but it was enabled by the awareness of British leaders that they could just, at that fleeting moment, cobble together a force that might be adequate to the task. The state of relevant British air power has been discussed earlier. But the presence of an adequate British invasion fleet offshore of the Falklands in just a few weeks would be just as much a miracle of industrial innovation and good fortune as it was for the RAF and Fleet Air Arm. The Royal Navy's nuclear attack submarines were critical assets, since they could get to the islands quickly, and the Argentines had little capability to find or attack them. By the time the Argentines walked ashore at Stanley, HM Ships *Spartan* and *Splendid* had been underway for a day. The *Conqueror*, *Valiant*, *Courageous*, and the conventionally powered *Onyx* followed by April 12. The first boats arrived in the war zone on April 11, allowing Britain to establish a maritime exclusion zone (MEZ) around the islands and impede further Argentine efforts to reinforce the islands by sea.[89] In addition to the two carriers, the Royal Navy gathered and dispatched some twenty-two destroyers and frigates. Drawing heavily on its Royal Fleet Auxiliary and its Ships-Taken-Up-From-Trade (STUFT) program, the Navy organized more than 100 other ships to fulfill the amphibious assault, troop transport, minesweeping, logistics, hospital, repair, tug, dispatch, and other tasks needed to move and support a division-size force, centered on the multi-arms 3rd Commando and 5th Infantry Brigades. Fortuitously for the British, the Royal Marines' 3

Commando Brigade had just completed its annual arctic warfare training and were well prepared to fight in the southern winter.[90] Ironically, a number of key ships providing amphibious support had been scheduled for retirement either before the conflict or soon after and were only available from the best of luck for the British.[91] The Army also rose to its own organizational, equipage, and organizational challenges as it prepared to fight in a harsh climate so far away.

U.S. support was a key element in Britain's confidence in preparing its response to the Argentine attack.[92] As discussed earlier, the American diplomatic posture was publicly neutral but privately committed to Britain. Neutrality was the posture of Secretary of State Haig, as he shuttled between London and Buenos Aires seeking an equitable settlement that British and Argentine diplomacy had failed to achieve over the preceding 150 years. But, reflecting guidance from President Reagan, Secretary of Defense Caspar Weinberger told his staff to give the British whatever they needed without any bureaucratic delays. The senior British military liaison in Washington, Air Vice Marshal Ron Dick, saw Weinberger's directive in action, when he visited the Pentagon on Monday, April 5. Every senior U.S. military official told him to just give them his list and they would take care of it. In short order, he had agreements for the British to reoccupy Wideawake Airfield on Ascension, U.S. Navy assistance in scheduling fuel tanker ships into Ascension, and access to American reserve fuel stocks on the island. Most of his weapons requests were satisfied, including for around 200AIM-9Ls, Stinger shoulder-launched antiaircraft missiles, and Vulcan close-in, air defense weapons for defense of the aircraft carriers. Dick even arranged for the U.S. Marines to give up enough aluminum runway matting to build a temporary airstrip.[93] The Americans were already cooperating with the British in intelligence matters and eventually would reposition a surveillance satellite to give them a timelier view of the battle area. The American commitment to Britain went as far as to include discussions of loaning the USS *Iwo Jima* helicopter carrier and "contract advisors" to the Royal Navy in response to a "what if" request from Britain in the event of a carrier being lost.[94]

Finally, on April 30, Haig declared failure to find the grounds of an agreement and expressed dismay at the disarray and illogic of the Argentine military officers running the country. In contrast, he praised the consistency and reasonableness of British leaders. He suggested, therefore that "we're not ... going to be able to be as even-handed in light of current Argentine attitudes."[95]

On May 14, the U.S. National Security Council cut off all direct and indirect sales of arms to Argentina. Left unsaid was the fact that the United States had been transferring arms to Britain since the first week of the war.[96] The extent of U.S. support was demonstrated by the estimation that British forces in the South Atlantic benefitted from the provision of in excess of $120 million of material during May.[97] Although the initial American diplomatic position caused disappointment in some quarters of Britain, Prime Minister Thatcher, knew from the start that she would enjoy U.S. support for the repossession of the Falkland Islands.[98]

More Escalation and Also Restraint—Argentina

For Argentine leaders, the outcome of the war had existential importance. As dictators whose popular support rested on their promises to improve the quality of life of Argentina's citizens and to restore the country's honor in the Malvinas, a defeat would cost them their holds on power and possibly lead to prison terms or worse. As indicted international criminals for their human rights violations, they also had no place to run. So, as Britain approached, they were "prepared to accept very high casualties to defend what they perceive as national honor."[99] Their problem, of course, was that Argentina's poorly prepared and conscript-heavy military forces offered little hope of escalating the conflict as necessary to defeat the juggernaut coming down the Atlantic.

The long British supply line and the British fleet itself offered opportunities to up the ante over the Malvinas. Ascension Island was an obvious center of gravity and "an early and constant concern" for British headquarters.[100] Overnight, Wideawake Airfield on Ascension had transformed from a moribund, one-flight-a-month backwater into one of the busiest airports in the world, with its parking ramps jammed with transports, tankers, and bombers. Less than a half mile from a number of beaches, and 3,000 nautical miles from Argentina, the airport was a potential target for commando raids, shelling from surface ships, submarine surveillance, and reconnaissance by Argentine Boeing 707s. The island's fuel supply was a particular vulnerability, since it came in from a small tanker ship anchored a half mile offshore and was then pumped through a floating pipeline into above ground storage tanks. Likewise, the steady flow of un-convoyed British logistics ships sailing past the island were a potentially lucrative target for Argentina's two modern Type 209 submarines. The submarines also could have been deadly against the SS *Canberra* and *Queen Elizabeth II*, the two main troop transports carrying 3rd Commando and 5th Infantry Brigades, respectively. The loss of either of these ships with their troops still on board likely would have brought the campaign to an end, at least for that year.

Similarly, Admiral Sandy Woodward, judged that the loss of either or both carriers "would almost certainly have proved fatal to the whole operation."[101] The timing of any such loss was critical. Later retrospection prompted Woodward to assess in 2002 that the loss of a carrier before the British "got a strip ashore, which was 6 June" would have precluded the invasion, an idea that was affirmed by Admiral Leach:

> It depended so much on the timing, did the loss or damage occur to one or to both, permanent or temporary, before, during or after the initial assault landing and so on . . . If both carriers had gone before the landing, then I think that serious consideration to cancelling the operation would have been given. If it had been after the landing . . . I think we would have pressed on and taken the risk.[102]

In the event, however, the technical and logistical limitations of the FAA and COAN precluded any serious escalations on their parts. FAA aircraft, particularly the Boeing 707s, did surveil British fleet elements as they steamed south, but made no attacks and, in return, the British refrained from attacking them.[103] Argentina's other long-range capabilities, mainly its Type 209s and the *Veinticinco de Mayo*, were mechanically too unreliable to push far out into the Atlantic. The carrier was probably limited to a week or two at sea and, in any case, its small squadron of Skyhawks would have been limited in its offensive power against defended ships. In combination, the FAA's two KC-130s and Exocet-armed Etendards provided what proved to be Argentina's greatest qualitative threat to the Royal Navy, though quantitatively it possessed only four operational air-to-surface versions of the missiles. During the war, three of these missiles sank HMS *Sheffield*, a destroyer, and the SS *Atlantic Conveyor*, carrying helicopters and cargo. The fourth missile and its carrying Etendard were lost during another attack. These operations highlighted the weaknesses of the Argentine air forces: mainly an acutely limited magazine of Exocets and inadequate long-range reconnaissance capabilities. Together, these weaknesses constrained the Argentines to make most of their attacks with unguided weapons and with knowledge of the positions of their targets only in the last minute or so of their run-ins. Consequently, they expended their "silver-bullet" Exocets on secondary targets. The Type 209s also proved impotent, with one lost in the retaking of South Georgia and the other immobilized in port by mechanical failures. The presence of a flight of Harriers and then of FGR.2 Phantoms also made any long-range attacks on Wideawake impractical for the Argentines.[104]

It is worth noting here that since the war, many authors have conjectured, usually based on circumstantial or hearsay evidence, that the Soviets were providing information on British movements gathered from satellites and long-range aircraft. But no hard details of what was provided have surfaced.[105] More important, as one early analyst pointed out, the Soviets would not have been able to assess, release, and deliver such strategic data in a timely enough manner to support tactical targeting by the Argentines. Otherwise, the Soviets had little to gain from the outcome of the conflict, other than to perhaps sell some weapons; the idea of allying themselves to the fervently anti-communist Argentine dictators would have been awkward at best, anyway.[106]

More Escalation and Also Restraint—Britain

For British leaders, the outcome of the war was vital to British honor, but personally not as existential as it was for their counterparts. PM Thatcher and her cabinet understood the war's political dangers included the fall of the Conservative government and losing their jobs. While personal and political interests certainly shaped their decisions about issues like escalation, they generally focused on making them in consideration of national interests, ideals, patriotism, and open discourse.[107] In contrast to Argentine leaders, British leaders had real escalation decisions to make. Their possession of useful aircraft carriers, nuclear submarines, Vulcan bombers, a war fleet at sea, high-caliber special operations forces, and other elements gave Britain numerous options to expand the scale and targeting of their operations.

As the fleet sailed southwards, the British kept their options open. They sent the fleet south slowly, to retain "the option to employ it or hold it back, depending upon the political turn of events, and to play for time if diplomatically necessary."[108] The slow rate of advance also gave late-departing ships time to catch up and join the fleet and more time to rectify matériel and training shortfalls. The aircraft carriers also, among other things, needed to install their new Vulcan/Phalanx Close in Weapon Systems and load munitions. Sea Harrier crews practiced attack procedures and low-level flying, and familiarized themselves with the new AIM-9Ls. Vulcan bombers had their aerial refueling equipment reinstalled, and their crews had to train in those and in low-level strike tactics.[109] And there were thousands of other tasks big and small to do as well.

As their capabilities to enforce them increased, British naval and air forces operated under incrementally permissive rules of engagement (ROE). On April 12, they (mainly submarines) were cleared to attack ships operating in a maritime exclusion zone 200 nautical miles around the Falklands and South Georgia. This increased to "guns free on any force believed to be a threat" on April 23, the day before operations to retake South Georgia began. Ultimately, the ROE allowed attacks on any Argentine vessels operating more than twelve miles from its coast, but never included air attacks against targets on the mainland.[110] Each of these steps reflected a British desire to put off declaratory escalations of the conflict until military necessity supplanted diplomatic flexibility as their primary concern.

For Margaret Thatcher and her ministers escalating to offensive operations in the retaking of South Georgia on April 24–25 had both political and military justifications. There was a political value, they perceived, in picking off an easy target to provide the British public with an early success. Militarily, the island's location could make it a useful platform for Argentine surveillance activities, and its sheltered bays could provide the British with refuge from exceptionally severe weather or for battle-damaged ships. The attack itself provided unexpected grist for the British press, in that it serendipitously resulted in the sinking of one of the Argentine Navy's older submarines, the ARA *Santa Fe*, in Grytviken harbor, and the victory was bloodless. After a short exchange of long-range rifle and British naval gunfire, British troops intimidated a larger Argentine force into surrendering with no casualties on either side.[111] Additionally, the recapture of South Georgia put the Junta on notice the British really did intend to fight.

The first three days of fighting over the Falklands, May 1–3, proved unexpectedly decisive. On the first night, the RAF conducted the first of several single-aircraft "Black Buck" raids. During this first raid a Vulcan bomber laid a string of 1,000-pound bombs across the Argentine base at Stanley Airport, damaging the runway enough to preclude any use for fighter operations. Subsequent air fighting demonstrated the superiority of Royal Navy air fighting tactics with the Sea Harrier, and of the AIM-9L. FAA aircraft losses to Sea

Harriers included a Canberra light bomber, a Dagger strike fighter, and two Mirage III all-weather interceptors. The Mirage III losses were particularly painful, since one small squadron of about seventeen, now fifteen, of them comprised the FAA's total all-weather interception capability. At 1557 the next day, HMS *Conqueror* put two torpedoes into the cruiser ARA *General Belgrano* as it maneuvered to make a night run on British ships around the islands. The *Belgrano* sank in minutes, taking 323 sailors down with it. The loss of its flagship was a major blow to the navy's combat capabilities, and an emotional one to the Argentinians, for whom the ship was a source of national pride.

These events robbed the Argentine military of any illusions it still possessed of holding the tactical and military initiatives in the war and forced them onto the tactical and campaign-level (operational) defensive. The appearance of a Vulcan over Stanley Airport implied that the RAF could strike bases or other targets near the Argentine coast, notably Buenos Aires. In response, the Argentines immediately withdrew their Mirage III's from the air battle in the south, to protect the capital over a thousand miles to the north. The deadly Sea Harriers sent a clear message that whenever the FAA chose to fight a decisive air battle, it likely would take heavy casualties and likely could do so only once. Thus, for the next three weeks, the FAA only sent sporadic, small-scale, and unescorted air attacks against the Royal Navy. These attacks produced the sinking of *Sheffield* and *Atlantic Conveyer* and cost the FAA and COAN six more fighters. Importantly, the ship sinkings were Exocet "kills" and the COAN expended the last of those missiles on May 30 without success. Otherwise, Argentine airmen held back from the air battle and husbanded their aircraft while they waited for the British landings to give them an opportunity to inflict maximum damage for the heavy casualties they would suffer, and were willing to suffer, in the defense of their nation.[112]

The disillusionment of Argentine forces was further indicated by the actions of the leaders of the Armada de la República Argentina. After the *Belgrano* went down, they pulled their ships into port and to all intents and purposes gave up the naval fight. Fearful of the power of the Royal Navy, particularly its submarines, and incapable of developing joint operational plans with the Air Force, they hid their ships in protected ports. Unlike the Air Force, they also made no unilateral plans to come out and expend themselves, if necessary, to sway the battle at a critical moment. In so doing, the Rattenbach Report found these leaders betrayed their responsibilities and the trust of their nation and left the forces on the Malvinas to wither on an inadequate logistical vine.[113] Further fighting by those forces, therefore, essentially became *pro honoris* or, more realistically, to protect the Junta from the public's wrath and the attentions of the courts.

Beyond the initial operations around the Falklands, the British were at pains to avoid any further escalations of the conflict. Perhaps most important, British leaders considered but then rejected proposals to launch Vulcan raids against military bases and other targets on the Argentine mainland. Given the existing British domination of the relevant air and maritime battles, such raids would have had only marginal military advantage, and could have undermined Britain's diplomatic interests in Latin America and elsewhere.[114] So, in general, unless Argentine aircraft or ships sortied against British forces, they were generally safe. Forces on the Falklands were fair game, however, and Harriers and armed helicopters kept up the pressure on Argentine air and ground forces. One of the more important events was a Special Air Service and naval gunfire raid on the night of May 14–15 on FAA aircraft operating from a grass runway on Pebble Island. The attack netted six Pucarás and four Turbo Mentor light attack aircraft and a light transport. Operation Mikado was a bolder concept, involving an SAS raid on Rio Grande Air Base on the mainland to destroy the Etendards based there and to kill their pilots. The raid was stymied by atrocious weather, forcing the commandos to escape by land into Chile. British commanders cancelled a second raid, when it became clear to them that the Argentines were alerted and waiting.[115] Finally, later in the war, when British submarines found the *Veinticinco de Mayo* traversing Argentine territorial waters, Secretary of State for Defence John Nott blocked an attack, assessing that the ship's military value no longer offset the diplomatic consequences of sinking it more-or-less gratuitously.[116]

Concluding Thoughts

Imbalances of forces and wills or at least perceptions of such imbalances drove the major escalatory decisions of the South Atlantic War. As long as British and Argentine leaders perceived that a war over the Falklands would be costly and uncertain in its outcomes, they talked—for 150 years. They settled no grievances and abandoned no objectives, but they curbed their frustrations and kept talking. However, when the Argentine Junta perceived that Britain had lost the will and ability to protect the islands, they acted on their nationalist delusions and political insecurities and invaded South Georgia and the Falklands. Recognizing that they were acting on a long chance, the British nevertheless began deploying ships southwards as soon as they were certain that the Argentines were launching their attacks. But Britain did not escalate to an open commitment to fight until their force capabilities began to coalesce as their fleet moved south, their numerous technical enhancement programs bore fruit, and the United States openly declared its support. Then, when the loss of the *Belgrano* and the heavy air casualties they suffered in the first days of fighting brought home their weaknesses in relation to the British, the Argentines de-escalated their fighting, holding back their fighters for the climactic battles that would come when the British invaded the Falklands. In contrast, the British restrained subsequent air operations—eschewing, for example, attacks on the Argentine mainland and sinking the *Veinticinco de Mayo*—once they were confident in their domination of the Falklands battle space.

The interactions of the geographic distances and technological characteristics of the aircraft involved largely determined the tactics of both sides. Given the potentially devastating consequences of losing a carrier, for example, the British were obliged to hold them well back from the Falklands and to accept the consequent limitations on the ability of their Harriers to fight for air control and to conduct air strikes. British bomber and long-distance surveillance operations were similarly hampered by the relationship of South Atlantic distances and the performance limits of their Vulcans, Nimrods, and Victors. Distance and fuel likewise forced the Argentines to employ low-level, hit-and-flee tactics, despite the limitations those tactics placed on their ability to find targets or to survive Harrier/AIM-9L attacks. Fortunately for both sides, neither could overcome the tyranny of the distances involved to hinder the ability of the other to flow forces into the theater or conduct operations. Though counterfactual, it is consequently interesting to consider how different the war would have turned out had either air force been able to persistently and effectively reach out just a few hundred miles further than it actually could.

Of course, personalities, national culture, military sophistication, and other factors shaped both escalation and tactics. British political dithering and unwillingness to make a clear commitment to defend their South Atlantic possessions reflected the political machinations and conflict aversions of democracies at work, and they sent a clear message to the politically insecure and military-minded Junta that war initiation likely would have no adverse consequences. The authoritarianism and wooden-headed refusal of the Junta generals and admirals to countenance contrary assessments and advice led them to precipitate a war without understanding their enemy's escalation triggers and will to fight. In what should be a thought-provoking juxtaposition for future war planners concerned with escalation management, the British democracy could not take logical action because it could not build consensus to pay the price, while the Argentine dictatorship arbitrarily inflicted the price on their country by suppressing consensus and taking an illogical action.

While the personnel in both air forces had no apologies to make for their courage and basic aircraft handling, it is clear that the British air arms were institutionally far more sophisticated as war fighting instruments than their Argentine counterparts. Though they entered the conflict with significant shortfalls in capabilities and training, the British quickly exploited a connected network of mature civil-military, military command, planning, technical-industrial, personnel management and training networks, and close alliance with the United States to mitigate their most significant shortfalls. This exploitation also presented the British with real escalation and escalation management opportunities. In contrast, the misguided senior commanders, inadequate logistics, and weak industrial base of the Argentine air arms robbed them of any substantive opportunity to escalate the scale and targeting of their operations against the British.

Following the conflict, the Rattenbach Report identified seven "deficiencies in joint action" that contributed to defeat. Of these, the lack of "balanced and harmonious" development of equipment, the lack of night-fighting capabilities, and the lack of diverse sources for obtaining weapons could be listed as "joint" or "army" issues. But, deficiencies in the submarine force, the lack of modernized aviation for war on land and sea, poor joint logistics, and insufficient training in electronic warfare generally related to shortfalls in the makeups of the Air Force and Navy.[117] Elsewhere, the assessment of the causes of defeat focused on the unwillingness and unpreparedness of service leaders to work together in a joint warfare context.[118] The point here is that the Argentine leaders were, as the saying goes, "writing diplomatic checks that the services, particularly their air arms, were not in the technical and professional positions to pay," and they did not give their services time to rectify the situation. Clear then and now, these shortfalls sealed Argentina's defeat, barring a miracle. As for the Junta, the Rattenbach Report laid the responsibility for ignoring these shortfalls and taking an unprepared country to war squarely in their laps.[119]

So a salient implication of the South Atlantic War would be the time-honored prescription to "know thy enemy." To know their enemies, future war planners should be inclined and intellectually equipped to contemplate their full range of leader predilections, civil-military command relations, military capabilities, and resilience attributes such as logistics, national characters, and so on. Capabilities and resilience attributes will be important to planning and executing operations. "Softer" elements of leader values and national character will be vital to understanding how enemy nations will respond to escalatory actions, such as war initiation, changing force balances, and operational expansions and restraints. It should go without saying that these understandings should be developed from the enemy perspectives as well as one's own. In the case of the South Atlantic War, these soft elements started and ended the war, while the combination of soft and hard elements allowed Britain to take a long chance and win. So leaders should not allow objective assessments of statistics to blind them to what people might actually do.

Notes

1. Anyone already familiar with this conflict will know that the word "Falklands" has political connotations, since that is the name given to the main island group discussed in this study by Britain and could, thereby, acknowledge and privilege British claims to the territory. Argentine readers almost certainly would prefer to see their name for the chain, "Islas Malvinas" used. While refusing to be drawn into or analytically hampered by that dispute, this study generally will use "Falklands" in all cases except where it is expressing Argentine perspectives, in which case it will use "Malvinas."

2. Ezequiel Mercau, *The Falklands War: An Imperial History* (Cambridge: Cambridge University Press, 2019), 183.

3. The issues have not changed. In response to renewed Argentine claims to the islands, the residents voted 1513 to 3 in March of 2013 to remain under the British government. Argentine president Cristina Fernandez de Kirchner responded that "the Falkland islanders wishes are not relevant in what is a territorial issue." See, "Falklands referendum: Voters choose to remain UK territory," *BBC News,* March 12, 2013, retrieved https://www.bbc.com/news/uk-21750909, June 1, 2020.

4. Steven Paget discusses British deception operations at length in "Target San Carlos: British Deception during the Repossession of the Falkland Islands," in *Weaving the Tangled Web: Military Deception in Large-Scale Combat Operations,* ed. Christopher M. Rein (Fort Leavenworth, KS: Army University Press, 2018), 193–208.

5. Lawrence Freedman and Virginia Gamba-Stonehouse, *Signals of War: The Falklands Conflict of 1982* (Princeton: Princeton University Press, 1991), 328.

6. Lawrence Freedman, *The Official History of the Falklands Campaign, Volume II: War and Diplomacy* (London: Routledge, 2005), 778–79.

7. Jeffrey L. Ethell and Albert Price, *Air War South Atlantic* (London: Schribner, 1984), 97.

8. The National Archives of the United Kingdom (TNA), ADM 202/924, Commodore, Amphibious Warfare, "Operation Corporate-Report of Proceedings," September 6, 1982.

9. TNA, PREM 19/630, "Statement by the Secretary of State for Defence," May 24, 1982.

10. TNA, ADM 201/276, Major General J. J. Moore, Headquarters, Commando Forces, Royal Marines, "Operation Corporate-Report of Proceedings," October 18, 1982.

11. Freedman, *Official History*, 778–79.

12. Richard Vinen, *Thatcher's Britain: The Politics and Social Upheaval of the Thatcher Era* (London: Simon & Schuster, 2009), 341.

13. John Harris Shields, *Air Power During the 1982 Falklands Conflict*, (PhD diss., King's College London, 2019), 230.

14. Ethell and Price, *Air War*, 184, 207, and 212–15

15. For an overview of the land campaign, see: Julian Thompson, *3 Commando Brigade in the Falklands: No Picnic* (Barnsley: Pen & Sword, 2013); Nicholas van der Bijl, *Nine Battles to Stanley* (Barnsley: Leo Cooper, 1999); Nicholas van der Bijl and David Aldea, *5th Infantry Brigade in the Falklands War* (Barnsley: Leo Cooper, 2003); Ewen Southby-Tailyour, *Reasons in Writing: A Commando's View of the Falklands War* (London: Leo Cooper, 1993).

16. The limited number of Sea Harriers available and their necessity in a defensive role meant that their offensive activities needed to be limited. Steven Paget, "Under Fire: The Falklands War and the Revival of Naval Gunfire Support," *War in History* 24, no. 2 (2017), 229.

17. For a general discussion of the Harrier deployment, see Ethell and Price, *Air War*, 174. David Jordan and John Shields discuss the RAF contingent in greater detail in, "'In at the Deep End: RAF Harrier Operations during Operation Corporate, 1982," *Air Power Review* 21, no. 2 (Summer 2018), 123–24.

18. Kenneth Warren, "Hansard HC Deb" (July 22, 1982) vol. 28, col. 582., retrieved https://hansard.parliament.uk/Commons/1982-07-22/debates/f94d9058-0213-4a57-a19e-57ef06d864f7/RoyalAirForce?highlight=falklands%20aircraft%20industry%20proud#contribution-c2a587f6-17b3-46b1-ba62-e3694c20671c, August 22, 2020.

19. Ethell and Price, *Air War*, 121–23 and 179; and Chris Hobson and Andrew Noble, *Falklands Air War* (Hinkley, UK: Midland Publishing, 1982), 20.

20. Carlo Kopp, "The Sidewinder Story: The Evolution of the AIM-9 Missile," *Australian Aviation*, April 1994, retrieved http://www.ausairpower.net/TE-Sidewinder-94.html, May 13, 2020.

21. Brigadier Horacio Mir Gonzalez, "An Argentinian Airman in the South Atlantic," in *The Falklands Conflict Twenty Years On: Lessons for the Future*, eds. Steven Badsey, Rob Havers, and Mark Grove (Milton Park, UK: Frank Cass, 2005), 80; and Philip D. Grove, "Falklands Conflict 1982—The Air War: A New Appraisal," in the same volume, 272.

22. Alejandro Luis Corbacho, "Predicting the Probability of War During Brinkmanship Crises: The Beagle and Malvinas Conflicts," working paper, *University del CEMA*, no. 244, 11–12; archived in SSRN, retrieved https://papers.ssrn.com/s013/papers.cfm?abstract_id=1016843, June 4, 2020.

23. Pedro Schwartz, interview with Martin Balza, "Declaraciones de BALZA en Tercera de Chile del 21dic2003," in *La Tercera*, December 21, 2003, retrieved *http://www.seprin.com/menu/notas6620.htm*, June 4, 2020.

24. História de la Fuerza Aerea Argentina: El Accionar de la Fuerza Aerea en Malvinas, Tomo VI, Volumen 1 (Buenos Aires, 1992).

25. René De La Pedraja, "The Argentine Air Force versus Britain in the Falkland Islands, 1982," in *Why Air Force Fail: The Anatomy of Defeat*, eds. Robin Higham and Stephen J. Harris (Lexington: University Press of Kentucky, 2006), 232–33; and Ethell and Price, *Air War*, 183.

26. Despite common perceptions, C-130s in the early 1980s were relatively small or light transports. KC-130s cruised at about 300 knots and carried about 65,000 pounds of fuel for flight and transfer to other aircraft. In comparison, KC-135 medium tankers cruised at about 460 knots and carried 200,000 pounds of fuel, while the KC-10 jumbo tanker cruised at about the same speed and carried 369,000 pounds of fuel.

27. Pedraja, "The Argentine Air Force versus Britain in the Falkland Islands, 1982," 234.

28. Shields, *Air Power During the 1982 Falklands Conflict*, 228.

29. Felipe Sanfuentes, "The Chilean Falklands Factor," in *International Perspectives on the Falklands Conflict: A Matter of Life and Death*, ed. Alex Danchev (New York: St. Martin's Press, 1992), 74.

30. Rubén Oscar Moro, et al, *Historyoria de La Fuerza Aerea Argentina: El Accionar de la Fuerza Aeria en Malvinas, tomo VI, Vol I* (Buenos Aires, Argentina: 1998, FAA), 87. This volume of the official history of the Argentine Air Force covers Malvinas operations.

31. Pradeep P. Barua, *The Military Effectiveness of Post-Colonial States* (Leiden: Brill, 2013), 48; Francisco Fernando de Santibañes, "The Effectiveness of Military Governments during War the Case of Argentina in the Malvinas," *Armed Forces & Society* 33, no. 4 (2007), 621.

32. *Historyoria de La Fuerza Aerea Argentina*, 182–402 presents a mission-by-mission record of FAA operations. Light civilian aircraft operated almost every day of the air war.

33. Mark S. Bell, "Can Britain Defend the Falklands?," *Defence Studies* 12, no. 2 (June 2012), 289; Pradeep P. Barua, *The Military Effectiveness of Post-Colonial States* (Leiden: Brill, 2013), 48.

34. James S. Corum, "Argentine Air Power in the Falklands War: An Operational View," *Air & Space Power Journal* (Fall 2002), 75.

35. *Rattenbach Report*, paragraph 617. The Junta chartered a team study led by Lieutenant General Benjamín Rattenbach in November 1982. Its full Spanish title was *Publicación oficial de Informe de la Comisión de Análisis y Evaluación de las responsabilidades políticas y estratégico militares en el conflicto del Atlántico Sur* (*Informe Rattenbach*) or, in English, *The Official Publication of the Report of the Commission of Analysis and Evaluation of the Political and Strategic Military Responsibilities of the Conflict of the South Atlan-*

tic. The report was harshly critical of the Junta's political, diplomatic, and military blunders and explicitly blamed them for starting an ill-conceived war that led to Argentina's defeat. Though completed in December 1982, the government did not declassify the report for restricted access until March of 2012.

36. Shields, *Air Power During the 1982 Falklands Conflict*, 238.

37. Ethell and Price, *Air War*, 7; and Freedman, *Official History*, 239; and Ethell and Price, *Air War*, 121.

38. Gonzalez, "An Argentinian Airman in the South Atlantic," 183; also see the *Rattenbach Report*, para 621, which declared that the effectiveness of the FAA's attacks were considerably diminished by the number of bombs that impacted and did not explode.

39. Mike Thompson, "How France helped both sides in the Falklands War," broadcast transcript, *BBC Radio 4*, March 6, 2012, retrieved https://www.bbc.com/news/magazine-17256975, January 31, 2021; Ewen Southby-Tailyour, *Exocet Falklands: The Untold Story of Special Forces Operations* (Barnsley: Pen & Sword, 2014), 43.

40. *The Times of Israel*, "UK opens files on Israeli arms sales to Argentina during Falklands War," August 25, 2016, retrieved *https://www.timesofisrael.com/uk-opens-files-on-israeli-arms-sales-to-argentina-during-falklands-war/*, December 20, 2020.

41. Interestingly, the authors consulted this issue with an experienced American A-4 pilot, Professor Joseph Clark of Embry-Riddle Aeronautical University, who reported that Stanley Airport's 4,000-foot-long runway would have supported operations, probably with slightly reduced loads of fuel and weapons. In corroboration, the Standard Aircraft Characteristics manual provided to the U. S. Navy by the manufacturer in 1967 (NAVAIR OO-110QQ4-2) calculated that, at its normal takeoff weight of 22,000 pounds and with a 25 knot headwind (not unusual at Stanley), an A-4B required a takeoff ground roll of 3,500 feet, while it could do the same thing at 18,500 pounds and no wind.

42. Pedro Schwartz, interview with Martin Balza, "Declaraciones de BALZA en Tercera de Chile del 21dic2003," in *La Tercera*, December 21, 2003, retrieved http://www.seprin.com/menu/notas6620.htm, June 4, 2020.

43. René De La Pedraja, "The Argentine Air Force versus Britain in the Falkland Islands, 1982," in *Why Air Forces Fail: The Anatomy of Defeat*, eds. Robin Higham and Stephen J. Harris (Lexington: University Press of Kentucky, 2006), 233 and 237.

44. Cedric Delves, in command of S Squadron 22 SAS, for example, acknowledged the bravery of the Argentine pilots. Lieutenant General Sir Cedric Delves, *Across an Angry Sea: The SAS in the Falklands War* (London: Hurst & Co., 2018), 105. Shields has taken a more dispassionate view, noting that the increased mission aborts during the final days of the Falklands Conflict due to the presence of Sea Harriers, demonstrated that "bravery is a finite resource": "Once the physical component is compromised, the moral component also diminishes." Shields, *Air Power During the 1982 Falklands Conflict*, 238-39.

45. Ethell and Price, *Air War*, 182.

46. Brigadier Horacio Mir Gonzalez. "An Argentinian Airman in the South Atlantic," 80.

47. Klaus Dodds, "The Antarctic Peninsula: Territory, Sovereignty Watch and the 'Antarctic Problem,'" in *Antarctic Security in the Twenty-First Century: Legal and Policy Perspectives*, eds. Alan D. Hemmings, Donald R. Rothwell, and Karen N. Scott (Abingdon: Routledge, 2012), 104.

48. Lord (Oliver Shewell) Franks, *Falkland Islands Review: Report of a Committee of Privy Counsellors* (London: HMSO, 1983), 109–13, retrieved https://api.parliament.uk/historic-hansard/commons/1983/jan/26/falkland-islands-franks-report, March 21, 2020.

49. Freedman, *Official History*, vol 1, 85; Francis Pym, "Remarks on Franks Report," Hansard HC Deb (January 26, 1983) vol. 35, col 916; and Franks, *Falkland Islands Review*, paragraph 60 and 338.

50. Freedman, *Official History*, vol 1, 132–33.

51. Geoffrey Sloan, "The Geopolitics of the Falklands Conflict," in *The Falklands Conflict Twenty Years On*, ed. Badsey, et al, 25; and Franks, *Falkland Islands Review*, 190.

52. Franks, *Falkland Islands Review*, 52–58.

53. Secretary of State for Defence, *The United Kingdom Defence Programme: The Way Forward* (London: HMSO, 1981), 5 and 10–11.

54. *Official Report, House of Lords*, June 30, 1981, col. 185, cited in Franks, 114–18.

55. Matthew Fehrs, "Too Many Cooks in the Foreign Policy Kitchen: Confused British Signaling and the Falklands War," *Democracy and Security* 10, no. 3 (2014), 240.

56. *Rattenbach Report*, 159, reported that at the beginning of planning, the principle military authorities believed that "a British reaction involving the massive employment of their military forces was impossible." See also, John Buckley and Paul Beaver, *The Royal Air Force: The First Hundred Years* (Oxford: Oxford University Press, 2018), 193.

57. Paul H. Lewis, *Guerillas and Generals: The 'Dirty War' in Argentina* (Westport, CT, Greenwood, 2001), 134–35.

58. Franks, *Falkland Islands Review*, 129–32.

59. Antonius C. G. M. Robben, "Combat Motivation, Fear and Terror in Twentieth-century Argentinian Warfare," *Journal of Contemporary History* 41, no. 2 (2006), 368.

60. Carolina Rocha, ed., *Modern Argentine Masculinities* (Chicago: Intellect Books, 2013), 8; and Franks, *Falkland Islands Review*, 263.

61. American Embassy Buenos Aires, "Message: Falklands Crisis: Prospective US Measures," April 3, 1982, 2; retrieved https://nsarchive.gwu.edu/document/21344-19820430-falklands-crisis-prospective-us-measures, June 01, 2021, and "Current Report: Falkland Islands Dispute," May 1, 1982; retrieved https://nsarchive.gwu.edu/document/21345-19820501-falkland-islands-dispute, June 1, 2021.

62. Freedman, *Official History*, vol 1, 132–33.

63. Daniel Schweimler, "Scrap dealer who accidentally set off the Falklands War," *BBC News*, April 3, 2010, retrieved http://news.bbc.co.uk/2/hi/8599404.stm, May 15, 2020.

64. *Rattenbach Report*, 235–38.

65. Franks, *Falkland Islands Review*, 213.

66. Freedman, *Official History*, vol 1, 161–76; and Franks, *Falkland Islands Review*, 244.

67. Barbara W. Tuchman, *The March of Folly from Troy to Vietnam* (New York: Alfred A. Knopf, 1984), 380. Also, for more detailed discussions of the Junta's group and individual calculi for starting the war, see Richard Ned Lebow, "Miscalculation in the South Atlantic: The Origins of the Falklands War," in *Psychology and Deterrence*, eds. Robert Jervis and others (Baltimore, MD: Johns Hopkins, 1985), 89–124; and Jessica L. P. Weeks, *Dictators at War and Peace* (Ithaca, NY: Cornell U. Press, 2014), 106–18.

68. The *Rattenbach Report*, 745–47, stated explicitly that the Junta should have and could have handled the South Georgia incident diplomatically. See also para 749–59 for discussion of the diplomatic failures that led to open war.

69. Christina Parajon, "War-Stopping Techniques in the Falklands," in *Stopping Wars and Making Peace: Studies in International Intervention,* eds. Kristen Eichensehr and W. Michael Reisman (Leiden: Martinus Nijhoff Publishers, 2009), 11.

70. UN Security Council Resolution 502 (1982), April 3, 1982.

71. American Embassy London, Message: Secretary's (Alexander Haig, au.) Meeting with Prime Minister Thatcher April 8: Falkland Islands Crisis," April 10, 1982; retrieved https://nsarchive.gwu.edu/document/21329-19820410-secretarys-meeting-prime-minister, June 01, 2021.

72. US National Security Council Meeting, SUBJECT South Atlantic Crisis, April 30, 1982; and *Rattenbach Report,* 305–96, with US offer acknowledged in paras 305–7.

73. *Rattenbach Report,* 304; "dinidad y el honor de la Nacion no se Negocian."

74. *Rattenbach Report,* 150–55.

75. *Rattenbach Report,* 167.

76. *Rattenbach Report,* 570.

77. Denis Healy, "Comments in the House of Commons," Hansard, HC vol. 35, col. 924–33 (January 26, 1983).

78. Alex Weisiger, *Logics of War: Explanations for Limited and Unlimited Conflicts* (Ithaca: Cornell University Press, 2013), 185.

79. Weeks, *Dictators at War,* 114.

80. Santibañes, "Effectiveness of Military Governments," 612.

81. Thomas Dolan, "Demanding the Impossible: War, Bargaining, and Honor," *Security Studies* 24 (2015), 549.

82. Dolan, "Demanding the Impossible," 554.

83. David Sanders, Hugh Ward, David Marsh, and Tony Fletcher, "Government Popularity and the Falklands War: A Reassessment," *British Journal of Political Science* 17, no. 3 (1987), 281.

84. Brian Lai and Dan Reiter, "Rally 'Round the Union Jack? Public Opinion and the Use of Force in the United Kingdom, 1948-2001," *International Studies Quarterly* 49 (2005), 258.

85. Andrew Gamble, "The Thatcher Myth," *British Politics* 10 (2015), 7.

86. American Embassy, London, message, "Falklands Dispute: British Political Mood," April 8, 1982, CONFIDENTIAL, released to the public June 17, 2008, National Security Archive, https://nsarchive.gwu.edu/document/21325-19820408-falklands-dispute.; and Sir John Nott, "A View from the Center," in *The Falklands Conflict Twenty Years On,* eds. Badsey, et al, 58.

87. John Nott, "Inside the War Cabinet: Reflections by Britain's Defence Secretary during the Falklands War," *The RUSI Journal* 152, no. 2 (2007), 74.

88. Gamble, "Thatcher Myth," 7; and Freedman, *Official History,* 13–17.

89. Steven R. Harper, *Submarine Operations During the Falklands War,* research paper, US Naval War College, June 19, 1994, 4, 5, 9, and throughout.

90. Ewen Southby-Tailyour, *Exocet Falklands: The Untold Story of Special Forces Operations* (Barnsley: Pen & Sword, 2014), xiv.

91. Ian Speller, "Delayed Reaction: UK Maritime Expeditionary Capabilities and the Lessons of the Falklands Conflict," *Defense & Security Analysis* 18, no. 4 (2002), 3–4.

92. See: John Lehman, "The Falklands War: Reflections on the 'Special Relationship,'" *The RUSI Journal* 157, no. 6 (2012), 80–85.

93. AVM Ron Dick, "The View from BDLS Washington," in *Royal Air Force Historical Society Journal* 30 (Northmoor, UK: Advance Book Printing, 2003), 29–35.

94. Sam LaGrone, "Reagan Readied U. S. Warship for '82 Falklands War," *USNI News*, June 27, 2012, retrieved https://news.usni.org/2012/06/27/reagan-readied-us-warship-82-falklands-war-0, January 18, 2021.

95. U. S. Congress, House Foreign Affairs Committee. Alexander M. Haig, Jr., "Secretary of State before Key House Leadership and House Foreign Affairs Committee," (April 29, 1982), 1–5 and 8.

96. U. S. National Security Council, "National Security Decision Directive Number 34: U. S. Actions in the South Atlantic Crisis," May 14, 1984.

97. Sally-Ann Treharne, *Reagan and Thatcher's Special Relationship: Latin America and Anglo-American Relations* (Edinburgh: Edinburgh University Press, 2015), 69–70.

98. For a discussion of the concerns caused by the initial American diplomatic position, see: Andrea Chiampan, "Running with the Hare, Hunting with the Hounds: The Special Relationship, Reagan's Cold War and the Falklands Conflict," *Diplomacy & Statecraft* 24 (2013), 640–60.

99. "Political Developments in the Falkland Islands Crisis," Director of Central Intelligence (DCI) Briefing Paper, May 19, 1982, originally TOP SECRET, released to the public on September 7, 2007, 9–12.

100. Air Vice Marshal George Chesworth, "A View from the HQ at Northwood II," *Royal Air Force Historical Society Journal* 30 (Northmoor, UK: Advance Book Printing, 2003), 21.

101. Alistair Finlan, *The Royal Navy in the Falklands Conflict and the Gulf War: Culture and Strategy* (London: Frank Cass, 2004), 70.

102. Shields, *Air Power During the 1982 Falklands Conflict*, 22.

103. Freedman, *Official History*, 54, 62–64.

104. Group Captain Peter W. Gray, "Air Power: Strategic Lessons from an Idiosyncratic Operation," in *The Falklands Conflict Twenty Years On*, eds. Badsey, et al, Routledge, London, 2005, 258.

105. For examples, see Tony Halpin, "Argentina had help from the Soviet Union during the Falklands's [sic] War," *The Times*, April 2, 2020, and Jaime Noguera, "The secret story of how Soviet satellites helped sink British warships in the South Atlantic," *Russia Beyond*, October 9, 2017; retrieved https://www.rbth.com/history/326350-soviet-satellites-sink-british-warships, June 21, 2026.

106. Vojtech Mastny, "The Soviet Union and the Falklands War," *U. S. Naval War College Review* 36, no. 2 (May–June 1983), 48 and throughout.

107. Peter Hennessy, " 'War Cabinetry': The Political Direction of the Falklands Conflict," in *The Falklands Conflict Twenty Years On*, eds. Badsey, et al, 131–42.

108. TNA, ADM 201/283, Lieutenant Colonel S. Pope and Lieutenant Colonel R. J. Ross to Commandant General, Royal Marines, December 14, 1982.

109. For a detailed look at what went into getting the Vulcans and their crews ready for the Black Buck raids, see David Jordan and John Shields, "The 'Most Daring Raid'? The Royal Air Force, Operation Black Buck and the Falklands Conflict, 1982," *Air Power Review* 21, no. 2 (Summer 2018), 96.

110. Harper, *Submarine Operations*, 9.

111. TNA, ADM 202/817, 148 (Meiktila) Commando Forward Observation Battery, Royal Artillery: Operation Corporate Report (Falklands Conflict), July 1, 1982–July 31, 1982 (hereafter Operation Corporate Report).
112. *Rattenbach Report,* 617–22.
113. *Rattenbach Report,* 611–16.
114. David Jordan and John Shields, "The 'Most Daring Raid'? The Royal Air Force, Operation Black Buck and the Falklands Conflict, 1982," *Air Power Review* 21, no. 2 (Summer 2018), 101–2.
115. Lawrence Freedman has indicated that a potential raid remained a source of debate and was still being discussed at the time of Argentina's surrender. Lawrence Freedman, "Air Power and the Falklands, 1982," in *A History of Air Warfare,* ed. John Andreas Olsen (Dulles, Virginia: Potomac Books, 2010), 166.
116. Sir John Nott, "A View from the Center," in *The Falklands Conflict Twenty Years On,* eds. Badsey, et al, 62. The potential sinking of the carrier was always a source of concern for a number of reasons, including the potential effect on public opinion. Lawrence Freedman, *The Official History of the Falklands Campaign, Volume II: War and Diplomacy* (London: Routledge, 2005), 261–68.
117. *Rattenbach Report,* 875.
118. *Rattenbach Report,* 870.
119. *Rattenbach Report,* 890.

6

India's Kargil War 1999

Conventional Air Operations under a Constant Nuclear Shadow

BENJAMIN S. LAMBETH

Ever since arch-rivals India and Pakistan acquired nuclear weapons and effective means for delivering them, the world has faced a localized bilateral standoff dominated by the omnipresent possibility of escalation to nuclear use during any conventional war between the two countries that might devolve into an imminent rout for either side. In light of this uniquely concerning source of regional instability with potentially global ramifications, most international security experts have tended to regard the likelihood of a war on the Asian subcontinent involving nuclear weapons by either India or Pakistan to be quite low. Moreover, given the highly undesirable implications of any such scenario in which either side might resort to nuclear weapons employment under duress, most also have tended to believe that any future conflict between the two countries may be intense but also most likely for limited stakes and not unduly prolonged. The principal concern of military planners in both countries with respect to combat readiness in any such circumstance has tended to focus on preserving the ability to operate effectively at a conventional level when both sides are within reach of a nuclear escalatory option. That said, it remains inescapable that the mere presence of the nuclear factor in any future test of strength between the two sides could weigh heavily in either side's decision to resort to force in a major way.

A revealing insight into this evolved dynamic between India and Pakistan and its potential impact on future conflict management can be gained from the instructive Kargil War that occurred in the high Himalayas in May, June, and July 1999 following a covert incursion by Pakistani troops into Indian-controlled Kashmir that was launched just a year after Pakistan's first demonstration of a nuclear weapons capability. That border clash for limited but important stakes, which ensued for seventy-four days at a cost of more than a thousand soldiers killed or wounded on each side, was overshadowed by NATO's higher-profile air war for Kosovo that occurred thousands of miles away in the Balkans at roughly the same time. In large part owing to that more internationally prominent and attention-getting conflict, the Kargil War remains only dimly appreciated by most Western defense professionals. Nevertheless, it was a milestone event in Indian military history that offers an exemplary case study in the use of airpower in a war between two nuclear-armed rivals conducted solely at a conventional level.[1] The conflict also was emblematic of a type of border skirmish that could recur anew between India and Pakistan, as well as possibly also between India and an even more nuclear-capable China, given the inhibiting effect of the nuclear overhang on more protracted and higher-stakes conventional engagements. As the late retired Air Commodore Jasjit Singh of the Indian Air Force aptly reflected on this point six years after the Kargil War's successful conclusion for India, the clash lasting nearly three months was "a typical example of a limited war in a nuclear weapons environment."[2] Especially in light of its uniqueness in that regard, Western analysts have much to gain from a closer look at this still little-known but notable chapter in the history of air warfare.

Prelude to a Showdown

Flare-ups along the border between India and Pakistan have had a long history, going as far back as 1947, when Great Britain finally abandoned its long period of colonial rule over the subcontinent, and the former British Indian Empire, known also as the British Raj for short, was subdivided into the newly independent Union of India and the Dominion of Pakistan. Ever since that fateful partition, the two newly spawned states have been in constant diplomatic and recurrent military conflict over control of the contested region of Jammu and Kashmir in between. An informed and thorough account of the heated passions that were unleashed on both sides in the partition's early aftermath aptly portrayed that tectonic shift as "one of the most violent transfers of power in the twentieth century. The widespread carnage and horror of sectarian warfare between Hindus and Muslims [that ensued in short order] was something that no one, including the British, had really anticipated.... [The end of British rule] would change the geopolitical landscape of the subcontinent forever and sow the seeds of unending violence in the beautiful state of Jammu and Kashmir and convert it into a proxy battleground to fulfill what [Pakistan] would repeatedly term as an unfinished agenda of partition."[3]

The first Indo-Pakistani war of 1947–1948 that followed in the partition's early aftermath ended with a United Nations (UN)-brokered ceasefire and the concomitant establishment of a formal Line of Control (LoC) demarcating a boundary through the portions of Jammu and Kashmir that were administered, respectively, by India and by Pakistan. Pakistan then started a second war over Kashmir less than a decade later in 1965 by invading the Indian-controlled portion of Kashmir with both regular and irregular forces. In the end, however, it failed to alter any of the realities on the ground or in the overall governance of the region. A far more intense and determined subsequent war in 1971 ended in a humiliating defeat for Pakistan. In that war's aftermath, aided by Indian military support, East Pakistan broke away from West Pakistan and became the new state of Bangladesh. Also out of that conflict came the Simla Agreement of 1972, in which India and Pakistan both agreed that the LoC "shall be respected by both sides [which shall] undertake to refrain from the threat or the use of force in violation of this line."[4] Tensions flared yet again in 1984 when India successfully preempted a planned Pakistani occupation of strategic positions on the disputed Siachen glacier.[5] Sporadic Indo-Pakistani fighting for control of the glacier then continued for more than a decade and a half, with the Indian army winning most tactical engagements and gaining control of the main strategic locations in its environs.

The most immediate and proximate seeds of the Kargil War were planted in March and April 1999 when small but determined units of the Pakistani Army's Northern Light Infantry (NLI) surreptitiously crossed the LoC into the Indian-administered portion of Kashmir in the remote and rugged Himalayan heights overlooking the town of Kargil between the Kashmir valley and the Ladakh plateau. The LoC running through Jammu and Kashmir that separates the Indian- and Pakistani-controlled portions of Kashmir is an abiding product of the third Indo-Pakistani war of 1971 noted above that

MiG-21s were reliable, if not advanced, war horses during the Kargil War. (Agnad Singh. Used by permission)

occasioned the newly established country of Bangladesh. It bisects some of the most forbidding terrain to be found anywhere in the world, with most of the main ridgelines being offshoots of K-2, the world's second highest mountain.

While preparations were under way for an upcoming meeting of India's and Pakistan's prime ministers, senior leaders in the Pakistani Army, led by the Army's chief of staff, General Pervez Musharraf, and the chief of the General Staff, Lieutenant General Mohammed Aziz, were conducting initial reconnaissance and laying the logistical groundwork for the impending cross-LoC operation. The most likely intent of the planned gambit, apart from seeking to internationalize the Kashmir issue in Indo-Pakistani relations, was to seize control of India's sole line of communications to troops on the Siachen glacier by obstructing the use of the key two-lane national highway NH-1A in Ladakh running from Srinagar through Kargil to Leh.[6] That highway provided the only access to the IAF's airfield at Thoise on the axis to Siachen.

The incursion's planners took full advantage of the relaxed atmosphere that had come to prevail in New Delhi after the visit of Prime Minister Atal Vajpayee to Pakistan to help promulgate the Lahore Declaration, which was signed by Vajpayee and his Pakistani counterpart, Nawaz Sharif, on February 21. With it, the governments of both countries swore their commitment to the vision of peace and stability embodied in the UN charter. The Pakistan Army leaders chose to exploit the nascent, and ultimately short-lived, feeling of goodwill that had emanated from that declaration in a way that might irreversibly change the status quo along the LoC to Pakistan's advantage.

Because of the capricious weather that predominates in the area, the Indian Army during the harshest winter months that immediately preceded the Kargil crisis had vacated its most inhospitable forward outposts—typically at elevations of 16,000 to 18,000 feet—that were normally manned on India's side of the LoC throughout the remainder of the year. Since substantial gaps existed in India's defenses in the segment of Kashmir that lay on both sides of the LoC, the Pakistani planners deduced that the vacated outposts made for lucrative targets for potential seizure. Adding even further to the attractiveness of the planned gambit, those outposts were situated on easily-defended high ground that Indian troops would have to attack from below in order to try to recapture them. A clever mix of regular combat troops and local civilian porters would infiltrate the area and present the Indian government with a fait accompli in Kashmir.

In planning this incursion, Pakistan's military leaders were all but surely emboldened by their country's public demonstration of a nuclear weapons capability within just the preceding year. They may also have been encouraged by a derivative belief that the awareness of that capability in key leadership circles in New Delhi would more than offset any conventional military advantage enjoyed in the region by India.[7] And even if the operation were to be detected by India while it was still in progress, the incursion's planners likely judged that the Indian Army's reaction to it would be slow and limited at best. Most important, they probably took it as a foregone conclusion that were India to seek to conventionalize the ensuing conflict, pressure from the international community would quickly intervene and force the government of Prime Minister Vajpayee to cease combat operations within a week, thereby leaving Pakistan "comfortably in possession of gains it would make by infiltration," in the words of retired Indian Army Major General G. D. Bakshi.[8]

Ultimately, in what turned out to be a phased infiltration in uniquely challenging mountainous terrain, Pakistani troops moving by foot and helicopter established a bridgehead across a 112-mile-wide frontage to a depth of five to six miles and occupying roughly 130 outposts on India's side of the LoC, thereby enabling forward observers to adjust artillery aimed at highway NH-1A for maximum effect before the intruders were first detected by local shepherds on May 3. Indian sources later reported that the occupying force numbered from 1,500 to 2,000 combatants, with perhaps four to five times that many troops mobilized to help supply the most forward elements on the Indian side of the LoC.[9]

The first phase of the insertion operation featured a covert movement of some 500 to 1,000 Pakistani troops in small groups of thirty or forty each, with multiple penetrations occurring along the ridgelines that passed through the LoC. The intruders were well trained in mountain warfare and were accustomed to operating at high elevations. They also were well-armed with AK-47 rifles, mortars, artillery tubes, antiaircraft guns, and U.S.-provided FIM-92A Stinger and Chinese-made Anza II infrared surface-to-air missiles (SAMs). The incursion's organizers sought plausible deniability of any culpability for their aggressive action through the use of a shrewd deception measure that generated indigenous militant Islamist radio traffic within Pakistani-administered Kashmir to convince Indian signals intelligence monitors that the incursion was an insurgent activity over which Pakistan had no control.[10] Finally, the intruders took special care to move only at times that would allow them to avoid detection by periodic Indian winter air surveillance operations.[11]

As the Indian Army units that had manned the temporarily vacated outposts began returning to their stations during the first week of May, they gradually discovered the full extent of the occupation of those positions by Pakistani troops that had taken place during their absence. One of the first of their patrols confirmed the infiltration but got ambushed, resulting in several Indian soldiers having been killed by the intruders. Later patrols that experienced unplanned encounters with the intruders suffered heavy casualties during their attempts to engage the enemy forces on their own. In the process, however, they were able to generate and pass up the chain of command valuable contact information that imparted greater clarity to the situation. The full scale of the intrusions was finally validated on May 8 by Indian Air Force (IAF) pilots in Cheetah light helicopters as they flew surveillance sorties along the Tololing ridge in the Dras subsector of the Kargil region.[12] Clearly local Indian Army commanders in Kargil and in Srinagar did not appreciate the full gravity of the Pakistani challenge at the start of the gathering crisis.

Once they understood more fully what had transpired along the LoC, the army's leaders finally responded by moving two infantry divisions, five independent brigades, and forty-four battalions from the Kashmir valley to the Kargil sector, ultimately mobilizing some 200,000 Indian troops in all, with around 30,000 of those soldiers actively deployed in the immediate war zone. Most of this buildup occurred during the three weeks between the initial detection of the incursion and the eventual start on May 26 of a major joint counteroffensive that the Indian Army code-named Operation Vijay (meaning "victory" in Hindi). The avowed objectives of the counteroffensive were to drive out the intruding forces and to restore the LoC to its previous status. This response was almost certainly more determined than anything the Pakistan Army's leaders had anticipated.

Enlisting the IAF's Involvement

After several early firefights with the entrenched Pakistanis that occasioned numerous Indian fatalities in an unsuccessful bid to recapture the closest of the occupied positions, the Indian Army finally approached the Indian Air Force (IAF) on May 11 and asked it to help turn the tide through a commitment of armed helicopters to support the embattled ground troops.[13] For its part, the IAF had already begun conducting initial reconnaissance sorties over the Kargil heights the day before, less than a week after the presence of the enemy incursion was first confirmed by Indian Army patrols. It also had begun deploying additional aircraft into the Kashmir valley in enough numbers to support any likely combat tasking, established a rudimentary air defense control arrangement there in the absence of any ground-based radars in the area, and started extensive practice of air-to-ground weapons deliveries by both fighters and attack helicopters at Himalayan target elevations over the service's weapons range located near Srinagar.[14] On May 12, an IAF helicopter was fired upon near the most forward-based intruder positions overlooking Kargil and landed uneventfully with a damaged rotor. That hostile act prompted the IAF's Air Headquarters to place Western Air Command, the IAF organization responsible for the Jammu and Kashmir sectors, on heightened alert and to establish quick-reaction aircraft launch facilities at

Although their payloads were reduced drastically by high-altitude operations, helicopters like this Mi-17 gave invaluable logistical support to Indian Army operations. (Agnad Singh. Used by permission)

the IAF's northernmost operating locations at Air Force Stations (AFS) Srinagar and Avantipur.

The next day, IAF Jaguar fighters launched on tactical reconnaissance sorties in the Kargil area to gather prospective target information using their on-board long-range oblique photography systems, and a forward direction center for the tactical control of combat aircraft was established at the IAF's highest-elevation airfield at AFS Leh. Concurrently, Canberra PR57 jet reconnaissance aircraft were pressed into service over Kargil, and electronic intelligence missions began to be flown regularly by the IAF in the vicinity of the detected intrusion and beyond.[15] Finally, on May 14, Air Headquarters activated the IAF's air operations center for Jammu and Kashmir and mobilized its fielded forces in that sector for a possible all-out air counteroffensive. At the same time, in close conjunction with their Indian Army 15 Corps counterparts, Western Air Command planners developed a tailored concept of operations for kinetic air attack in the Kargil heights that included target selection procedures, force deconfliction and other safety criteria, and an arrangement for conducting and communicating prompt battle damage assessment. These and related activities well attested to the IAF's clear expectation from the very start that it would be engaged in earnest against the intruders just as soon as a final course of action for it was agreed upon in the joint arena. As the air officer commanding-in-chief (AOC-in-C) of the IAF's Western Air Command at the time, Air Marshal Vinod Patney, later affirmed, "we were ready for a full-fledged war and had been for some days before May 25, 1999, when government clearance to commit the IAF to combat was received."[16]

In the end, during the pivotal chiefs of staff committee meeting on May 25 that was chaired by Prime Minister Vajpayee, General Ved Malik, the chief of staff of the Indian Army, explained the seriousness of the situation in the Kargil sector and the need for the IAF "to step in without delay." At that, Vajpayee reportedly said: "OK, get started tomorrow at dawn." The IAF's chief of staff, Air Chief Marshal Anil Tipnis, then asked the prime minister for permission to cross the LoC while attacking targets only on India's side of the LoC. To that request, no doubt with the disturbing possibility of escalation by Pakistan all the way to the nuclear level at least in the back of his mind, Vajpayee responded adamantly: "No. No crossing the LoC."[17] With that rule of engagement firmly stipulated by the civilian leadership, the die was finally cast for full-scale IAF involvement in the counteroffensive.

Initial Air Operations

Less than a week before the start of Operation Vijay, the IAF had launched a Canberra PR57 on May 21 to conduct a reconnaissance of the besieged area that overlooked highway NH-1A and the adjacent town of Kargil. While descending to 22,000 feet just two miles from the LoC in a racetrack pattern over Batalik, which put the aircraft as low as 4,000 feet above the highest ridgelines, the Canberra sustained a direct hit in its right engine by what was later determined to have been a Chinese-made Anza infrared SAM, with the SAM having possibly been fired from the Pakistani side of the LoC. Fortunately, the Canberra's pilot succeeded in making a safe emergency landing at AFS Srinagar. From that moment onward, the IAF's leadership knew without question that it was nearing the brink of a major combat involvement.

Kinetic air operations began in earnest at 0630 on May 26, just a little more than two weeks after the initial detection of enemy infiltration into Indian-administered Kashmir, with six attacks in succession by two-ship elements of MiG-21s, MiG-23s, and MiG-27s against intruder camps, matériel dumps, and supply routes in the general areas of Dras, Kargil, and Batalik. These early attacks marked the first time that the IAF had expended ordnance in anger in Kashmir since its Vampire jet fighters destroyed Pakistani bunkers in the Kargil sector twenty-eight years before in December 1971. The IAF fighters that were pressed into these initial strikes conducted 57mm rocket attacks and strafing passes against enemy targets. A second wave of air attacks began at 1430 that afternoon, followed by high-altitude reconnaissance overflights by Canberra PR57s and subsequent low passes by MiG-21Ms to conduct near real-time battle damage assessment.[18]

Nearly all of the targets selected for attack in those initial strikes were on or near jagged ridgelines at elevations ranging from 16,000 to 18,000 feet. The stark backdrop of rocks and snow made for uncommonly difficult visual target acquisition, complicated further by the small size of the enemy troop positions dispersed against a vast and undifferentiated snow background. That unique terrain feature yielded a sight picture from the cockpit that inspired the code name assigned to the IAF's contribution to the campaign, Operation Safed Sagar (Hindi for "White Sea").[19]

During the second day of surface-attack operations that began at 0600, the IAF lost two fighters in close succession. The first, a MiG-27, experienced an engine failure due to gun gas ingestion while coming off a target after its pilot had just conducted a successful two-pass attack with 80mm rockets and 30mm cannon fire on one of the enemy's main supply dumps. The ensuing in-flight emergency resulted in the pilot ejecting safely after several unsuccessful air start attempts, only to be captured by the Pakistani intruders almost as soon as he reached the ground. The downed pilot was released and repatriated on June 3 after having been held prisoner of war for about a week. The second IAF fighter downed, a MiG-21M providing top cover for the attacking jets, sustained an infrared SAM hit while its pilot was flying over the terrain at low level to assist in the search for the downed MiG-27 pilot. Its pilot also succeeded in ejecting safely but was executed shortly after having been captured following his landing, since his body was subsequently returned bearing fatal bullet wounds and clear signs of torture.[20] On the third day of air operations, an IAF Mi-17 helicopter carrying four pods of air-to-ground rockets was downed by an enemy shoulder-fired SAM while conducting a low-level attack, with all four crewmembers on board being killed as a result.

The ability of the IAF's Mirage 2000s to drop precision-guided munitions was a game changer in the rugged terrain of the Kargil region. (Agnad Singh. Used by permission)

In performing these initial low-level strike operations during the first three days of Operation Safed Sagar, the IAF's pilots quickly relearned what the Israelis had learned at great cost during the Yom Kippur War of 1973, when Egyptian and Syrian SAMs and antiaircraft artillery downed nearly a third of the Israeli Air Force's fighter inventory (102 aircraft in all) before the three-week war finally ended in victory for Israel. At that point, the IAF moved with dispatch to equip all of its participating fighters with flares in order to provide an active countermeasure against the heat-seeking SAMs. It also called a halt once and for all to any further use of slow-moving and vulnerable Mi-17 helicopters in a fire-support role and directed that all target attacks by IAF fighters henceforth be conducted from outside the lethal threat envelopes of enemy shoulder-fired SAMs. In all, enemy forces fired more than one hundred SAMs at IAF aircraft throughout the conflict. After the service's first three days of combat operations, however, not a single one of its aircraft ever again was downed or sustained battle damage from enemy fire.[21]

Along with American F-16s, the Pakistan Air Force relied on Chinese-built Chengdu F-7s to patrol its side of the Line of Control. (United States Air Force. https://en.wikipedia.org/wiki/File:Pakistani_Chengdu_J-7.JPG)

Throughout the campaign, whenever IAF reconnaissance or ground attack operations were under way in the immediate combat zone, Western Air Command ensured that IAF MiG-29s or other air-to-air fighters were also airborne on combat air patrol (CAP) stations over the ground fighting on India's side of the LoC to provide top cover against any possibility of an attempt by the Pakistani Air Force (PAF) to enter the fray in a ground attack role. PAF F-16s on opposing CAP stations to the west typically maintained a safe distance of ten to twenty miles on the Pakistani side of the LoC, although they occasionally approached as close as eight miles away from the ongoing ground engagements. The PAF's director of operations during the Kargil War later reported that there had been isolated instances of IAF and PAF fighters locking on to each other with their onboard fire control radars, but that caution had prevailed throughout on both sides and that "no close [air-to-air] encounters took place."[22] IAF fighters never joined in aerial combat with the PAF F-16s due to the Vajpayee government's strict injunction that Indian forces not cross the LoC.[23]

In all, the IAF flew some 460 fighter sorties throughout the campaign dedicated exclusively to maintaining battlespace air defense.[24] These medium- and high-altitude defensive CAPs and offensive fighter sweeps, typically entailing four-ship flights of MiG-29s, took place not only in the immediate area of ground fighting in the Kargil sector, but throughout Western Air Command's entire area of responsibility. As Operation Vijay's air component commander later recalled in this regard, he was not just concerned about Kargil or the Kashmir region but "was working on a much bigger canvas.... I was fully conscious that as we hit and killed enemy soldiers, there was every possibility for escalation, possibly outside the immediate combat area, and it was my job to be ready with adequate remaining resources for that eventuality."[25]

Increasingly as the joint campaign unfolded, most Indian Army operations were preceded by preparatory air strikes, each of which was closely coordinated beforehand between 15 Corps planners and the IAF's forward air operations center for Jammu and Kashmir.[26] Because of their rudimentary bomb sights, MiG-21, MiG-23, and MiG-27 pilots typically achieved only limited effectiveness when attempting to provide close air support (CAS) against enemy point targets owing to the resultant inaccuracy of their unguided weapons and the added constraint imposed by the government's ruling against crossing the LoC. Had it not been for the latter ruling, the IAF could have spared the Indian Army the need for its costly frontal assault against the intruders by leveraging its asymmetric advantage to attack their source of resupply in Pakistani-administered Kashmir, in effect imposing an aerial blockade. That, however, would have risked escalation to a wider war, to include possibly bringing the PAF into play against India's ground forces with manifold unforeseeable consequences. The Vajpayee government was determined to avoid such an occurrence at every reasonable cost.

Accordingly, on May 30, just four days after the start of Operation Safed Sagar, Air Chief Marshal Tipnis decided to commit Mirage 2000Hs capable of delivering laser-guided bombs (LGBs) to ground attack operations in the Kargil sector. By way of implementing this directive, Air Headquarters launched an accelerated drive at AFS Gwalior, where the IAF's Mirage 2000Hs were based, to configure a number of those aircraft for delivering LGBs. By that time, the Aircraft System Testing Establishment (ASTE) in Bangalore was well along in a program to integrate the Israeli-made Litening electro-optical and infrared targeting pod onto the Mirage 2000H and Jaguar. To support the accelerated effort at Gwalior, ASTE began a full court press to prepare selected Mirage 2000Hs to be fitted with Litening pods for use over Kargil. At the same time, it helped to modify the Mirage 2000H's centerline weapon station to carry a British-made 1,000-pound bomb fitted with a U.S. Paveway II laser guidance kit instead of the French Matra LGB that was prohibitively expensive. By June 12, the upgraded Mirage 2000Hs were ready to commence precision strike operations for the first time in IAF history.

A Successful Endgame for India

By the time Operation Vijay had reached full momentum in early June, the Indian Army had marshaled nearly a corps' worth of dedicated troop strength in the Kargil area. The overriding objective of those forces was to recapture the high ground from which the intruders had a direct line of sight to highway NH-1A, allowing them to lay down sustained artillery fire on it and on adjacent targets. Toward that end, after more than a week of hard fighting, units of the army's 8th Mountain Division recaptured the strategically important Tololing ridge complex and an adjacent point in the Batalik sector on June 13, in what one informed account later described as "probably the turning point" in India's land counteroffensive.[27]

Four days later, on June 17, another important breakthrough in the joint campaign was achieved when a formation of Mirage 2000Hs struck and destroyed the enemy's main administrative and logistics encampment at Muntho Dhalo by means of accurately placed 1,000-pound general purpose bombs delivered in high-angle dive attacks using the aircraft's computer-assisted weapon aiming capability. For this pivotal attack, the IAF waited until the encampment had grown to a size that rendered it strategically ripe for such targeting. Air Marshal Patney, the AOC-in-C of Western Air Command at the time, affirmed later that the essentially total destruction by the IAF of the NLI's rudimentary but absolutely life-sustaining infrastructure at Muntho Dhalo "paralyzed the enemy war effort, as it was their major supply depot." Patney called that depot "*the* logistics and administrative center for the Pakistanis," adding: "After this attack, it was all downhill."[28] In characterizing the attack as "perhaps the most spectacular of all the [campaign's air] strikes," a still-serving IAF air commodore reported at the end of 1999 that it resulted in as many as 300 enemy casualties within just minutes.[29]

A second major milestone in the air contribution to the campaign was passed a week later, on June 24, when a two-ship element of Mirage 2000Hs, in the first-ever combat use of LGBs by the IAF, struck and destroyed the NLI's command bunkers with two 1,000-pound Paveway II laser-guided munitions. In all, a total of nine LGBs were said to have been employed eventually against NLI targets during the campaign's final weeks, eight by Mirage 2000Hs and one by a Jaguar.[30] However, those two were the only ones needed against the enemy's command and control complex in the Kargil heights. As Air Marshal Patney later remarked in this regard: "Unfortunately, there were not enough targets [of sufficiently high value there] to merit laser-guided bombing. Hence only two [LGBs in toto] were dropped over Tiger Hill."[31] In these LGB attacks, the target was acquired through the Litening pod's electro-optical imaging sensor at about twelve miles out, with weapon release occurring at a slant range of about five miles and the aircraft then turning away while continuing to mark the target with a laser spot for the weapon to guide on.[32] Air Marshal Patney later recalled that this attack "caught the imagination of many because of the [IAF's hitherto unprecedented combat] use of LGBs," but that "its impact on the war was less important" than was the more stunningly successful attack on Muntho Dhalo the week before, which "turned the tables irrevocably and permanently."[33]

The same day, other Mirage 2000Hs struck additional targets on Tiger Hill with unguided bombs. From that high vantage point, the intruders had previously directed artillery fire on the Indian Army's brigade headquarters at Dras. The following day, Mirage 2000Hs and Jaguars initiated around-the-clock bombing of enemy positions throughout the Batalik and Dras subsectors. In all, Mirage 2000Hs struck as many as twenty-five separate designated aim points toward the campaign's end, including the enemy's logistical nerve center at Muntho Dhalo in the Batalik sector.[34]

On June 29, 15 Corps captured two vital posts on the high ridgelines near Tiger Hill. On July 2, it launched a more massive three-pronged attack from Kargil, finally recapturing Tiger Hill on July 4 after an exhausting 11-hour battle, during which the attacking troops climbed fixed ropes at night and in freezing rain to scale vertical mountain faces reaching more than 1,000 feet high. By July 8, 15 Corps reported that its units had recaptured 99 percent of the Batalik-Yaldor subsector and 90 percent of the Dras area, leading Prime Minister Vajpayee to declare that Operation Vijay had finally reached a turning point and that "there is going to be a great victory."[35] The following day, the IAF received this congratulatory message from the Indian Army's field headquarters: "You guys have done a wonderful job. Your Mirage boys with their precision laser-guided bombs targeted an enemy battalion headquarters in Tiger Hill with tremendous success . . . . The enemy is on the run. They are on the run in other sectors also. At this rate, the end of the conflict may come soon."[36] As was well attested by that spontaneous accolade, the air support provided by the IAF almost instantly boosted the morale of India's beleaguered ground troops and facilitated an early recapture of their outposts at Muntho Dhalo and Tiger Hill.

In all, other than for an inconsequential brief delay due to weather, IAF combat operations continued without interruption for seven weeks under the operational control of the AOC-in-C for Western Air Command, Air Marshal Patney, and his senior air staff officer, Air Marshal Michael McMahon, both headquartered in New Delhi. At the height of Operation Safed Sagar, the IAF was generating more than forty fixed-wing combat sorties a day in both direct and indirect support of 15 Corps. Notably, however, Western Air Command was not the sole provider of IAF assets to conduct these daily missions. Because of its depth with respect to India's western border, the service's Central Air Command headquartered at Allahabad in Uttar Pradesh has traditionally been the repository of such major IAF strategic assets as the since-retired Mach 3-capable MiG-25R high-altitude reconnaissance aircraft and the Mirage 2000Hs. It was under Central Air Command's direction that the MiG-25R was eventually pressed into a unique medium-altitude tactical reconnaissance role to meet the needs of Operation Safed Sagar. The Mirage 2000Hs were also Central Air Command's assets and were seconded to the operational control of Western Air Command for their use in the Kargil fighting. As the parent command's AOC-in-C later recalled: "Initially there was great reluctance to use Mirage 2000Hs in the strike role in Kargil, the idea being to preserve them to cater to the needs of a possible higher level of escalation to all-out war. It took a lot of convincing for their use in the Kargil operation, but the lingering feeling . . . still prevented their full-fledged use, which otherwise would have brought about even better results than achieved in Operation Safed Sagar."[37]

By July 12, when aerial strike operations ended, IAF fighters had flown more than 1,700 strike, reconnaissance, and CAP and escort sorties in all, including around forty at night during the campaign's final weeks. Although the IAF's Mi-17 helicopters were not used in an armed role after one was lost to an enemy SAM during the air offensive's third day, they continued to play a vital part throughout the remainder of the campaign in conducting airlift, casualty evacuation, and reconnaissance missions. IAF helicopters flew a total of 2,474 sorties, evacuating 441 casualties and airlifting some 2,000 infantry troops and 105mm field guns into position. They also airlifted close to 300 tons of matériel to the war zone.[38]

At long last, "yard by bloody yard," as a retired Indian Army general later described the effort, the Kargil ridgelines were recaptured from the intruders through a heroic Indian infantry counteroffensive facilitated from its first days onward by supporting IAF air power.[39] By July 26, Indian forces had reclaimed a majority of their seized outposts above Kargil and driven the enemy troops that had occupied them back to their own side of the LoC, with all remaining Pakistani forces subsequently vacating the still-occupied positions under the weight of diplomatic pressure from the United States. In the end, by its official after-action count, the Indian Army suffered 471 troops killed in action and 1,060 soldiers wounded during the Kargil fighting. For their part, the occupying Pakistani forces were said by Indian sources to have lost more than 700 troops killed in action with around a thousand more wounded, although much disagreement and uncertainty still surround the latter figures.[40]

Assessing the IAF's Performance

In facilitating Operation Vijay's ultimately successful outcome for India, both the Indian Army and the IAF were essential players in a genuinely joint counteroffensive in which it would be hard to deem either as having been the more pivotal contributor toward determining the ultimate victory for India's forces. To be sure, from a simple weight-of-effort perspective, 15 Corps artillery was the main source of direct fire support throughout the fighting, and massive barrages of it provided sustained suppressive cover under which Indian infantry teams eventually moved up the daunting terrain to recapture their former posts. In all, 15 Corps committed fifteen artillery regiments and more than 300 artillery pieces to what one account called "one of the most bitterly fought mountain battles of all times."[41] Throughout the campaign, those weapons expended more than 250,000 rounds of ammunition in a sustained laydown of fire on a scale not seen anywhere in the world since World War II.

Yet that said, although the enemy's small and generally well-concealed individual troop positions were often sufficiently resistant to visual acquisition and targeting that the IAF's pilots "did not provide reliable and consistent close support" to 15 Corps' engaged units, the IAF performed more than effectively in servicing enemy headquarters complexes, supply dumps, and other assets that were more readily accessible to aerial attack from standoff ranges.[42] Furthermore, in marked contrast to what the IAF's air component commander during the Kargil fighting later characterized as 15 Corps' "profligacy in the use of artillery in a carpet-bombing mode," the IAF dropped only around 500 general-purpose bombs in all during the seventy-four-day campaign, none of which were released indiscriminately and most of which were deemed to have been effective against their assigned interdiction targets. As Air Marshal Patney recalled in this regard, "after every mission, the army would give us the results of the attack. In about 70 percent of the missions, we were told 'bombs on target.'"[43]

There are two compelling explanations for why close-quarters CAS delivery was so problematic for the IAF throughout most of the Kargil fighting. First, the enemy targets that presented themselves in the Kargil heights were nothing like the more conventional target array that fighter aircraft typically engage in providing support to ground combat operations. As one IAF airman later pointed out in this regard, the target complex did not consist of troop concentrations, command posts, and logistical supply lines, but rather "near-invisible humans well dug into hideouts . . . on various hilltops and slopes," where "only their tents and earthwork structures were identifiable" from the air when not masked by the natural camouflage that was provided by "the ubiquitous black and white color combination of the terrain." By this informed account, the largest target struck by the IAF during Operation Safed Sagar, the enemy's supply camp at Muntho Dhalo, "would normally have been the smallest target considered for the use of air power during a normal all-out war."[44]

Second, the IAF's combat operations were hampered from the very start by multiple constraints on their freedom of action. As noted before, the Indian government's refusal to countenance any crossing of the LoC by friendly forces made for a substantial limiting factor on the IAF's flexibility, in that fast-moving fighters were driven to employ target-attack tactics using ingress and egress headings that were not optimal or, in many instances, even safe. With respect to the harmful impact of this politically imposed constraint on the IAF's tactical flexibility, India's minister for external affairs during the Kargil War later recalled in his memoirs: "There were but two routes for the air force to operate on, and both were extremely narrow funnels. Our missions could fly in this narrow corridor either west or east or reverse." He further recalled: "The fact of the LoC not being a visibly marked line on the ground compounded difficulties."[45] Relatedly, because the decree prevented the IAF from operating on the Pakistani side of the LoC, the conduct of Operation Vijay remained limited to the immediate terrain from which the Indian Army sought to evict the intruders, while the most lucrative targets associated with providing logistical sustenance to the intruders enjoyed an inviolate sanctuary in Pakistani-administered Kashmir.

In addition to the two situational limitations outlined above, the IAF experienced a predictably slow start in the Kargil campaign and rode a steep learning curve at first as its pilots and planners gradually adapted to unfamiliar operating conditions and steadily improved their performance over time. As a former IAF air marshal frankly conceded on this score, the service "took some time before honing the [needed] skills and becoming effective" in a high mountain combat setting that no air force had ever experienced before.[46] Until that happened, the PAF's director of operations during the Kargil crisis was on firm ground in remarking retrospectively that "the results achieved by the IAF in the first two days were dismal."[47] In a similar vein, some Indian Army field commanders later complained that for the campaign's first three weeks, the effectiveness of the IAF's strikes was "near negligible."[48]

Be that as it may, however, it overstated the impact of the IAF's operational shortcomings by a considerable margin to suggest that on balance, the service turned in a "poor showing" during the Kargil War, as one otherwise insightful campaign assessment observed two years after the conflict ended.[49] On the contrary, as a more richly informed review of Operation Vijay concluded some time thereafter, the IAF's entry into action on May 26 and its gradual improvement in performance over time in fact "represented a paradigm shift in the nature and prognosis of the conflict."[50] Granted, it was only natural that India's leading airmen would lend their voices to such a self-congratulatory conclusion. For example, a decade after the war ended, the chief of the air staff at the time, Air Chief Marshal Fali Homi Major, suggested that the IAF's entry into the Kargil equation had "immediately altered the nature of the conflict."[51] By the same token, during his tenure as the AOC-in-C of Western Air Command, Air Marshal Pranab Barbora volunteered at roughly the same time that "the conflict in Kargil would have gone on and on if air power ... had not come into play."[52]

It was not, however, just the IAF's leaders who rendered such laudatory judgments regarding their service's performance. Senior Indian Army officers were likewise generous in voicing their appreciation of the IAF's combat contributions. For example, retired Major General G. D. Bakshi characterized the IAF's innovative use of air power as "one of the excellent features of the Kargil operations," adding that "the complete domination of the sky by the IAF over the area of intrusion . . . served to demoralize the [NLI] troopers" and, "in combination with artillery, served to mass effects and generate an element of shock and awe."[53] If the IAF was unable to provide consistently effective on-call CAS in close combat conditions for all of the extenuating factors addressed above, it certainly was effective in other air applications no less pertinent to the ongoing fighting. As a U.S. Army officer rightly observed in this regard, the IAF's contribution to the joint fight "grew as the campaign wore on," and fighter aircraft armed with LGBs and well-placed unguided munitions "eventually destroyed virtually all of the Pakistani supply lines and played a major role in the battle for Tiger Hill."[54]

Finally, it bears stressing here that since Pakistan just a year before had publicly demonstrated the capability to detonate a nuclear device, the IAF's ability to adapt to an unnatural rules-of-engagement limitation imposed by top-down civilian decree and to work effectively within the Vajpayee government's ban against any crossing of the LoC by Indian forces may well have been the determining factor in keeping the PAF out of the fighting and hence in maintaining escalation control throughout the seventy-four-day war. After the surviving intruders were driven back into Pakistani-administered territory and the Indian Army reclaimed and secured its positions in the Kargil heights, the AOC-in-C of Western Air Command, Air Marshal Patney, reflected in this regard: "It is the nature of air power that escalation is inherent in its use, unless its use is one-sided, as happened this time . . . . Before May 26, when we went into action, one of our apprehensions . . . was the degree of enemy resolve and to what extent we could expect such escalation." Patney added: "We had not planned for this kind of war. We had planned that we would use air power in this particular area, but certainly not in the way we were required to do so . . . . If we were to apply air power in its classical sense, in which we had done all our training, we would have crossed the LoC well before and crossed the [international border] as well."[55] In the end, however, neither development ever occurred.[56]

Viewed in hindsight, as one of the best Western accounts of the Kargil fighting from an operational perspective later observed, "the unprecedented use of the IAF in a situation short of all-out war had a dramatic shock value."

To begin with, it severely undermined the morale of the NLI infiltrators, "adding a psychological blow to complement whatever physical damage was inflicted. At the very least," this account noted, "the NLI soldiers would have to ask: 'Where is our own air force?'" The reassuring presence of IAF combat aircraft directly above the contested battlefield from the campaign's first days onward also boosted the fighting spirit of those Indian troops who otherwise faced rough going until the campaign's final breakthrough toward victory at the very end. At the same time, the asymmetrical use of India's air power allowed the Vajpayee government to telegraph an unmistakable signal of its seriousness to key audiences both in Pakistan and worldwide.[57] In the early aftermath of Operation Vijay's successful ending, the Indian government's formal after-action assessment of the campaign released on December 15, 1999, likewise found the intervention of the IAF to have been both "unnerving" and "a significant development with far-reaching consequences.... Not only did this decision send a signal to Pakistan that India would use all available means to evict the intruders, it also had a strong impact on the course of the tactical battle in terms of the interdiction of Pakistani supply lines within Indian territory... and the lowering of the morale of the intruders."[58]

A Preview of More to Come?

In a brief but consequential reaffirmation that the long-seething tensions over Kashmir that triggered the Kargil War of 1999 had scarcely abated in the years that followed, something of a replay of the Kargil experience—fortunately, this time only in microcosm—occurred nearly two decades later when the air arms of *both* India and Pakistan went head-to-head during an eventful two-day period in late February 2019. The fuse for that renewed flare-up was lit nearly two weeks before on February 14 when a vehicle-borne suicide bomber driving through the Indian-administered portion of Kashmir assaulted a convoy of vehicles transporting Indian Central Reserve Force paramilitary troops along Highway NH-1A between Jammu and Srinagar in what one account later described as "the largest-ever terrorist attack on Indian security forces in Kashmir."[59] Some forty-six Indian soldiers were killed in that incident, in the most provocative cross-border attack to have occurred in the region since the Kargil War. The Pakistan-based terrorist organization Jaish-e-Mohammad (JeM) promptly claimed responsibility for the attack. In response, the government of India's Prime Minister Narendra Modi promptly blamed Pakistan for the provocation and vowed that India would retaliate in an appropriate manner in due course.[60]

In a gathering of the nation's most senior leaders not long thereafter, the IAF's chief of staff, Air Chief Marshal Birender Dhanoa, personally briefed Modi and his national security adviser on the IAF's options for striking back against terrorist camps both in the Pakistani-occupied portion of Kashmir and also more deeply into sovereign Pakistani territory. Unlike in the cases of earlier terrorist attacks staged in the Indian-administered portion of Kashmir and emanating from Pakistani-controlled terrain close to the LoC, this time the attack was thought to have been planned from farther back within Pakistan itself. Dhanoa took care to caution his political superiors that the IAF's striking at any targets on Pakistan's side of the LoC and beyond might well prompt a retaliation in kind by the PAF, and he expressly asked if India's civilian leaders would be willing to run the risk of such a possible escalation. In response, Modi directed Dhanoa to plan and deliver an effective retaliatory blow against an appropriate JeM target within relatively easy reach but to ensure that no collateral harm would occur in the process either to Pakistan's military assets or to innocent Pakistani civilian lives and infrastructure.[61]

Duly honoring that tasking, the IAF began considering alternative target options. India's National Technical Research Organization, an intelligence arm reporting to the prime minister's national security adviser, had provided the IAF with satellite imagery and other information regarding some thirty known Islamist terrorist training facilities within Pakistan. The most appropriate target for an air attack would have been the personal headquarters of JeM's leader, Masood Ashar, located in the city of Bahawalpur in Pakistan's Punjab province. That option was ruled out, however, because the headquarters complex was protected by the Pakistani army and by local air defenses. The IAF's eventual choice of a more symbolic but also more easily serviceable target was JeM's Syed Ahmed Shaheed paramilitary training camp in Balakot, situated more than forty miles west of Pakistani-administered Kashmir and well inside sovereign Pakistani territory itself. The town's outskirts had long harbored one of Pakistan's oldest terrorist training camps dating back to the rule of President Zia-ul-Haq, who had arranged for the training of Afghan *mujahideen* there who had been resisting Soviet forces in the 1980s. Ashar himself was known to have visited the Balakot facility the previous February 5.[62]

In its planning for the upcoming strike, the IAF could have opted to use dedicated MiG-27 or Jaguar ground-attack fighters fielded most closely to the Pakistani border. In the end, however, it chose to go instead with its Mirage 2000Hs based farther inland at AFS Gwalior, since that multirole combat aircraft was equipped with onboard electro-optical and infrared targeting pods, the most sophisticated avionics, and the ability to deliver 2,000-pound general-purpose bombs configured with Israeli-designed SPICE [for "smart precise-impact cost-effective"] guidance kits that allowed them to attack targets accurately while causing a minimum of undesirable byproduct damage. Once that decision was reached, Dhanoa's office contacted the IAF's 7 Squadron at Gwalior that operated the Mirage 2000Hs and assigned the mission to that unit. By then, the IAF had already developed a suitably refined plan for the mission under the combined aegis of Western Air Command and Central Air Command, with the latter having 7 Squadron under its direct organizational purview and the former with the required assets to provide overhead air surveillance, air defense cover, fighter escorts, and as-needed inflight refueling with the IAF's Il-78 tankers.[63]

With only a week within which to sharpen their combat edge before launching on the upcoming mission, 7 Squadron's assigned pilots, along with supporting MiG-29s and Su-30MKIs orbiting on CAP stations overhead, flew "hundreds" of rehearsal sorties near the LoC. Also, in a timely coincidence just two days after 7 Squadron had been tapped to conduct the strike, the IAF conducted its annual firepower demonstration, called Vayu Shakhti, which had long before been scheduled to take place in India's Pokhran Test Range in Rajasthan. Unbeknown to all but a few who were watching the ongoing series of live-fire target attacks from the grandstand, a few of the Mirage 2000Hs taking part in that event were actually fine-tuning portions of the mission they would fly into Pakistan soon thereafter.[64]

Finally, at 0200 on February 26, 2019, as was later reported by a retired IAF air vice-marshal and experienced fighter pilot, a "surprise and deception element of Su-30MKI decoys" conducted a calculated misleading feint toward JeM's headquarters in Bahawalpur.[65] Concurrently, the main strike force of three four-ship flights of Mirage 2000Hs took off from Gwalior on their scheduled mission against the real preplanned target at Balakot. The latter group of strike fighters later descended to a ground-hugging altitude for their final target ingress so as to make the most of terrain masking to minimize their exposure to enemy radar. They then split up into three separate four-ship attack packages at 0342 to bomb three designated aim points from different directions over a time span of eight minutes. By then fully alerted to the incoming attack, the PAF reportedly scrambled a contingent of F-16s to intercept the IAF fighters, but the latter by that time had already left the target area and pressed homeward, with all twelve having safely landed at Gwalior by 0430. Later that morning, India's foreign secretary, Vijay Gokhale, declared to a gathering of reporters: "In an intelligence-led operation in the early hours of Tuesday, India struck the biggest training camp of JeM in Balakot. In this operation, a very large number of JeM terrorists, senior commanders and groups of jihadis who were being trained for fedayeen action were eliminated." In response to that statement, a Pakistani spokesman adamantly denied that the attack on Balakot had caused any fatalities or had otherwise occasioned any significant damage, maintained that PAF F-16s had successfully fought off the attacking IAF fighters and forced their pilots to jettison their bombs prematurely, and added sternly: "India has started the wrong game, and Pakistan will respond two times [over] to any provocation."[66]

Sure enough, at around 1000 the following morning, as had been promised the day before and in a response codenamed Operation Swift Retort, the PAF launched a contingent of its own fighters that assumed CAP stations over Pakistani-controlled Kashmir near the LoC, after which some two dozen additional PAF fighters, said to have included F-16s, JF-17s and Mirage 5s, crossed the LoC heading eastbound, with the Mirage 5s reportedly tasked with bombing six assigned targets in the Indian-administered portion of Kashmir, including the headquarters of the Indian Army's 25th Division and a nearby ammunition and logistics depot.[67] Having fully anticipated such a counterstrike, the IAF in response scrambled a number of its own fighters to intercept the incoming PAF jets, including Su-30MKIs, Mirage 2000Hs, and a supporting formation of its most advanced MiG-21 Bisons from nearby AFS Avantipur. The latter aircraft were said to have chased off four attacking PAF F-16s, during the course of which one IAF MiG-21 was confirmed to have been downed by a PAF fighter. The pilot ejected successfully and was promptly taken prisoner by Pakistani troops after having landed safely on Pakistan's side of the LoC.[68] Several subsequent press accounts characterized that aerial incident as a "dogfight," although there is no basis on which to confirm that either of the involved fighters actually engaged in close-in air combat maneuvering.[69] The IAF's fighter pilots have long been rightly regarded as being among the world's most proficient in air-to-air combat, and it is entirely possible that the downed pilot in this instance was the hapless victim of an unobserved PAF air-to-air missile shot.

Whatever the case, Pakistan's Ministry of Foreign Affairs later that day insisted that the PAF had struck solely at nonmilitary targets, with Prime Minister Imran Khan himself adding that the retaliatory attacks had been intended principally "to send a message to India."[70] Expanding further on the PAF's reprisal, Pakistan's military spokesman, Major General Asif Ghafoor, declared later that "when PAF [aircraft struck their] targets, the IAF's two [intercepting] planes violated the line of control and entered Pakistan. The PAF was ready, and there was an engagement." Ghafoor added that the PAF had not violated sovereign Indian airspace but had attacked a military installation on the Indian side of the LoC.[71] The next day, the U.S. government urged that prompt steps be taken by both sides toward de-escalation, at which point Prime Minister Khan allowed that Pakistan would soon release the downed Indian pilot as "a gesture of peace."[72] Tension in the region on both sides quickly abated after the IAF pilot's repatriation.

Even before the smoke had cleared, however, a confrontation of countervailing narratives began unfolding between the two countries with studied efforts being made by both sides to manipulate worldwide perceptions regarding what had just occurred. To begin with, it was by no means clear what the IAF's initial retaliatory strike into Balakot had yielded by way of actual combat results, with Indian claims of mission effectiveness offset by counterclaims from Pakistan that any JeM facilities that may have been in the area had remained unharmed by the attack. As for Pakistan's ensuing Operation Swift Retort and the IAF's response to it the following morning, Indian officials claimed at first that the IAF had downed a Pakistani F-16, as had allegedly been confirmed by telltale "electronic signatures," with Pakistan replying that it had lost no aircraft in the encounter and claiming for its part that it had downed two IAF fighters.[73] India then denied in response that the PAF had downed an IAF Su-30MKI, calling that a "false" claim to mask the alleged loss of one of its own F-16s.[74] Pakistan, in turn, denied that it had lost an F-16 and noted that its own fighter that had downed the IAF's MiG-21 had been not an F-16 but a JF-17.[75] Summed up in a nutshell, the only fact known for sure from these conflicting claims up to now is that the IAF lost a MiG-21 while seeking to break up the PAF's counterstrike. Beyond that, the absence of clarity that has pervaded the continuing claims and counterclaims put forward by both sides regarding this latest confrontation over Kashmir has made it all but impossible to arrive at a conclusive assessment as to how the two air arms actually performed during that two-day evolution.

The Balakot Reprisal in Broader Context

All of that said, this latest Indo-Pakistani dust-up was enough of a precedent-setter to prompt a former Pakistani ambassador to the United States, Husain Haqqani, to declare during the course of it that "we [i.e., the two countries] are [now] in unchartered waters."[76] In a significant air-warfare first in nearly five decades, *both* countries crossed the hitherto-inviolate LoC to strike at targets on the other side's proclaimed terrain, and in the IAF's case on sovereign Pakistani territory itself. And it was the first time *ever* in which two nuclear-armed states had conducted conventional air attacks against one another under an umbrella of mutual nuclear deterrence. That eventful but also fortunately brief and limited confrontation, which pitted some of the most advanced IAF and PAF fighters against one another, raised tensions between the two countries to a level not seen since the Kargil War nearly two decades before. It also featured the first air-to-air encounter between the IAF and PAF since the Indo-Pakistani war of 1971.[77]

Interestingly, of special note in this regard, a well-informed and thoughtful retired IAF air vice-marshal remarked several months later that the Indian defense establishment had likewise "entered uncharted territory" as a result of this latest use of force by the two sides and had come to face "some hard imperatives" making it necessary for India to explore both possibilities and opportunities for sharpening its air options now that "a new normal has been established by [India's] calling Pakistan's nuclear bluff and hitting Pakistan-backed terrorists in their own backyard."[78] Even before then, that same observer had already portrayed the Balakot reprisal as "an act of political signaling that India is willing to raise the price that the Pakistani state has to pay in order to support terrorism." He added on this key point that while there remains "no room [in the region] for a conventional three-dimensional war as we know it," there is now "immense space among stressed frontiers with both our western and northern neighbor [i.e., Pakistan and China] for short, limited and high-intensity conflicts, skirmishes and encounters that can be limited in both time and space, with a significant element of surprise."[79] Even as the dust from the two days of air action was still settling, he also suggested that the IAF's Balakot strike and its timely counter to Pakistan's wholly anticipated aerial response had "dramatically changed the predominant thinking about the Indian Air Force and [about] the strategic diffidence that had [previously] come to define India's use of air power until now." He suggested that a conscious choice of "escalating to de-escalate" had now become the essence of India's new strategy.[80]

Fortunately in this latest case, in the immediate aftermath of the reciprocal IAF and PAF air attacks that occurred in late February 2019, the situation in Kashmir pretty much reverted to the status quo ante, suggesting that the leaders on both sides fully appreciated the omnipresent risk of escalation that has long dominated their bilateral nuclear relationship. To offer just one example of this important and salutary awareness, even as the results of the PAF's riposte following the IAF's attack on Balakot were still being sorted out, Pakistan's Prime Minister Khan sought to lower the temperature when he said: "History tells us that in wars, there are miscalculations. Shouldn't we consider that if it escalates from here, where will it go? I ask India: With the weapons you have and the weapons we have, can we really afford a miscalculation? Let's sit down and settle this with talks."[81]

Looking back on the experience nearly two months after it had taken place, one U.S. press report suggested that the crisis had "threatened to escalate to all-out war." That was all but surely an overstatement of the actual facts. That same report, however, was most definitely on safe ground when it rightly observed also how the initial affront posed by JeM's terrorist foray into Indian-administered Kashmir the previous February 14 "could raise questions both inside and outside of India about the IAF's conventional advantage if it [i.e., India] is unable to punish a weaker adversary to reestablish deterrence," which in turn might "encourage Pakistan to behave more aggressively in a future India-Pakistan crisis," thereby raising "deeper concerns about the risks of escalation and a mushroom cloud over the subcontinent."[82] Offsetting that concern, however, a fair-minded appraisal offered by the independent European Foundation for South Asian Studies heralded the IAF's Balakot strike as a testament to the fact that "India has definitely changed the rules of the game as far as its response to Pakistan-backed terrorism is concerned. Pakistan's calculation that a low-cost asymmetrical war fought by terrorist proxies would keep India tied down and its assumption that the threat of nuclear war will inhibit India from retaliating in a conventional manner can now be consigned to history. India has finally discarded its policy of strategic restraint and unveiled a new security doctrine in which Pakistan can no longer export terror to India without paying a heavy price for it."[83] A similar observation offered just days later by an Indian analyst suggested that since such retaliatory air strikes "have [now] been established as an acceptable use of force, it may become politically difficult for any Indian government [in the future] to refrain from using them or even to resist opting for deadlier strikes."[84]

As if to further underscore that important latter point, the chief of staff of the Indian Army, General Bipin Rawat, warned Pakistan the following August that it would receive an even "bloodier nose" should it ever seek another such confrontation with India, advising that country's leaders to avoid repeating its past "misadventures." For his part, Air Chief Marshal Dhanoa likewise added that the IAF "is always alert on the border . . . . The recent offensive strike against terrorist outfits in our neighborhood speaks volumes about the reach and lethality of the formidable arm of the Indian armed forces."[85] Without question, much as in the case of the protracted Kargil War that had preceded them by nearly two decades, the events that ensued in Kashmir in February 2019, in response to the JeM's terrorist provocation earlier that month, roundly belied the proposition put forward by Pakistan's military spokesman, General Ghafoor, that since Pakistan went overtly nuclear in 1998, "our stance is that this capability eliminates the possibility of conventional war between the two states."[86]

Most press reporting in the early aftermath of this latest Indo-Pakistani set-to suggested that India was the more supported of the two protagonists in the eyes of Western diplomacy. By one informed account, U.S. President Donald Trump's national security adviser at the time, John Bolton, tacitly acceded to India's going ahead with its planned retaliatory attack against JeM after having considered the various arguments and issues at stake.[87] For his part, Secretary of State Mike Pompeo spoke to the foreign ministers of both countries immediately after hostilities ended and urged Pakistan not to retaliate anew to the Indian response to the PAF's initial counterstrikes, adding: "I expressed to both ministers that we encourage India and Pakistan to exercise restraint and avoid escalation at any cost."[88] In a subsequent statement that was largely sympathetic to India, however, Pompeo also studiously characterized the IAF's strike into Pakistan as a "counter-terrorism action" and expressly enjoined Pakistan's leaders to take "meaningful action against terrorist groups operating on its soil."[89]

As to the question of ultimate winners and losers in this latest round of conflict between two nuclear-armed regional rivals, neither side can lay convincing claim to have emerged from the clash as having achieved a strategically decisive outcome. On one hand, by any reasonable standard, Prime Minister Modi was well within the bounds of propriety in having responded in force to the wanton attack by a Pakistani terrorist operating within the Indian-administered portion of Kashmir that killed forty-six Indian servicemen. True enough, Modi's ruling Bharatiya Janata Party was facing a tight upcoming election season at precisely the time of JeM's provocation, and for that reason he may have felt an added urge to project an image of strength in that gathering situation. But even absent such a possible added motivation, India had previously shown remarkable forbearance for years following the 1999 Kargil War in refraining from responding with force to repeated subsequent Pakistani-inspired terrorist acts on Indian soil. This time, with India's leaders apparently having run out of patience at long last, the IAF's retaliatory strike into Balakot most definitely seemed directed toward deterring any future Pakistani government support for such terrorist attacks. On this important count, one of the most widely respected Western experts on Southeast Asian security affairs, Ashley Tellis, offered as a key takeaway from the IAF's precedent-setting Balakot reprisal the entirely reasonable proposition that India's security establishment as a whole had finally become "simply tired of being the punching bag for Pakistani terrorism and decided [at long last] to send a signal that conspicuous attacks would not go unanswered [and that] Pakistani territory would not remain immune [any longer] from Indian retaliation."[90]

Without question, the IAF's reprisal showed a clear Indian willingness this time to accept greater risk by not only violating the LoC for the first time in nearly five decades but also striking beyond Pakistani-administered Kashmir into Pakistan itself. At the same time, however, the IAF's response also showed commendable restraint in limiting its initial strike to a largely symbolic target directly associated with JeM, and in a way carefully limited so as to cause no byproduct harm to Pakistani military assets or to innocent Pakistani civilians. As for the underlying strategic rationale that may have informed the Modi government's decision to respond with force this time, India's minister of external affairs, Sushma Swaraj, later remarked that the initial IAF strike into Balakot was meant to show just enough resolve against JeM to forestall any further terrorist attacks by it into India.[91] Inescapably, such a strike would also show Pakistan by force of example that its mere possession of nuclear weapons in no way precluded India's resort to a nonnuclear retaliatory option if deemed appropriate.

On the downside for India, the loss of an IAF MiG-21 at the hands of a PAF fighter pilot, whatever the actual tactical circumstances of that event may have been, was plainly embarrassing, especially when one considers that the IAF's airmen have long enjoyed a well-deserved reputation for excellence in aerial combat on a par with that of the best Western air arms. As one American press account aptly noted shortly thereafter, that experience was also "an inauspicious moment for a military the United States is banking on to help keep an expanding China in check."[92] Another observer commented in a similar spirit: "It is far from clear that India's actions in 2019 . . . brought major strategic gains. The Balakot strike, intended to be a bold and signature operation, quickly became bogged down in competing claims and overt politicization during the [subsequent Indian] election campaign, while leading to suboptimal global headlines about the capture of the [downed] Indian pilot."[93]

As for the more positive side of the experience, however, in the nationwide general election that took place the following April and May, Modi and his party won in an unanticipated landslide, thereby even further strengthening his hand in the Indo-Pakistani relationship. As if to underscore this emerging image of renewed Indian forcefulness, the following August the Modi government surged security forces into the Indian-administered portion of Jammu and Kashmir and revoked the region's former special status as a contested area, resulting in the emergence of a new security order in the region featuring detentions and new restrictions. As one commentator portrayed this new Indian stress on toughness and boldness, the new order in that region seemed dominated by an increased "emphasis on risk-taking and assertiveness, the fusing of domestic and international politics, and the use of unrelenting spin to hold critics at bay."[94]

Viewed on balance, the Modi government's undeniable determination this time to go beyond India's self-imposed restraint during the Kargil War by not only violating the LoC intentionally but also striking directly into Pakistan itself for the first time since 1971 showed that it may now be less hesitant about doing the same yet again, perhaps with even greater forcefulness and sought-after strategic effect, in the event of any future terrorist provocation on Indian soil that might originate from Pakistan. If only by having gained clear diplomatic support for its latest gambit in Kashmir from the United States, the United Kingdom, France, Australia and Japan through the combined insistence of those five countries that Pakistan crack down more firmly on its terrorist organizations and their activities, that outcome led another commentator to suggest, reasonably enough, that although the IAF's air strike into Balakot "did not indicate a total victory, . . . it was relatively successful for India."[95]

Lessons and Implications

The foregoing discussion leaves still unanswered the most basic question as to whether the Kargil experience of 1999 offers an instructive prototype for the most probable near-term future threats that may face the Indian defense establishment along India's borders with Pakistan and China. Without question, the unusually demanding combat challenges presented by Operation Safed Sagar made for a sobering wake-up call for the IAF, which had not given much prior thought to such a scenario and had not routinely trained at such high mountain elevations until it was forced to do so by operational necessity. Not long after the fighting ended, Indian defense experts began contemplating such limited engagements in time and scale as the most likely wave of the future with respect to any provocations of that sort that might arise anew along the volatile LoC running through Jammu and Kashmir. In that regard, retired IAF Air Commodore Singh voiced the opinion of many when he called Kargil "a template for limited war and future options if war becomes inevitable."[96]

Viewed in hindsight, the Kargil War is replete with instructive insights into the dynamics of deterrence in the Indo-Pakistani relationship. Especially important in this regard, Pakistan's military leaders miscalculated badly in their apparent belief that the international community would press immediately for a ceasefire in Kashmir out of concern over a possible escalation of the fighting to the nuclear level, with the net result that Pakistan would be left with the easy *fait accompli* of a new slice of terrain on the Indian-administered side of the LoC. As for other planning assumptions that most likely underlay the miscalculations of those who concocted the incursion gambit, India's General Malik later suggested, plausibly enough, that they had erroneously convinced themselves that a stable deterrent relationship between India and Pakistan at the nuclear level would enable a Pakistani conventional offensive into Kashmir with virtual impunity, on an expectation that India would not counter the provocation with an all-out conventional response that would risk either escalation or ending in a costly stalemate.[97]

In the end, both of those likely Pakistani assumptions proved unfounded. The nuclear balance between the two countries did *not* deter a determined Indian conventional response, and the successful reaction that India ultimately mounted on the Kargil heights fell well short of being all-out in scale. Since the Vajpayee government scrupulously kept its combat operations confined to Indian-administered Kashmir, the international community had no compelling reason to intervene. As a result, a remote but high-intensity and high-stakes showdown was allowed to run on for more than two months, something the Pakistani Army's leaders all but certainly did not anticipate when they first conjured up their incursion plan. Indeed, in the view of a retired Indian Army major general, Pakistan's military leaders "had not thought beyond the first week or ten days" in their approach to planning the confrontation. They also, the retired Indian general suggested, all but surely did not bargain on the combat involvement of Indian air power or on the aggressive forward deployment of the Indian Navy.[98]

As to the first count, an informed and insightful former Pakistani Army brigadier later well characterized the introduction of IAF fighter aircraft into the conflict on May 26 as an effective asymmetric vertical escalation that Pakistan could not counter without running unbearable risks of a larger and more consequential confrontation.[99] As to the maritime dimension of India's response, in a determined anticipatory move to help deter Pakistan from escalating the fighting into a larger war once India was fully engaged against the NLI intruders, the Indian Navy went on full alert as early as May 20 and readied itself to blockade Pakistan's ports, principally Karachi, should an assessed need for such action arise. Toward that end, surface combatants configured for conducting missile firing and antisubmarine and electronic warfare were deployed in the North Arabian Sea. In the ensuing Operation Talwar (Hindi for "Sword"), India's eastern and western fleets joined assets and blocked the Arabian Sea routes to Pakistan. Later, Pakistan's former Prime Minister Sharif disclosed that Pakistan had been left with just six days of fuel remaining to sustain combat operations had a full-scale war broken out.

Expanding further on Pakistan's short-sighted military leadership going into the Kargil imbroglio and on the latter's resultant adverse consequences for Pakistan over time, the PAF's director of operations during the conflict later recalled, in an article published in an Indian defense journal, that in an effort to keep its plan secret, "the army trio [of planners] led by Army chief of staff General Pervez Musharraf took no one into confidence" and presided over a "closed-loop thought process" that engendered "a string of oversights and failures." These included a "failure to grasp the wider military and diplomatic ramifications of a limited tactical operation that had the potential of creating strategic effects, failure to correctly visualize the response of a powerful enemy to what was, in effect, a major blow in a disputed sector," and "failure to appreciate the inability of the [Pakistani] army officers to evaluate the capabilities and limitations of an air force."[100] More or less concurrently, this same well-informed PAF air commodore writing in a Pakistani forum later recalled even more expansively that Musharraf and his closest confidants had kept the PAF completely in the dark until their incursion into India's Himalayan highlands was well under way. Once curious PAF planners requested a briefing after they had learned that "something big was imminent," they were assured by a three-star deputy to Musharraf that any needed "air support was not envisaged and that his forces could take care of enemy aircraft if they intervened," declaring confidently: "I have Stingers on every peak." The PAF air commodore then added that "the [army] corps commander's smug appreciation of the situation" wrongly assumed that "the Indians had been strait-jacketed in the situation" and lacked any resort to "an alternate action . . . given the nuclear environment."[101]

Among other things, the Kargil experience suggested the value of New Delhi's creating and sustaining an appreciation by both Pakistan and China of overwhelming Indian conventional force preponderance in the region as a deterrent against any such provocations in the future. Such a realization ultimately led to a new Indian declaratory policy toward that end that was enunciated in January 2000 by then-Minister of Defence George Fernandes.[102] At a seminar in New Delhi that month, Fernandes observed that in precipitating the Kargil War, Pakistan "had not absorbed the real meaning of nuclearization—that it can deter *only* the use of nuclear weapons, but not all and any war." The overarching teaching of the war experience, he added, was that nuclear weapons had not rendered war in the region obsolete or made "covert war by proxy . . . the only option." A no less important teaching, Fernandes said, was that "conventional war remained feasible, but with definite limitations [now] if escalation across the nuclear threshold was to be avoided."[103]

A related question concerns the extent to which the IAF's role in helping to enable India's successful outcome in Operation Vijay may offer a central ingredient of *conventional* deterrence against future such provocations. In this regard, the same reflective IAF warrior/scholar quoted earlier suggested that the IAF's "never-done-before" high-elevation interdiction operations during the Kargil fighting contributed significantly to the achievement of the government's ultimate strategic goal of evicting Pakistan's forces from the positions that they had occupied. He further observed that its telling strikes against enemy troop emplacements and supply dumps "created a strategic effect" by forcing Pakistan's leadership to reassess its strategy of conducting an open-ended proxy war against India. This senior airman added that those operations "also silenced critics within India who [previously had] felt that air power was essentially escalatory in nature."[104]

Without a doubt, the bilateral air balance throughout the Kargil War stood markedly in India's favor, with an overall fighter force ratio of 750 to 350. With respect to the most cutting-edge fighters then fielded by the two sides, Pakistan's inventory of just twenty-six U.S.-provided F-16As was greatly outmatched numerically, and perhaps qualitatively as well, by the IAF's 145 highest-performance aircraft (seventy MiG-29s, forty-five Mirage 2000Hs, and thirty Su-30MKIs).[105] Air Commodore Singh suggested that this advantage in India's favor "clearly deterred Pakistan from using its air force to come to the rescue of its soldiers, whose large numbers were being killed by the Indian Army and Air Force [and were] being denied critically needed supplies like ammunition, rations, and reinforcements."[106]

Yet at the same time, prudent Indian defense planners will likely find themselves shortchanged in their preparations for the full spectrum of possible challenges to their country's security in years to come if they draw undue comfort from the happy ending of the Kargil experience and accept that conflict as their *only* planning baseline for hedging against future contingencies along the LoC. For one thing, much like NATO's air war for Kosovo that unfolded in the Balkans at roughly the same time, the Kargil War offered a poor test of India's air warfare capability. Because many, if not most, of the targets were small and difficult to acquire, attack, and destroy, the IAF's fighter pilots were consigned to do what they could rather than what they might have done in a less restricted engagement in which they would not have been bound by such operating constraints as the government's directive not to cross the LoC in reversing Pakistan's incursion and 15 Corps' need for the IAF to service target types that offered the least tactical payoff for the effort invested. Moreover, like NATO's roughly concurrent Operation Allied Force against Serbia, the enemy had the initiative throughout most of the Kargil War, and both the nature of the operational challenge the IAF faced in the Kargil heights and the targeting requirements that ensued from that challenge necessarily dictated an unconventional and suboptimal use of India's increasingly capable air weapon.[107]

How might another Pakistani armed challenge along the LoC in years yet to come end up presenting a more demanding test of the IAF's strength that would require a more exacting approach to air power employment? A decade after Operation Safed Sagar's successful conclusion, the AOC-in-C of Western Air Command and de facto joint force air component commander during the Kargil War, Air Marshal Patney, observed that "Pakistan had a reasonably good air force but elected not to use it or was wary of the consequences of its use . . . . [It] handed over air dominance to India without a fight. Had Pakistan offered [aerial] combat, . . . the pattern of air activity would have been very different. We would have had to fight for air dominance, even if it was at the cost of other air operations of the war."[108] That suggests that a bolder Pakistani risk calculus, or even an inadvertent escalation dynamic emanating from misjudgment on either side, could have resulted in a higher-intensity showdown over the same initial stakes that, in turn, would have demanded a far more robust and sustainable Indian conventional force posture than that which prevailed well enough over Pakistan in 1999. Ultimately, one can only speculate as to what kept a major aerial clash between the IAF and PAF from occurring at any time during the Kargil fighting. However, insofar as India's clear preeminence in the bilateral air balance was a contributing factor in accounting for that nonoccurrence, the IAF should have every incentive henceforth to sustain a no less pronounced combat edge over Pakistan, as well as at least a local preponderance of air capability along India's border with China, in its future force development.

A similar logic seems to have governed the also limited but more than just symbolic Indo-Pakistani tit-for-tat air exchanges that followed on the heels of JeM's terrorist provocation in Indian-administered Kashmir on February 14, 2019, when the IAF responded with "a calibrated, decisive and yet restrained show of force" that ultimately converted Prime Minister Modi's "promise of punitive action into reality." As the previously-quoted former IAF air vice-marshal reflected on that experience more than a year later, a succession of previous Indian governments following the 1999 Kargil War had "failed to bite the bullet and [had] continued with reactive response strategies [in answering subsequent Pakistani-inspired terrorist acts against India] that eschewed the use of air power because of a lack of understanding of what air power could and could not do." During the years that followed, he suggested, those governments' assessed need for India to be viewed by the world as a "responsible but restrained" power had caused the country to "balk at the use

India's Kargil War 1999   201

of force." In marked contrast, he went on to say, Modi's unhesitating approval of the IAF's retaliatory attack on an assessed JeM target, and one located not just on Pakistan's side of the LoC but within Pakistan itself, suggested "an emerging understanding within the [Indian] strategic community and the political establishment that offensive air power can [now] be employed as a credible tool of punitive or proactive deterrence," a policy that he clearly ascribed to "the more muscular national security posture of the Modi government."[109] In previous years, he recalled, India's willful show of restraint in the face of repeated Pakistani terrorist provocations had "emboldened Pakistan-based jihadi networks like . . . JeM and [had] allowed them to proliferate and to grow into powerful entities and strategic assets of Pakistan's deep state." Yet with the IAF's kinetic strike into Pakistan in response to the latest JeM provocation at long last, "India's mask of restrained deterrence it has worn for decades may have come off," he suggested, with the clear and welcome result that the country's "strategic restraint and responsibility" may have finally been complemented with "a third 'R,' and that is resolve."[110]

In all, for students of air warfare, the IAF's combat experience during the 1999 Kargil War reaffirmed a number of abiding characteristics of modern air arms around the world today. It showed, for example, that innovation and adaptability under the stress of confining rules of engagement (in this case the Vajpayee government's strict injunction that the IAF not cross the LoC under any circumstances) is a generic hallmark of modern airmanship. It further showed that professionalism in such operationally crucial matters as campaign planning, presentation of forces, accommodating to new and unique tactical challenges (in this instance the need to engage hard-to-see targets in unprecedentedly high-elevation Himalayan battlespace), and effectively underwriting the needs of a joint force commander is scarcely a monopoly of more familiar Western air arms. It demonstrated yet again how the effective application of air-delivered firepower, particularly if unmatched by the opposing side, can shorten and facilitate the outcome of an engagement that might otherwise have persisted much longer.

As for the broader implications of the Kargil War as a benchmark for international security, that war was the first serious border conflict of sustained duration between two nuclear-armed antagonists that ended with a clear winner and loser at the conventional level. Although it is always risky to try to generalize from a singular and, in many ways, unique case of that sort, the Kargil War nonetheless offers much food for creative thought regarding such generic issue areas as the escalation dynamics that govern a bilateral nuclear relationship of major tension, the importance of avoiding such escalation-prone thresholds as India's crossing of the LoC to carry the fighting into Pakistan and Pakistan's engagement of IAF fighters servicing NLI targets on India's side of the LoC, and the ever-present possibility that inadvertent leadership misjudgment on either side regarding the other's limits of tolerance could lead to a breach of the nuclear taboo that neither side either wanted or could possibly profit from.

With regard to plausible lessons learned by both sides from that pioneering experience at intrawar nuclear deterrence, the confrontation showed for India the downside strategic consequences of an avowed nuclear no first-use policy that necessarily put the country's government in a reactive mode when it came to the prospect of inadvertent nuclear escalation. By the same token, for Pakistan's leaders, the unexpected—and unexpectedly sharp, intense, and effective—response that their provocation prompted on the part of the Indian Army and IAF should have had a tempering influence on their initial presumptions about the extent to which merely having a credible nuclear attack capability, in and of itself, empowered them to try conventional acts of territorial acquisition with impunity. To that extent, it should have instilled a healthy once-burned, twice-shy mindset among those leaders and their successors who might be tempted to undertake a reprise of that gambit some day in the future—particularly in light of the persistent regional imbalance of conventional air power in India's pronounced favor.

Viewed against that backdrop, the most recent Indo-Pakistani air exchanges that followed JeM's latest terrorist outrage in Indian-administered Kashmir two decades later may well have reflected what one might cautiously regard as a perceptible growth in the maturity of the bilateral nuclear balance between the two countries. As one Indian analyst insightfully noted in this respect, for nearly thirty years following its accession to nuclear status, Pakistan had, in effect, "been playing the nuclear madman." Yet the IAF's determined air strike into Balakot in February 2019 represented "the most emphatic challenge" to such Pakistani posturing to date, making it "undeniable that the old red lines no longer exist, [that] a door has been opened, and [that] space has [now] been created by India to raise the ante in the face of a grave provocation from Pakistan." Thanks to this sea change in the Indo-Pakistani standoff, the analyst concluded, "the more serious players in Pakistan [now] know that the rules of the game have changed," in that this time India "not just crossed the

LoC but also the international border and struck in Pakistan proper . . . . All those who were warning of a nuclear holocaust suddenly seemed to be piping down." It made for a true pivot point, he added, in that "the likelihood that Modi's 'madness' (and this is not meant in a pejorative sense but a positive sense) has set a new benchmark for all future [Indian] governments."[111]

Finally, for both protagonists, the Kargil War of 1999 arguably represented a real-world battle laboratory for reconfirming, just as the leaders of NATO and the Warsaw Pact came to learn during the height of the Cold War in Central Europe a generation before, that a stable bilateral nuclear deterrence relationship at the strategic level can markedly constrain in intensity and scale, if not inhibit entirely, recurrent flash points that might otherwise have every chance of erupting into an open-ended conventional showdown for the highest stakes in the absence of such a relationship. It also, on the other hand, showed for both sides in the specific Indo-Pakistani context that the mere presence of such mutual nuclear deterrence at the strategic level has in no way foreclosed the persistent possibility of future conventional wars of major consequence beneath that abiding threshold.

Notes

1. For the most thorough retrospective assessments of this war, see Air Commodore Jasjit Singh, IAF (Ret.), ed., *Kargil 1999: Pakistan's Fourth War for Kashmir* (New Delhi: Knowledge World, 1999); Ashley J. Tellis, C. Christine Fair, and Jamison Jo Medby, *Limited Conflicts Under the Nuclear Umbrella: Indian and Pakistani Lessons from the Kargil Crisis* (Santa Monica, Calif.: RAND Corporation, 2001); and Peter R. Lavoy, ed., *Asymmetric Warfare in South Asia: The Causes and Consequences of the Kargil Conflict* (Cambridge: Cambridge University Press, 2009).

2. Air Commodore Jasjit Singh, IAF (Ret.), "Kashmir, Covert Wars, and Air Power," *Air Power Journal* (New Delhi, Summer 2005), 79.

3. Air Vice-Marshal Arjun Subramaniam, IAF (Ret.), *India's Wars: A Military History, 1947–1971* (Annapolis, Md.: Naval Institute Press, 2016), 107, 114.

4. "Gandhi-Bhutto Pact Text," *The New York Times*, July 4, 1972.

5. See D. P. Ramachandran, "Siachen Glacier: Battling on the Roof of the World," *Indian Defence Review* (New Delhi, June 20, 2015), n.p.

6. Preeti Kumar, "Sustaining Air Bridges," *Strategic Affairs* (New Delhi, October 2008), 8. These two top military leaders were said to have obtained an "in-principle" go-ahead from Pakistan's Prime Minister Nawaz Sharif without having offered him any specifics regarding the planned incursion. For an informed account of the motivations that most likely underlay this Pakistani initiative by a since-retired Pakistani Army brigadier, see Shaukat Qadir, "An Analysis of the Kargil Conflict 1999," *Journal of the Royal United Services Institution* (London, April 2002), 24–27.

7. Such a presumption could have animated the Pakistani incursion's planners even if, as seems most likely, the possibility of actual nuclear weapons use in the worst case never figured seriously in their calculations.

8. Major General G. D. Bakshi, Indian Army (Ret.), "Kargil: Dynamics of a Limited War Against a Nuclear Backdrop," *CLAWS Journal* (New Delhi, Summer 2009), 43. The journal is a publication of the Centre for Land Warfare Studies.

9. Government of India, National Security Council Secretariat, Kargil Review Committee, *From Surprise to Reckoning: The Kargil Review Committee Report* (New Delhi: Sage, 2000), 96–97.

10. Bakshi, "Kargil: Dynamics of a Limited War Against a Nuclear Backdrop," 44.

11. Kargil Review Committee, *From Surprise to Reckoning*, 227.

12. Pushpindar Singh, *Himalayan Eagles: History of the Indian Air Force* (Volume III: World Air Power, New Delhi: The Society for Aerospace Studies, 2007), 108.

13. Air Commodore Arjun Subramaniam, IAF, "Kargil Revisited: Air Operations in a High-Altitude Conflict," *CLAWS Journal* (New Delhi), Summer 2008, 186.

14. Comments on an earlier draft of this chapter by Air Marshal Vinod Patney, IAF (Ret.), August 16, 2011. See also Air Marshal Vinod Patney, IAF (Ret.), "1999 War in Kargil and Its Aftermath," (New Delhi: Centre for Air Power Studies, briefing to a group of successor-generation IAF officers, September 8, 2011).

15. Patney, "1999 War in Kargil and Its Aftermath."

16. Ibid.

17. Air Chief Marshal A. Y. Tipnis, IAF (Ret.), "Operation Safed Sagar," *Force* (New Delhi, October 2006), 12.

18. Singh, *Himalayan Eagles: History of the Indian Air Force*, 111.

19. Air Commodore Ramesh V. Phadke, IAF, "Air Offensive in the High Himalayas," *Strategic Analysis* (New Delhi, December 1999), 1606.

20. Comments on an earlier draft of this chapter by Air Marshal Vinod Patney, IAF (Ret.), August 16, 2011.

21. Subramaniam, "Kargil Revisited: Air Operations in a High-Altitude Conflict," 187.

22. Air Commodore Kaiser Tufail, PAF (Ret.), "Kargil 1999: The PAF's Story," *Vayu Aerospace and Defence Review*, no. 3 (New Delhi, 2009), 98.

23. On this point, as the AOC-in-C of Western Air Command at the time later recalled: "I think my insistence to mount CAPs across the [command's entire area of responsibility] at different heights and times to give the message that I was ready and angling for an enlarged conflict helped. It was akin to throwing a glove, but it was not picked up." Comments on an earlier draft of this chapter by retired Air Marshal Vinod Patney, IAF, August 16, 2011.

24. Group Captain D. N. Ganesh, IAF, "Indian Air Force in Action," in *Kargil 1999: Pakistan's Fourth War for Kashmir*, ed. Jasjit Singh, 183.

25. E-mail to the author from Air Marshal Vinod Patney, IAF (Ret.), August 27, 2011.

26. Colonel M. Sabharwal, Indian Army, "Joint Operations in Modern Warfare," *Air Power Journal* (New Delhi, spring 2006), 19.

27. John H. Gill, "Military Operations in the Kargil Conflict," in *Asymmetric Warfare in South Asia*, ed. Peter Lavoy, 114.

28. E-mails to the author from Air Marshal Vinod Patney, IAF (Ret.), August 27 and 29, 2011

29. Phadke, "Air Offensive in the High Himalayas," 1608.

30. Singh, *Himalayan Eagles: History of the Indian Air Force,* 125, reported that number of LGBs delivered during the campaign's endgame.

31. E-mail to the author from Air Marshal Vinod Patney, IAF (Ret.), August 22, 2011. Air Marshal Patney personally regarded that successful precision attack on the enemy's vital command post atop Tiger Hill as "the real turning point" in the campaign. "One mission," he recalled, "was all that was necessary." Ibid. As an indication of the effectiveness of the LGB attack, he further noted that once 15 Corps' troops reached their objective on Tiger Hill, "the place was manned by only seven [surviving enemy] soldiers." Comments on an earlier draft of this chapter by Air Marshal Vinod Patney, IAF (Ret.), August 16, 2011.

32. Singh, *Himalayan Eagles: History of the Indian Air Force,* 125.

33. E-mail to the author from Air Marshal Vinod Patney, IAF (Ret.), August 27, 2011.

34. Prasun K. Sengupta, "Mountain Warfare and Tri-Service Operations," *Asian Defence Journal* (October 1999), 25.

35. Ibid., 121.

36. Ganesh, "Indian Air Force in Action," 184.

37. Comments on an earlier draft of this chapter by Air Marshal V. K. "Jimmy" Bhatia, IAF (Ret.), August 18, 2011. On this point, in the retrospective view of another IAF leader who headed the initial integration of the Litening pod with the Mirage 2000H and Jaguar and who flew most of the associated fight test sorties, "the Mirages with the LGBs should have been used from Day One," since the integration had been essentially completed and declared fit for operational use three months before, in January 1999. A duly conservative final certification of the pods for actual combat employment, he added, might have required as much as a week to complete once the start of Operation Safed Sagar was clearly imminent, but "ego hassles" and other sources of bureaucratic pushback occasioned a needless—and costly—delay in the first use of LGBs until June 24. (Comments on an earlier draft by a still-serving IAF leader who was closely involved in preparations for the IAF's entry into the war at the tactical level, December 4, 2011.)

38. Singh, *Himalayan Eagles: History of the Indian Air Force,* 122, and Air Marshal R. S. Bedi, IAF (Ret.), "Kargil Controversy: An IAF Response," *Indian Defence Review* (New Delhi), January-March 2010, 152.

39. Bakshi, "Kargil: Dynamics of a Limited War Against a Nuclear Backdrop," 45.

40. For a well-documented account of the various conflicting casualty numbers on both sides, see Gill, "Military Operations in the Kargil Conflict," 122.

41. Sayan Majumdar, "The IAF's M-MRCA Requirement: The Mirage Factor," *Vayu Aerospace and Defence Review,* no. 5 (New Delhi, 2005), 30.

42. Captain Marcus P. Acosta, USA, "High-Altitude Warfare: The Kargil Conflict and the Future," thesis submitted in partial fulfillment of the requirements for the degree of Master of Arts in National Security Affairs, Monterey, Calif.: Naval Postgraduate School, June 2003, 2.

43. Comments on an earlier draft of this chapter by Air Marshal Vinod Patney, IAF (Ret.), August 16, 2011.

44. Ganesh, "Indian Air Force in Action," 178–79.

45. Jaswant Singh, *In Service of Emergent India: A Call to Honor* (Bloomington, Indiana: University of Indiana Press, 2007), 203.

46. Bedi, "Kargil: An IAF Perspective," 151.

47. Tufail, "Kargil 1999: The PAF's Story," 97–98.

48. Bedi, "Paying to Keep the High Ground," 31.

49. Tellis, Fair, and Medby, *Limited Conflicts Under the Nuclear Umbrella*, 71.

50. "1999 Kargil Conflict, webpage, anonymous," at http://www.globalsecurity.org/military/world/war/kargil-99.htm/, n.p.

51. Air Chief Marshal Fali Homi Major, IAF, "National Defence and Aerospace Power," *Air Power Journal* (New Delhi, Spring 2009), 3.

52. "I Do Not See China to Be a Major Concern in My Area of Responsibility," interview with Air Marshal P. K. Barbora, IAF, Air Officer Commanding-in-Chief, Western Air Command, *Force* (New Delhi), October 2008, 28.

53. Bakshi, "Kargil: Dynamics of a Limited War Against a Nuclear Backdrop," 48, 50.

54. Acosta, "High Altitude Warfare: The Kargil Conflict and the Future," 58.

55. Singh, *Himalayan Eagles: History of the Indian Air Force*, 108–9.

56. It should be added in passing here that senior officers from all three Indian services have since opined that the Vajpayee government's insistence that Indian forces not cross the LoC under any circumstances during the Kargil War constituted a major "lost opportunity" in the country's systemically conflicted relationship with Pakistan. (Comments on an earlier draft by retired Air Marshal Vinod Patney, IAF, August 16, 2011.) For example a former Indian Army vice chief wrote in 2009: "There was no great captain in the Indian military who could urge the political executive to let him seize the opportunity offered by Pakistan to take the bull by the horns . . . . Instead, the army chief acquiesced to troops being condemned to frontal attacks . . . . Our timid response at Kargil laid the foundation for future terrorist attacks . . . ." (Harwant, "Kargil Controversy: Mismanagement of Higher Defence.") In a similar vein, a former Indian Navy chief also characterized Kargil as "the last battle of World War II fought with massive frontal attacks and artillery barrages," adding that "had there been some cool-headed, joint, and strategic thinking when the Kargil intrusions were detected, we could have widened the conflict, kept the Paks engaged on land, and blockaded them by sea. Already in dire economic straits, they would have come to their knees soon. Of course, this would have required political will." (E-mail to the author from former Chief of Naval Staff Admiral Arun Prakash, Indian Navy [Ret.], August 18, 2011.)

57. Gill, "Military Operations in the Kargil Conflict," 107–8.

58. Kargil Review Committee, *From Surprise to Reckoning*, 22, 105.

59. Srinath Raghavan, "The India-Pakistan Crisis Is More Dangerous Than Ever," report from Carnegie India (New Delhi), March 6, 2019.

60. Maria Abi-Habib, Sameer Yasir, and Hari Kumar, "India Blames Pakistan for Attack in Kashmir, Promising a Response," *The New York Times*, February 15, 2019.

61. R. Prasannan, Namrata Biji Ahuja, and Pradip R. Sagar, "Inside Story of India's Airstrike and Pakistan's Counter-Attack," *The Week*, March 2, 2019.

62. Ibid.

63. Ibid.

64. Ibid.

65. Air Vice-Marshal Arjun Subramaniam, IAF (Ret.), "Balakot and After: IAF Demonstrates Full-Spectrum Capability," *Firstpost* (New Delhi), March 11, 2019.

66. Ibid.

67. Naveed Siddiqui, "PAF Response to Indian Aggression Will Be Remembered as Operation Swift Retort: Air Chief," *Dawn* (Karachi), May 1, 2019.

68. In an unrelated event, an IAF Mi-17 helicopter was also shot down, evidently by inadvertent friendly fire, killing all six crewmembers who were aboard.

69. See, for example, Maria Abi-Habib, "After India Loses Dogfight to Pakistan, Questions Arise about Its 'Vintage' Military," *The New York Times*, March 3, 2019, and Laura Seligman, "India's Dogfight Loss Could Be a Win for U. S. Weapons Makers," *Foreign Policy*, March 5, 2019.

70. " 'Won't Be in My Control or Narendra Modi's If This Escalates:' Imran Khan," NDTV (New Delhi), February 27, 2019.

71. Michael Safi, Mehreen Zahra-Malik, and Azhar Farooq, "Pakistan Says It Has Shot Down Indian Jets after Kashmir Cross-Border Attack," *The Guardian*, February 27, 2019.

72. Prasannan, Ahuja, and Sagar, *The Week*, March 2, 2019.

73. "Shot Down in Indian Battle: Report," *Reuters World News*, April 5, 2019.

74. "We Didn't Lose Any Su-30 Jet, Pakistan's Claims False: Defence Ministry," *The New Indian Express* (Chennai), March 5, 2019.

75. "JF-17, Not F-16, Used to Shoot Down Indian Aircraft, Says ISPR DG," *Pakistan Today* (Lahore), March 25, 2019.

76. Soutik Biwas, "India Pakistan: Kashmir Fighting Sees Indian Aircraft Downed," *BBC News*, February 27, 2019.

77. For an informed and thorough assessment of air operations in that war, see Subramaniam, *India's Wars: A Military History, 1947–1971*, 337–438.

78. Air Vice-Marshal Arjun Subramaniam, IAF (Ret.), "The Indian Air Force, Sub-Conventional Operations and Balakot: A Practitioner's Perspective," ORF Issue Brief, New Delhi: Observer Research Foundation, May 13, 2019.

79. Air Vice-Marshal Arjun Subramaniam, IAF (Ret.), as quoted in Archana Masih, " 'It Is Not So Much about Dropping Bombs on a Target, It Is the Effect That That Bomb Creates,' " *Rediff.com* (Mumbai, India), March 6, 2019.

80. Air Vice-Marshal Arjun Subramaniam, IAF (Ret.), "Escalating to De-escalate Is India's New Strategy with an Irrational Pakistan," *The Print* (New Delhi), February 28, 2019.

81. Associated Press, "Pakistan Says It Downed Indian Warplanes and Captured Pilot in Major Escalation between Nuclear Rivals," *NBC News*, February 26, 2019, and Saeed Shah and Rajesh Roy, "India-Pakistan Clash Intensifies with Downed Jets, Captured Pilot," *The Wall Street Journal* February 27, 2019.

82. Sameer Lalwani and Emily Tallo, "Did India Shoot Down a Pakistani F-16 in February? This Just Became a Big Deal," *The Washington Post*, April 17, 2019.

83. Quoted in EFAS commentary, "India's Bold Counter-Terrorist Air Strike Deep within Pakistan Marks a Paradigm Shift in Its Security Strategy," Amsterdam: European Foundation for South Asian Studies, March 1, 2019.

84. Srinath Raghavan, "The India-Pakistan Crisis Is More Dangerous Than Ever," report from Carnegie India (New Delhi), March 6, 2019.

85. "Air Force Chief Dhanoa Warns Pakistan, Says IAF Always Alert along Indo-Pak Border," *India Today*, August 20, 2019.

86. "JF-17, Not F-16, Used to Shoot Down Indian Aircraft, Says ISPR DG," *Pakistan Today*, March 25, 2019.

87. Sameer Lalwani and Emily Tallo, "Did India Shoot Down a Pakistani F-16 in February? This Just Became a Big Deal," *The Washington Post*, April 17, 2019.

88. Shah and Roy, *The Wall Street Journal*, February 27, 2019.

89. Safi and Zahra-Melik, *The Guardian*, February 27, 2019.

90. Quoted in European Foundation for South Asian Studies, web page, anonymous, "India's Bold Counter-Terrorist Air Strike Deep within Pakistan Marks a Paradigm Shift in Its Security Strategy," Retrieved https://www.efsas.org/commentaries/india%E2%80%99s-counter-terrorist-air-strike-within-pakistan-marks-a-paradigm-shift-in-its-security-strategy/.

91. Associated Press, "Pakistan Says It Downed Indian Warplanes and Captured Pilot in Major Escalation between Nuclear Rivals," *NBC News*, February 26, 2019.

92. Abi-Habib, *The New York Times*, March 3, 2019.

93. Paul Staniland, "India's New Security Order," *War on the Rocks*, December 17, 2019.

94. Ibid.

95. Satoru Nagao, "Who Won the Battle? India or Pakistan?" *Ceylon Today*, April 3, 2019.

96. Singh, "Kashmir, Covert Wars, and Air Power," 83.

97. General V. P. Malik, Indian Army (Ret.), "The Kargil War: Some Reflections," *CLAWS Journal* (New Delhi), Summer 2009, 2.

98. Bakshi, "Kargil: Dynamics of a Limited War against a Nuclear Backdrop," 45

99. Qadir, "An Analysis of the Kargil Conflict 1999," 27.

100. Tufail, "Kargil 1999: The PAF's Story," 99.

101. Air Commodore Kaiser Tufail, PAF (Ret.), "Kargil Conflict and Air Force," *Defence Journal* (Pakistan), May 2009.

102. Group Captain T. D. Joseph, IAF, *Winning India's Next War: The Role of Aerospace Power* (New Delhi: KW Publishers, 2008), 155.

103. Quoted in Singh, "Kashmir, Covert Wars, and Air Power," 86–87, emphasis added.

104. Air Commodore Arjun Subramaniam, IAF, "The Strategic Role of Air Power: An Indian Perspective on How We Need to Think, Train, and Fight in the Coming Years," *Air and Space Power Journal* (Fall 2008), 64.

105. Singh, "Kashmir, Covert Wars, and Air Power," 80.

106. Ibid., 81.

107. These points are developed in Patney, "1999 War in Kargil and Its Aftermath."

108. Air Marshal Vinod Patney, IAF (Ret.), "Air Dominance: Concept and Practice," *Air Power Journal* (New Delhi, Summer 2009), 133, 144.

109. Air Vice-Marshal Arjun Subramaniam, IAF (Ret.), "IAF Operation Has Established Air Strikes as an Effective Tool of Deterrence in Sub-Conventional Warfare," *The Indian Express* (New Delhi), September 10, 2020.

110. Air Vice-Marshal Arjun Subramaniam, IAF (Ret.), "The End of Diffidence: India Has Moved from Restrained to Robust Deterrence of Terror. Can It Sustain This Shift?," *The Times of India* (New Delhi), March 19, 2019.

111. Sushant Sareen, "Balakot Air Strikes: The End of the Madman Theory," ORF Issue Brief, New Delhi: Observer Research Foundations, March 5, 2019.

7

Escalation Management in Practice

Forrest E. Morgan and Robert C. Owen

This study has reinforced the expectation that the question of whether peer opponents can conduct limited air warfare has a complex answer. In each of the cases examined, the calculi of the leaders making escalatory decisions for their air forces included mixtures of considerations unique to their circumstances. Included in these considerations were the predilections, characters, and self-interests of the leaders involved; cultural norms and mythologies; estimations of the likely reactions of enemies and important external powers; geospatial relationships of combatants and battlefields; relevant technologies and force structures; and unfolding events. In all cases examined here the weight assigned by leaders and leader groups to these various considerations evolved as conflicts progressed.

It follows, then, that the general value of this study is that it reinforces two common-sense insights of importance to students and practitioners of air warfare; that escalation is influenced by many factors and that the mixes and balances of those factors evolve in the process of war. Taken together, these insights warn that cookbook recipes of how escalation works and how enemies will react to escalatory actions likely won't bake well in future conflicts. Indeed, the very notion of escalation *control* is naively mechanistic. Future leaders making war-initiation and subsequent escalation decisions should, therefore, lean toward informed caution in their presumptions about their enemies and make sure that their plans objectively incorporate the full range of operational, cultural, human intelligence, and diplomatic knowledge such as are available to them and that allow them to respond flexibly to the unexpected. Escalation *management* should be among their objectives as they weigh the operational advantages expected in any prospective escalation against the risks of how adversaries and third parties might react to it.

Discussion

In the cases discussed in this study, the range and lethality of their air forces gave all combatants opportunities to escalate the scale and targeting of their operations. In the South Atlantic War, Britain had the capability to strike at air, naval, and economic targets in Argentina proper. Argentina's options were materially more limited, but it accepted the cease fire while its Air Force still had the capacity to continue operations. Over Angola and Namibia, the South African and Cuban Air Forces were gaining strength and capabilities when their governments agreed on peace. India and Pakistan ended the Kargil War with both in possession of powerful air forces capable of expanding their conventional and even nuclear attacks on military forces and civil targets for strategic effect. If, as new nuclear powers, Indian and Pakistani leaders had followed the logic of the planners of Exercise Sagebrush, they should have anticipated a nuclear exchange by launching all-out, preemptive strikes on each other to neutralize opponent retaliatory capabilities. But they did not, even when evidence emerged that the Pakistani military was shifting some nukes to forward employment positions, perhaps without the knowledge of its civilian leaders. So, after initiating or being forced into bitter conflicts, and having in most cases engaged in some escalations in subsequent fighting, all of these combatants stood down with air options still on the table, and that is at the heart of the opening question of this study.

Technology and force structure limitations were principal factors in the decisions of most countries to not escalate their air operations and to terminate them when they did. The short range of their strike aircraft, exacerbated by the weakness of their air refueling capabilities, were the Achilles' heels of Britain and Argentina over the Falklands. The RAF had the Vulcan, of course. But the maximum air refueling effort required for each Vulcan sortie was an unsurmountable barrier to conducting more than salutary attacks on the Argentine mainland had Britain chosen to escalate in that direction. Similarly, the inability of the South African Air Force to patrol and strike deep into Angola obviated its ability to support Operation Savanah and thereafter restricted its operations to the immediate south of Angola and left the Cubans with sanctuary bases farther to the north. The Pakistani and Indian air forces could reach each other during the Kargil War. But in an all-out conflict, the limited number of Indian AF bases in the battle zone and the short ranges of their Mirage and MiG fighters would have restricted their ability to concentrate forces and fly deep into Pakistan. Pakistani F-16s would have been less handicapped, but they had fewer of them than the Indians had MiGs and Mirages. Weapons technology further shaped escalation opportunities. Although precision guided munitions had been around since World War II and were available in much-improved forms, most of the countries discussed here entered their wars either with very limited magazines of such weapons or none at all. Air-to-air and surface-to-air missile technologies also played key roles in Angola (the AA-7), in the South Atlantic (AIM-9L), and over Kargil (Stingers). Further, as aggressive as they might have been in intent, many of these air forces were simply too small to consider escalations beyond the battlefield operations they were conducting. To be decisive, escalated air strikes must be of appropriate weight in scale, intensity, and weapons effects in relation to objectives sought. Escalating *without* enough force to win at a new level of fighting, it follows, likely will only prolong operations, continue attrition, and give enemies opportunities to respond in kind or to up the ante.

Geospatial realities also played a role in checking escalation in these conflicts between peer or near-peer air forces. Most obvious, the weight of attack and freedom of maneuver available to an air force is inversely proportional to the distance between its air bases or final air refueling points and the battle zone. Over the Falklands, for example, poor logistics and an operating distance right at the radii of action of most of its aircraft, restricted the Argentine Air Force to something like one sortie per aircraft every *other* day. Better maintained and launching closer to the fight, Royal Navy and RAF Harriers, in contrast, flew two to three sorties *per day* and, with their AIM-9Ls, dominated the air battle. Given the impact of distance on the battle, it is an interesting exercise to ponder how differently the South Atlantic air battle might have gone in chronology and casualties, had the islands been a hundred miles closer to Argentina or had Britain kept HMS *Ark Royal* in service. The shorter operating ranges of the Kargil and Angolan conflicts should not obscure the reality that the combatants had targets that they wished to strike, but could not, in part, because their aircraft lacked the range.

Fear of consequences restrained escalation in all of the conflicts examine here. During the Angolan and South Atlantic wars, where the engaged air forces were operating near the limits of their capabilities from the start, decisions not to escalate reflected diplomatic and strategic concerns more than immediate shifts in military balances. Regarding the Angolan conflict, South African airmen and political leaders understood that bombing some targets and even just rattling their nuclear weapons late in the war could provoke potentially overwhelming diplomatic, economic, and military responses from the US, the Soviet Union, and other outside powers. On his part, Fidel Castro had good reason to worry about similar consequences, should he push his forces into Namibia in 1988. Likewise, British calculations to eschew attacks on Argentina's mainland reflected both their limited capabilities to conduct such operations and the likely responses of Latin American governments and the United States to them. Indicative of the sensitivity of international diplomacy to the employment of air power, the British were willing to consider employing commandos but not Vulcans to attack Etendards and assassinate their pilots at Rio Gallegos Air Base. In contrast, it is doubtful that diplomatic considerations carried much weight with the Argentine dictators as they considered the one escalatory decision left to them after the fall of Stanley—continuing the air war. Given the political and personal risks they were then facing, the degraded state of the Argentine air force, and the British now in possession of the operationally critical Stanley airport, their situation was hopeless militarily and mandated surrender. The Kargil War presents the case where the danger of *nuclear* escalation overtly and immediately restrained escalation decisions on both sides. Both India and then Pakistan kept their combat aircraft on their sides of the Line of Control for fear that air battles and air strikes in their homelands would prompt one or both countries to preempt with nuclear attacks, perhaps on large scales to blunt enemy retaliations. Thirty-five years earlier, the Generals conducting Exercise Sagebrush had come to essentially the same conclusion: Countries stepping across the nuclear threshold were not starting down a slippery but incremental escalatory slope; they more likely were falling over a cliff, or about to have the cliff fall on them—all or nothing, or stay away from the game.

Leaders tended to be a complex and difficult-to-predict variable in the employment of their national air forces. The air power assessments of the Argentine Junta, particularly General Galtieri and Admiral Anaya, and of the rogue Pakistani general, General Musharraf, were driven by personal issues of political survival and nationalist vengefulness rather than objective assessments of capabilities and likely enemy responses. Indeed, they deluded themselves regarding the probable responses of their enemies and, since air power would be important or even decisive elements of those responses, they quarantined themselves from the advice of professional airmen. Then, when things went bad, they turned to their consequently unprepared air forces for salvation. In the case of Musharraf, once the full scope and risks of his disastrous actions became public, his civilian leaders held back the Pakistani Air Force from crossing the Line of Control and kicking off a full-scale war. In contrast, the consultative democracies assailed by these petty tyrants handled their air forces much more skillfully and rationally. Prime Minister Thatcher and Prime Minister Vajpayee both had the good sense to set operational boundaries for their military commanders and then let them work out the tactical details.

The obedience of the air leaders to the boundaries set for them was crucial to keeping their countries on the diplomatic high ground in world opinion and, crucially, with key allies. Britain's policy of not striking the Argentine homeland gave the American government freedom to continue the flow of crucial weapons, such as the AIM-9L, Shrike anti-radar missiles, and so on. Vajpayee's proscription of strikes across the Line-of-Control may have frustrated his air commanders and probably cost the lives of some Indian soldiers. But it also preserved India's moral position and gave Pakistan no excuse to escalate the air war. For their part, South African politicians and generals tended to be a closer-knit group than their equivalents in the other cases discussed. Consequently, their story in the long Angolan War reveals few internal conflicts over escalation and de-escalation—both groups were ready and did escalate several times, but only up to the point that might prompt outside intervention. Finally, Exercise Sagebrush stands in this study of an example of the logic of escalation between powers in possession of air forces wielding weapons of mass effect, if that logic is untempered by other values, such as the moral compass of war and national survival.

Morgan's Taxonomy: Deliberate, Inadvertent, and Accidental Escalations

The empirical discussions in this study give credence to the deliberate-inadvertent-accidental escalation taxonomy put forth by Forrest Morgan in his opening chapter. As a group, these studies present several instances of all three types of escalations, along with careful accounts of their outcomes. Importantly, the historical evidence also bears out the truth of Morgan's argument that subjectivity and chance play a role in many (all?) escalatory decisions. As he explains himself, Morgan's useful linkage of escalation and "threshold(s) considered significant by one or more of the participants" illuminates the inevitability of subjectivity, since participants in conflicts tend to view escalation thresholds through differing political, strategic, cultural, and self-interested lenses. When combined with the certain uncertainty of the future, these differing appreciations of escalation thresholds virtually guarantee that few if any escalatory decisions in war will produce results that precisely match the expectations of their makers.

Certainly, none of the deliberate war-initiations of the conflicts examined here delivered on the expectations of the leaders making them. South Africa plunged into Angola in 1976 expecting to secure its borders. Instead, the Angolan war became a twelve-year drain on the country's financial resources and the moral underpinnings of Apartheid in the eyes of its own white population. The Argentine Junta's military and political debacle in the South Atlantic War is a classic case of a deliberate escalatory action (from negotiation to active conflict) that went badly. The Kargil War was another case in point. Perhaps President Anwar Sadat's decision to launch the 1973 War was the only war-initiation action that eventually helped to produce a desired result, namely greater respect for Egypt's strength and increased international pressure for Israel to withdraw from the Sinai. Through the Camp David Accords (1978) he shared in the normalization of Egyptian-Israeli relations and the start of a phased Israeli withdrawal from the Sinai.

Consistently, the outcomes of many of the *tactical* escalations undertaken in the conflicts discussed here were unpredictable. The South Africans, for example, launched Operation Reindeer to break up SWAPO formations before they could launch their annual incursions into Northern Namibia. The operations did that, but it also reenergized South Africa's direct confrontation with Cuba and Angola and brought down upon it the diplomatic opprobrium of most of the world. A successful tactical effort to shape the battlefield, in other words, expanded the scope and the stakes of the war in a manner inimical to South Africa's strategic interests. In contrast, Britain's successful attacks on the Stanley airport and the *Belgrano* had limited tactical effects, but they unexpectedly changed the strategic character of the war by starting the decline of Argentine popular and military morale and intimidating the rest of the Argentine

Navy to flee back into its ports, from which it conducted only limited active operations thereafter. In this case, then, deliberate tactical actions had their intended effects, but also *de*-escalated the war's potential at the strategic level.

Inadvertent escalations, defined by Dr. Morgan as deliberate actions that escalators do not consider escalatory but opponents do, were frequent events in all of the wars discussed. The most egregious examples of culturally and politically stupid escalations were the war-initiation decisions of all of the leaders involved. In all the cases discussed in this study, authoritarian governments with heavy military influence chose to ignore the advice from better informed quarters that their planned actions would initiate major conflicts. Driven by their egos, political interests, and woodenheaded misreadings of the willingness or abilities of their opponents to fight, these leaders initiated conflicts that common sense would have suggested put them at risk of suffering decisive defeats. The Argentine Junta stands as a case study of willful self-delusion regarding an opponent's, in this case Britain's, willingness to fight for the Falklands on the basis of principle, rather than accede on the basis of the political and military expediencies that drove its own decision processes of the dictators. The leadership cohorts of Egypt and Pakistan made similar miscalculations reflecting their need to believe they were undertaking limited actions against irresolute enemies when, in fact, they were pushing them across vital thresholds, namely national sovereignty, political credibility, and broader strategic interests.

These leaders also deluded themselves on the global diplomatic and economic reactions to their actions. In their anticipation of American support for their invasion of Angola, for example, the South Africans were way behind the times in their understanding of the willingness and ability of American political leaders to support the aggressive actions of a government wedded to long-discredited racialist theories and a racist domestic political setup. Similarly, Pakistani leaders anticipated that, fearing the possibility of a regional nuclear war, the United States and the world in general would force India to acquiesce to their aggression in the Kargil region. Instead, the bald illegality of the invasion and India's astute mix of powerful conventional military actions and respect for the Line of Control handed Pakistan a resounding military and diplomatic defeat. Characteristic of his self-imposed strategic myopia, Argentine President Galtieri actually believed that U.S. President Ronald Reagan's praise for his anti-communism equated to a willingness of the United States to endorse Argentina's aggression against a treasured ally—Great Britain.

America's decisive logistical support for Britain quickly disabused a surprised Galtieri of such silliness.

By their very nature—unintended and often the consequences beyond the control of belligerents—accidental escalations happened in these conflicts, though they are often overlooked in subsequent analyses. By essentially demilitarizing its presence in the South Atlantic, for example, the British government made the classic error of creating a power vacuum in the presence of enemies interested in expanding into it. Convinced that Britain no longer had the means or will to defend its kindred so far away, Argentine leaders saw a virtual written invitation to regain their political credibility and satisfy their patriotic aspirations by invading the Falklands and South Georgia. In the case of the Kargil War, the mere rumor that the Pakistanis might be moving some of their nuclear weapons was enough to increase international pressure on them to withdraw back across their border. Likewise, during the 1973 Yom Kippur War, a vague and unelaborated threat by Soviet Premier Leonid Brezhnev to take unilateral action to force a cease fire galvanized American leaders to intensify their diplomatic and military postures, which intimidated the Soviets and increased the pressure on all sides to move toward a cease fire. None of the initiators of these conflicts could have anticipated these sorts of actions by outsiders, but they happened and they shaped their outcomes nearly or as much as did the actual clashes of arms.

This discussion of deliberate, inadvertent, and accidental escalations highlights two of Morgan's most important insights into escalation theory. First, the many uncertainties involved render the concept of escalation control largely moot. It is a reassuring idea for governments and militaries facing relatively powerful opponents, but the evidence indicates that the outcomes of escalatory actions are almost always, perhaps always, skewed from expectations by unknown and unknowable elements of context and unpredictable futures. Indeed, and this is the second salient point, even the more tempered notion of escalation *management* tends to be easier in theory than in practice. The leaders on any side of a conflict should understand that their abilities to accurately predict the results of their efforts to escalate or deescalate conflicts will be restrained by ultimately unbridgeable cultural, emotional, strategic, and other differences between them and their enemies. They may think that they are taking prudent actions to coerce or calm their opponents, but they should not be surprised to discover that they guessed incorrectly about how they would perceive and respond to those actions.

Implications

The complex dynamics observed in these cases have several important implications for managing the risks of escalation when employing airpower in war. First, this study tends to confirm findings that other analysts have reached regarding the inability to deter conventional wars with nuclear threats, or even to deter conventional escalation in those wars . . . at least, up to a point. As early as 1965, Glen Snyder identified what he called the "stability-instability paradox," maintaining that "the greater the stability of the strategic balance of terror, the lower the stability of the overall balance at its lower levels of violence."[1] In other words, the stability imposed by fears of nuclear war makes actors freer to engage in lower level conflicts. This study suggests that the shared fear of nuclear war does indeed make implicit threats of nuclear escalation hollow, allowing belligerents to escalate conventional air operations without fear of tripping over an adversary's nuclear threshold. This is clearly evident in initial stages of the Kargil crisis, where India engaged in intense conventional air operations against Pakistani forces in that province for the first time since 1971, despite both states being emergent nuclear powers. Yet the freedom to escalate conventional operations against a nuclear-armed state is not unlimited. The aggressiveness of the Indian response startled Pakistan, prompting it to put at least some nuclear units on alert and explicitly threaten to use the "ultimate weapon" should India cross the line of control. This undoubtedly caught New Delhi's attention. Indian ground forces had driven deep into Pakistan in previous conflicts and could have done so again in this one, but they did not. Threats of nuclear escalation may not be credible in limited conventional war, but when a vital interest, such as territorial integrity of the homeland, is put at risk, such threats carry more weight.

On a more interesting note, this study's findings indicate that the presence of nuclear weapons does not deter conventional airstrikes even when there is no "balance of terror" between the specific belligerents. In the Falklands, Middle East, and Namibia conflicts, only one of the states involved had nuclear weapons, yet the other side commenced or escalated air attacks in apparent disregard of them. One reason for this might be that the nonnuclear belligerent had a nuclear-armed patron that could be relied upon to intervene, should the adversary cross the nuclear threshold. That is probably the case in the Middle East wars, where the Soviet Union extended a deterrent umbrella over its client state, Egypt, and perhaps in the Namibia conflict. But it was not a factor in the Falklands case. With the United States backing Britain, Argentina had no nuclear-armed ally to deter nuclear escalation in response to its conventional airstrikes on British forces. Yet Argentina attacked aggressively without fear that Britain would respond with nuclear weapons.

To understand why Britain did not escalate to nuclear brandishing in response to Argentine air attacks, we must look at escalation decision making more broadly than just at the operational level of war. British forces were heavily dependent on U.S. logistical support to project power into an operational theater so far from Britain's shores. Just as importantly, Britain relied on the United States for political support in international forums for its action against a state that was ostensibly a U.S. ally in the Organization of American States. Had London begun threatening the use of nuclear weapons, Washington might have curtailed that support, and it almost certainly would have done so had British forces resorted to their use. Buenos Aires understood what was obvious to London and Washington: the threat of nuclear use was neither politically *nor morally* acceptable. It simply was not even a credible *idea* in a limited conflict over territory of questionable importance to Britain.

Taken together, these insights suggest several implications for future planners. First, decisions of whether to escalate air attacks in a conflict should not be made by air planners alone, even at the operational level of air war, where targets are prioritized and weapons are selected. That is where the decision process must begin, of course, based on whether planners believe the prospective escalation will affect the campaign in a way that is advantageous for friendly forces and make victory more assured. But a key part of deciding whether to escalate the scope or intensity of airstrikes is to consider what the adversary might do in response. What escalation thresholds will the proposed action cross? To what degree will it threaten enemy leaders, and how might they react? The proposed escalation should be weighed in terms of the degree to which it is expected to contribute to military success while not tempting or even compelling the enemy to escalate in ways that are unacceptable in response.

It follows from this, of course, that escalatory decisions should not be made by civilians alone. As Ben Lambeth pointed out, the inability of Indian politicians in the years following the Kargil War to understand the nature and capabilities of air power hamstrung their abilities to formulate effective responses to Pakistani enabled terrorism. Likewise, the failure of Army General Galtieri and Navy Admiral Anaya to appreciate the likely importance of the Argentine Air Force in a fight over the Falklands caused them to leave their Air Force counterpart, General Dozo, out of the planning process until almost too late for that service to get ready to make an effective contribution. In contrast, Israeli leaders may have grumbled at the expense of maintaining a first-class air force, but the benefits of doing so far outweighed its costs in 1973. It follows from this that, while Carl von Clausewitz famously said that war is a continuation of politics by other means, it is also fair to say that politics often are continuations of wars by less violent means. If both sides of that coin are true, then the strategic questions of escalation and de-escalation must be made in cooperation between political and military experts who are knowledgeable and respectful of what each brings to the table.

In closing, escalation management is about keeping limited wars limited. It requires both deterrence *and* restraint. One cannot expect enemy leaders to be deterred from doing everything in their power to fight if they are convinced that their power, visions of their country's best interest, their own self-interests, or even survival are at stake. Granted, war is war, so the prospective course of action should be aimed at defeating the opponent's conventional forces, but only to the extent needed to obtain the conflict's limited objectives. The plan must respect the opponent's higher-level interests and thresholds, while holding them at risk as part of a carefully crafted escalation management strategy.

Note

1. Glenn Snyder, "The Balance of Power and the Balance of Terror," in *Balance of Power*, ed. Paul Seabury (San Francisco, Calif.: Chandler, 1965), 184–201. For more on the stability-instability paradox as it relates to new nuclear states, see: Peter Lavoy, "The Strategic Consequences of Nuclear Proliferation," *Security Studies* 4, no. 4 (Summer 1995), 739–40; Michael Krepon, "The Stability-Instability Paradox, Misperception, and Escalation Control in South Asia" in *Escalation Control and the Nuclear Option in South Asia*, eds. Michael Krepon, Rodney W. Jones, and Ziad Haider (Washington, D.C.: Henry L. Stimson Center, November 2004), 1–24.

About the Authors

Lazar Berman is the senior diplomatic correspondent at the *Times of Israel*. From 2015–2020 he was Head of Joint Learning at the IDF/J3 Dado Center for Interdisciplinary Military Studies. Berman commanded a Bedouin unit during his active IDF service and is currently a reserve captain in the 89th Commando Brigade. He taught at Salahuddin University in Erbil in Iraqi Kurdistan and studied the Kurdish language. Berman is also a PhD student in War Studies at King's College London. He holds an MA in military operations from Georgetown University's Security Studies Program, where he wrote his thesis on IDF innovation. He has published in *The Journal of Strategic Studies*, *Small Wars Journal*, *Weekly Standard*, *Mosaic*, and other journals.

Benjamin S. Lambeth is a nonresident Senior Fellow with the Center for Strategic and Budgetary Assessments, a position he assumed in 2011 following a thirty-seven-year career as a Senior Research Associate at the RAND Corporation. A long-time specialist in international security affairs and air warfare, he holds a doctorate in political science from Harvard University and has flown or flown in more than forty different types of combat aircraft with the U.S. Air Force, Navy, Marine Corps, and eight foreign air forces. In 2002, he was elected an honorary member of the Order of Daedalians, the national fraternity of U.S. military pilots. Among his many previous books and other publications, he is the author most recently of *Airpower in the War against ISIS*, Annapolis, Md.: Naval Institute Press, 2021.

Forrest E. Morgan is a lecturer at the Carnegie Mellon University Institute for Politics and Strategy. In 2019 he retired from the RAND Corporation where he had been a senior political scientist since 2003. At RAND he did strategy and doctrine research for the Air Force, Army, and other national defense clients and held a faculty appointment to the Pardee RAND Graduate School. Morgan's work focused on deterrence, escalation management, crisis stability, military applications of artificial intelligence, and space policy, strategy, and operations. Morgan joined RAND in 2003 after retiring from a twenty-seven-year career in the U.S. Air Force. His service there included duty as a signals intelligence analyst and as a space operations officer in various operations and staff positions. Toward the end of his Air Force career he served on the strategy and policy staff at Headquarters, U.S. Air Force, Pentagon, and as professor of comparative military studies at the Air University School of Advanced Air and Space Studies (SAASS). Morgan holds a PhD in policy studies from the University of Maryland, College Park.

Robert C. Owen is a professor in the Department of Aeronautical Science at Embry-Riddle Aeronautical University, Daytona Beach Campus. He holds an MA in African Studies (UCLA-1973) and a PhD in History (Duke-1991). In his current position, he teaches courses in manned and unmanned aviation operations, law, and history and conducts research in national defense policy issues. Professor Owen joined the Embry-Riddle faculty in 2002, following a twenty-eight-year career with the United States Air Force. His military career included a mix of operational, staff, and advanced education assignments. He is a USAF Command Pilot and a commercial pilot, and has logged over 4,500 hours of flight time in around twenty-five different aircraft. Professor Owen also served on the HQ U.S. Air Force staff and the HQ staff of the Air Mobility Command as a doctrinalist and strategic planner. His academic assignments included tours as an assistant professor of History at the U.S. Air Force Academy, Dean of the USAF's School of Advanced Airpower Studies, the service's graduate school for strategic planners, and as chair of the Aeronautical Science Department at Embry-Riddle. In addition to numerous articles and monographs, his book publications include the *Chronology* volume of the *Gulf War Air Power Survey* (1995), *Deliberate Force: A Case Study in Effective Air Campaigning* (2000), and *Air Mobility: A Brief History of the American Experience* (2013).

Steven Paget is the University of Portsmouth's Director of Academic Support Services (International Security) at Royal Air Force (RAF) College, Cranwell.

In addition to leading the University of Portsmouth team at Cranwell, he oversees the academic component of the Initial Officer Training Course and several individual courses. Professor Paget also serves as a member of the editorial board of the *RAF Air Power Review*. Following positions teaching defense and security studies at the New Zealand Defence Force (NZDF) Command and Staff College and at the Centre for Defence and Security Studies at Massey University, Dr. Paget took his current position at Portsmouth. His many publishing credits include *The Dynamics of Coalition Naval Warfare: The Special Relationship at Sea* (Abingdon: Routledge, 2017), and a range of articles and monographs on amphibious warfare, interoperability, naval warfare (particularly naval gunfire support) and professional military education published in *War in History, Small Wars and Insurgencies, The RUSI Journal, Mariner's Mirror,* and *Naval War College Review*. He currently is analyzing multinational air power and RAF operations throughout the history of the service.

Index

A-4 Skyhawk aircraft, 64, 82, 128, 134, 136, 138
AA-7 missile, 106, 114, 115, 119, 211
AIM-9L Sidewinder air-to-air missile, 131, 138, 153, 156, 211, 213
airlift, 44, 47–57, 81–86, 99, 107, 130, 181
air superiority, 47, 111, 116
Anaya, Admiral Jorge (Argentina), 134, 139, 141, 143, 212, 219
Anza II missile, 171, 174
Apartheid, 101, 103, 113, 119, 214
Argentine Junta, 127, 133, 134, 140–47, 153, 155–58, 212–15
Argentine Naval Aviation (COAN), 128, 136, 139, 140, 151, 154
Ascension Island, 127, 130, 131, 142, 149, 150
atomic field test army, 41
atomic simulators, 38, 40, 44
atomic weapons/attacks, 21, 36–51, 57, 113

B-26 aircraft, 36, 37, 39, 43
B-57 aircraft, 39
Balakot strike, 187, 188, 189, 190, 191, 192, 194, 195, 196, 202
Belgium, 19
Belgrano (Argentine navy cruiser), 154, 156, 214
Black Buck raids, 153
Bosnia, 20

Brazil, 133
Brezhnev, Soviet Premier Leonid, 84, 86, 216
brinkmanship, 12, 13, 14, 55

C-119 aircraft, 39
C-124 aircraft, 39, 44
C-130 aircraft, 82, 96, 130, 134
Calueque Dam incident (1988), 111, 112
Cambodia, 11, 23
Canberra aircraft, 96, 103, 134, 138, 154, 173, 174
Castro, Premier Fidel (Cuba), 91, 94, 99, 100–119, 121–22nn42–43, 212
Chile, 98, 133, 155
China, 2, 3, 7, 12, 15, 16, 54, 167, 191–98, 200
Clausewitz, Carl von, 6, 10, 26, 219
Commonwealth and Foreign Office (CFO), 141
compact air strike force, 41
Crespo, AF General Ernesto (Argentina), 134, 136, 137
Comando de la Aviación Naval Argentina. *See* Argentine Naval Aviation (COAN)
Crocker, Asst. Secretary of State (U.S.), 110
Cuba, 13, 22, 34n41, 55, 91–100, 106, 108, 112–23, 214
Cuban Revolutionary Air and Air Defense Force (DAAFAR), 92–96, 104–19

226   Index

Cuito Cuanavale, Battle of, 105–10, 114, 116

Dayan, Defense Minister Moshe (Israel), 71, 73, 74, 79
Del Pino, General Rafael del, 94, 95
Dick, RAF AVM Ron, 149
dispersal of air operations, 44, 47, 51
Dobrynin, Ambassador Anatoly (USSR), 13, 32n25
Douhet, Giulio, 3
Dozo, AF General Lami (Argentina), 134, 139, 141, 219
Dulles, John Foster, 8, 50

Eighteenth Air Force (troop carrier), 44
Eisenhower, President Dwight (U.S.), 7, 50
Elazar, IAF Chief of Staff David, 67–77, 80–84, 87
escalation, 5–9, 11, 17–21, 101, 209–19; accidental escalation, 24–26, 213; deliberate escalation, 20–23; escalation dominance, 7–13, 16, 27; escalation ladder, 7–11, 22, 104; escalation management, 1–8, 14–17, 30, 32n19, 32n21, 32n24, 33n30, 33n32, 33n37, 33nn39–40, 34n43, 34n46, 35n48, 38–39, 56, 62, 63, 129, 157, 216, 219, 222; escalation thresholds, 2, 3, 4n2, 12, 14, 17–30, 198, 202, 203, 212–19; inadvertent escalation, 15, 23–24, 25
Exercise Sagebrush, 36–58
Exercise Swarmer, 44

F-4 aircraft, 71, 82, 115
F-4 Phantom II aircraft, 65
F-16 aircraft, 190
F-84F aircraft, 36, 37, 39
F-86D aircraft, 36, 39, 42
F-86H aircraft, 37
Falkland Islands Committee, 141
FAPA (People's Air Force of Angola), 92–96, 104–8, 114, 119
5th Infantry Brigade, 148, 151
FIM-92A Stinger missile, 107, 149, 171

Fleet Air Arm, 130, 148
flexible response strategy, 55
FNLA (National Liberation Front of Angola), 90, 91, 99, 100, 102
France, 22, 24, 98, 113, 195

Galtieri, President Leopoldo (Argentina), 133, 134, 139, 141, 143, 146, 212, 215, 216, 219
Granada, 12

Haig, Secretary of State Alexander (U.S.), 145, 146, 149
Harpoon anti-ship missile, 131
Harrier aircraft, 127, 128, 130, 131, 132, 140, 153, 156
Hiroshima, 21, 45, 113
HMS Ark Royal, 130, 211
HMS Endurance, 142, 144
Hod, General Motti, 64, 66, 68, 76, 87

IADS (integrated air defense system), 93, 107, 109, 116, 117
IAF Operational Plan Dugman, 67, 70, 74–78, 85
IAF Operational Plan Srita, 67, 71, 77
IAF Operational Plan Taggar, 67, 73–80, 85
Iklé, Fred, 11
India, 16, 166–203, 205n37, 206n56, 210–217
Indian Air Force, 167, 169, 171–203, 205n37, 206n56, 207n68, 210–211, 217
Israeli Air Force (IAF), 62–88,
Israeli Defense Forces (IDF), 62–87, 221

Jaguar aircraft, 173, 178, 180, 187, 205n37

Kahn, Herman, 7–13
Kennedy, President John F. (U.S.), 13, 22, 55
Kennedy, Robert, 13, 32n25
Khrushchev, Premier Nikita (USSR), 13
Kissinger, Secretary of State Henry (U.S.), 30, 80, 81, 84, 87, 92

Lambeth, Benjamin, 115
Laos, 11, 18, 23
laser-guided bomb (LGB), 179, 180
LoC (India-Pakistan Line of Control), 168–203
Lorenzo, Colonel Orestes, 94–96, 121n18

massive retaliation strategy, 8, 50, 51
Matador missile, 37, 43, 44
Matra 550 air-to-air missiles, 105, 115
Mavinga, Angola, 107, 109
MiG-17 aircraft, 92
MiG-21 aircraft, 95, 98, 104–8, 117, 178, 189, 190, 194
MiG-23 aircraft, 93, 96, 107, 108, 114–19, 178
Military Airlift Command (MAC), 81
Mirage-5 aircraft, 132, 134, 154
Mirage 2000 aircraft, 178–81 198, 222
Mirage F1 aircraft, 95, 105, 110, 114–20
Mirage III aircraft, 74, 107, 115–17, 132, 134, 211
Mitchell, William, 3
Mossad, 69, 82
Muntho Dhalo, 179–83
Musharraf, General Pervez (Pakistan), 169, 197, 198, 212, 213

Nagasaki, 21
National Liberation Front of Angola. *See* FNLA
New Look policy, 7, 50
Nickel Grass, 81, 82
Nixon, President Richard M. (U.S.), 35n47, 80, 81
North Korea, 8, 12, 16, 22, 23
Nott, Secretary of State for Defense John, 142, 148, 155
nuclear attack/strategy, 7–19, 22–30, 36–57, 81, 84, 86, 98, 112, 113, 124n98, 124n101, 144, 166, 167, 170, 174, 185, 191–219. *See also* atomic weapons/attacks
nuclear weapons, 2–9, 18, 19, 29, 37–51, 55, 56, 112, 113, 166, 194, 198, 204n7,

212, 216, 217, 218. *See also* atomic weapons/attacks

Operation Agony (1980–1982), 105
Operation Askari (1983), 106, 118, 119
Operation Carlota (1975), 99
Operation KWÊVOËL planning (1988), 111, 124n94
Operation Protea (1981), 104, 119
Operation Reindeer (1978), 102, 104, 118, 119, 214
Operation Rolling Thunder (1965–1968), 21
Operation Safed Sagar (1999), 175, 176, 178, 181, 183, 196, 200, 205n37
Operation Saludando Octubre (1987), 109
Operation Savannah (1975), 96, 99, 102, 118
Operation Sceptic (1980), 104
Operation Vijay, 172, 174, 178–86, 198

Pakistan, 16, 113, 166–70, 185–217
Patney, Air Marshal Vinod (India), 174, 179–81, 183, 185, 200, 204n23, 205n31, 206n56
Peled, IAF Chief of Staff Benny, 68–77, 80, 81
People's Air Force of Angola / Air and Antiaircraft Defense (FAPA), 92
Posen, Barry, 14
proxy wars and conflicts, 14, 56, 168, 198, 199
Pucará aircraft, 134

RAF, 34n46, 127, 130, 131, 138, 142, 148, 153, 154, 210, 211, 222, 223
RAF Special Air Service (SAS), 155
Rattenbach Report, 154, 157, 158
Reagan, President Ronald (U.S.), 15, 145, 149, 215
Russia, 2, 3, 8, 12, 15, 16, 54, 92, 93, 99, 106, 112, 113

Sadat, President Anwar (Egypt), 78, 79, 214

San Carlos Island, the Falklands, 128
Schelling, Thomas C., 12
Sharif, Prime Minister Nawaz (Pakistan), 170, 197, 203
Shazly, Chief of Staff Saad El (Egypt), 76
Shrike anti-radar missile, 131
Siachen Glacier, 168, 169, 203
Simla Agreement (1972), 168
Sinai Desert, 64, 70–72, 76–78, 214
Six-Day War (1967), 62–65, 68, 78
Somalia, 7, 27
South African Air Force (SAAF), 92–119
South African nuclear strategy, 112–14
South Georgia Island, 126, 127, 140, 143, 144, 152, 153
South Sandwich Islands, 126, 129, 140
South Thule Island, 142, 144
strategy, 62–87
Suez Canal, 66, 69, 73, 76, 77, 80, 82, 84, 86
SWAPO (South West African People's Organization), 91, 99, 101, 102–6, 111, 118, 214

Tactical Air Command, 38, 39, 41
Taiwan, 8, 15, 98
Taylor, General Maxwell D., 46, 52, 55
Thatcher, Prime Minister Margaret (Great Britain), 142, 145, 147, 148, 150, 152, 153, 213

3rd Royal Marine Commando Brigade, 148–49, 151, 221
Tiger Hill, 180, 181, 185
Timberlake, General E. J., 43, 46
Tipnis, Air Chief Marshal Anil (India), 174, 178
Tololing ridge, 172, 179
transnational threats, 16

UNITA (National Union for the Total Independence of Angola), 91, 93, 94, 100–109, 114, 116

V3B missile, 97, 116
Vajpayee, Prime Minister Atal (India), 170, 174, 177, 178, 180, 185, 186, 197, 201, 206n56, 213
Vergooi tactics and weapons, 107
Victor K2 aircraft, 130
Vietnam War, 2, 10, 11, 18, 21–26
Vulcan B.2 aircraft, 127, 130, 131, 152–55, 210

Warsaw Pact, 8, 15, 203
weapons of mass destruction, 38
weapons of mass effect, 38
Wells, H. G., 3
Weyland, General O. P., 41, 48–50, 56
Wideawake Airfield, 149, 150, 152

Zaire, 98, 99, 100

A Mitchell Institute Book
Aviation and Air Power
Series Editor: Brian D. Laslie

In his work *Winged Defense*, Brigadier General William "Billy" Mitchell stated, "Air power may be defined as the ability to do something in the air." Since Mitchell made this statement, the definition of air power has been contested and argued about by those on the ground, those in the air, academics, industrialists, and politicians.

Each volume of the Aviation and Air Power series seeks to expand our understanding of Mitchell's broad definition by bringing together leading historians, fliers, and scholars in the fields of military history, aviation, air power history, and other disciplines in the hope of providing a fuller picture of just what air power accomplishes.

This series offers an expansive look at tactical aerial combat, operational air warfare, and strategic air theory. It explores campaigns from the First World War through modern air operations, along with the heritage, technology, culture, and human element particular to the air arm. In addition, this series considers the perspectives of leaders in the US Army, Navy, Marine Corps, and Air Force, as well as their counterparts in other nations and their approaches to the history and study of doing something in the air.